Guy Debord

Revolutionary

Len Bracken

FERAL HOUSE

Feral House
2532 Lincoln Blvd. Suite 359
Venice, CA 90021

The author can be contacted at:
POB 5585
Arlington, VA 22205

Designed by Linda Hayashi

First edition 1997
10 9 8 7 6 5 4 3 2 1

Dedicated to Mi-Lun Chow

with heartfelt thanks

for her love and support...

Acknowledgements

Very special thanks to Eddie Lee for his generous contribution to this book. His knowledge of the material and keen editorial eye were a big help. Indeed, several of the phrases that he suggested are sprinkled throughout the book. That said, the author takes full responsibility for any lapses of form or content. Thanks go to Jean-Noel Clement for furnishing me with important recordings, documents and books, to Nadine Poupart for assistance with French language texts and recordings, and to Sandrine for luring me to France several times. I'm grateful to Jean Heriot of *Kaspharaster* fame for her invaluable computer searches for material related to Debord, and to Lucy Forsyth and Michel Prigent for sharing their insights. Thanks to Richard Greeman for his anaylsis of *Theses on the Paris Commune.* The International Institute of Social History and the Silkeborg Kunstmuseum came through with relevant documents—thanks to them. And I'd also like to acknowledge the excellent work done by Ken Knabb—perhaps more than anyone else, he has brought Debord and the S.I. to the English-speaking world. Thanks too, to the many friends who gave their moral support to this project, either by mail or walking and talking WDC style, especially Gabriel Thy who proofed and pre-pressed the book. Above all, I would like to thank my publisher, Adam Parfrey, for having the courage to publish this subversive book.

N.B. I didn't want to bog the text down with translator citations, and it was necessary edit many translations; but I should acknowledge all Debord translators—good and bad—for their efforts. The book contains numerous previously untranslated documents.

Contents

Introduction

I'll limit my introductory remarks to a quick sketch—a lure for those who are unfamiliar with the adventurous life and profound insights of this writer, cinematographer, strategist and revolutionary.

Who was Guy Debord? He is only now appreciated by a wide circle of academics in the English-speaking world so don't feel surprised if you haven't heard much about him or if what you've heard is wrong). Revolutionaries around the world have long recognized the value of his unified critique of the totality of social relations that emerged in the journal *Situationist International* (1958–1969), which he founded and edited; and in his radical classic *Society of the Spectacle*. Although much of Debord's superb form is lost in often-flawed translations, the clarity of his style is still very striking, particularly in his latter books, Comments on the *Society of the Spectacle* and his autobiographical fragment *Panegyric*. This rarefied style, acclaimed by many as one of the finest in the French language, is especially unique if one considers what he wrote. He was a poet of revolutionary theory.

Debord took this poetry to the walls of Paris during it's historic upheaval in 1968 as well as to the silver screen; and finally, he took it to the pages of books published by the most prestigious publisher in France, Gallimard. But more than being a mere man of letters, he was a founding member of the influential revolutionary group, Situationist International, known for its intellectual intensity, systematic use of insults and ability to create big affects with small gestures and few people. Despite his attention-getting derision of authority and other avant-gardes, Debord eschewed celebrity status and remained in the margins. In what is almost unimaginable in these days of shameless self-promotion, Debord indulged his creative impulses, but he did so in ways calculated to combat the fame he garnered during the events of Paris in May 1968.

"Some of my reasons for drinking are estimable. I can proclaim, like Li Po, this noble satisfaction: 'For thirty years I've hidden my fame in taverns,'" Debord proclaimed in his lyrical autobiographical fragment *Panegyric*. In the same way Thucydides' account of the Peloponnesian war towers over all other histories of the war, we're told *Panegyric* is the authoritative work on Guy Debord. With his characteristic tone of icy melancholy, Debord describes the society of the spectacle as one where the beloved tastes of yesterday are gone, leaving only industrially produced wines, beers and spirits. It's symptomatic of the spectacle that the bottles retain their labels so that, "one can photograph them as they used to be, not drink them [...] In drunken memory, no one has ever imagined that drinks would disappear from the world before the drinker."

To oppose the past to the present and the real to the false is an ancient method, even older than the cliché of new wine in old bottles. Debord applied this lost art masterfully in his prescient critique of modern capitalism. *Society of the Spectacle* is a Heraclitian text that can be read many ways—a critique of the planned *separation* of individuals, a very intense expression of Hegelian Marxism, an incisive summation of world history and radical praxis. Some commentators have gone so far as to call it "the secret play book of power." In *Society of the Spectacle,* Debord brings us into an Orwellian world where the organized system of appearances dominates everyday life by enforcing isolation and alienation. Separation is the alpha and omega of the spectacle, and the spectacle is the essential trait of contemporary capitalism. Don't worry if you haven't grasped the definition of the spectacle because there isn't one—there are a dozen complementary ones that apply to commodities, capital, celebrities, urban planning, etc. (delineated below). Here it might simply be suggested that all quality of life is ruined in the spectacle because banal, quantitative values are at its base. In his later works, Debord takes justifiable pride in seeing his theory confirmed by history, and he gloats by dismissing his detractors with the witty invective of a caustic drunk.

Faced with this misery of the modern world, drinking became Debord's dominant characteristic and his greatest consolation. Like Winston Smith languishing at the bar in *1984,* Debord spent a great deal of his time in his latter years in the dives of the seedier districts of Paris. Consoled by the Machiavelli, Sun Tsu, Clausewitz, Chateaubriand and Shakespeare, he's quick to comment, "Even though I've read a lot, I've drunk even more." This hiding out in bars was Debord's formula for retaining his military distinction with dignity. The masks of gravity and discretion, borrowed from those whom he considered to be masters, such as Baltasar Gracian, enhanced Debord's reputation for genius in letters. Debord explicitly states that he wanted to give the impression of possessing great talents, which he withheld from his contemporaries.

Despite his refusal of all interviews with the press and writing only six slim volumes ("I wrote much less than most people who write, but I drank much more than most people who drink"), Debord earned a reputation for greatness among the cognoscenti. Only his suicide, his final creative act of destruction, seemed designed to stun the mass of spectators into recognizing his worth. The headline could almost read like the title of a bad detective novel: *Triple Suicide on the Left Bank.* Debord shot himself in the heart on November 30, 1994. Within a week, two more Left Bank notables killed themselves: Roger Stéphane, an aging writer, producer and provocateur; and Gérard Voitey, publisher of Éditions Quai Voltaire. Stéphane shot himself in his Paris apartment and was perhaps ripe for death. Voitey was once the notary of Debord's very wealthy publisher and the film producer Gérard Lebovici (himself the victim of an ambush in 1984). Voitey was discovered at the wheel of his Porsche near a deserted lake with one round from a revolver in his head.

Although no evidence of a suicide pact was found, *Le Monde* reports that, "The proximity of their gestures takes on the meaning of a lofty protest in the setting of the carnival of vanities found in public life." If this triple suicide wasn't enough to rock the spectacle, Debord had a parting shot for it in the form of an anti-television movie. He made the film in collaboration with Brigitte Cornand, a producer at one France's racier television channels, a film that begged comparisons to the XIXth Century French writer Gerard Nerval who hanged himself from a lamp post for public inspection. The film *Guy Debord—His Art and Time* was shown during prime time a few days after his death. As if to add more mystery to the enigma of his being, this player of human chess went into the unknown with a great burst of creativity that drenched the spectacle in his blood. As his story unfolds, we quickly discover that he foresaw this last move while still in his youth.

Part I

The Formative Years 1931–1956

Guy Debord as a young boy
from *Spectacular Times*

**All my life I have seen only
troubled times, extreme divisions
in society, and immense destruction;
I have joined in these troubles."**
Panegyrique

Chapter One

Excessive debt, overproduction and widespread layoffs in the United States engendered the infamous Wall Street crash (1929) that sent shock waves of financial panic rippling around the globe. Largely because France had a big share of widely dispersed family industries that weren't overly indebted to banks, the economic depression that eventually engulfed the world reached the shores of France later than most other industrial countries. Guy Ernest Debord was born in Paris, at the height of the crisis, on December 28, 1931.

Debord tells us that his bourgeois family was ruined by the Great Depression—

these were desperate times when rents went unpaid and bankruptcy was declared. Honest people turned into con artists overnight out of sheer desperation; the already corrupt, namely the stock brokers and bankers, turned to suicide. Corruption was so generalized that France actually experienced widespread riots in 1934 due to the machinations of a con artist—a promoter of fraudulent bonds and other speculations who was shown to have been protected by corrupt ministers. The Fascist Leagues took advantage of the affair to attack the IIIrd Republic, and the workers of France responded with a general strike that united several unions in an anti-fascist alliance. The country was polarized, and everyone was forced to choose sides.

Debord grew up in the crumbling streets of Paris trodden by these workers who felt the menacing rise of Hitler in Germany and fascism in Spain. Leon Blum (1872-1950) brought these workers together under the trade union alliance know as the C.G.T. (General Confederation of Labor), and as a Socialist he was able to form a political alliance with Communist and Radical parties in the reformist Popular Front government. This left-wing coalition whose "popular culture" movement certainly must've effected the young Debord, made a huge effort to bring culture to the people in a participatory way.

The Undersecretary of Sport and Leisure in the Popular Front government reject-ed what he called the "sport-spectacle" in favor of leisure activity—tourist, cultural and sporting. Later, Debord would write that he and his friends would be "satisfied to work anonymously in the Ministry of Leisure of a government preoccupied with changing the way people live," and affirmed that his preoccupation with leisure and complete neglect for productive activity were what qualified him for the avant-garde. Of course, the Popular Front goals of promoting health, hygiene and cultural improvement wouldn't coincide with the future revolutionary whose idea of leisure would have much more to do with heavy drinking and idling in cafes with underage women; but then who could reasonably argue with the logic of total leisure when overproduction was a primary cause of the economic crisis.

When Debord was four, his father died, perhaps as an indirect result of the stress-es of the Depression (much the same way Nietzsche's father died in the immediate wake of the Revolutions of 1848 when Nietzsche was roughly the same age). Debord was still four when, in 1936, General Franco's faction of the Spanish military revolted against the Republic governed by the Popular Front. Most of the French population wanted Leon Blum to support the Popular Front in Spain—many workers protested his non-intervention policy in the street and sent provisions. In Spain, the Popular Front crumbled into bitter factions that undermined the war. Debord would later call for starting the Spanish Civil War over again—his support being for the dissi-dent (non-party) Marxist P.O.U.M. depicted in Ken Loach's excellent film *Land and Freedom*.

"The Land is Yours"
P.O.U.M. (Partido Obrero
de Unification Marxista)

Debord was still six when, in 1938, France found itself without a government and Hitler had his Anschluss with Austria. The following year, Hitler occupied Czechoslovakia (breaking the Munich Agreement), and invaded Poland. Panzers, stukas, messerschmitts, Luftwaffe—these were the first German words that Debord learned. Using these arms and their offensive doctrine, the Germans rolled over neutral Belgium in 1940, and then France. Pétain (1856-1951) conceded victory to the Germans and collaborated with them, convinced that all of Europe would become German. Debord, still a young boy, left Paris by car with his mother and sister—all the churches along the way sounded their bells, warning of dis-aster as the Debord family raced south. They waited out the war in Pau and Cannes.

Like all the children of his time, he witnessed the newsreel images of rocket trac-
ers and the sound of air raid sirens. Many of the situations he experienced later in
life, such as his war with the institution of art and his war against society, undoubtedly drew on this experience of war in his youth. It's interesting to note that Debord,
the future cinematographer, would live in Cannes during the war and immediate
post-war years. The city's international film festival certainly enabled him to recognize, early on, that film was the language of his generation.

In his film *In Girum Imus Nocte et Consumimur Igni* Debord evokes occupied
France by using fragments of the Marcel Carné's classic *The Children of Paradise*,
which was clandestinely filmed under the Nazi's noses. Although he was never a
"thief," Debord clearly identifies with the film's portrayal of Lacenaire (1800-1836),
the notorious literary bandit who wrote some excellent poems and killed a few people in cold blood. In his film *In Girum...*, made when he was forty-seven, Debord
frames the following clips from Carné's *The Children of Paradise* with quotes from
Pascal (1623-1662) and Hobbes (1588-1679) and with his own chiseled prose. In
the *In Girum Imus Nocte et Consumimur Igni* excerpt cited below, which shows
Debord's use of *The Children of Paradise* (in plain italics), the synthesis of Debord's
prose and Pascal and Hobbes' lines are is bold.

In vain it's been said: "He's old; he's changed"; he has also remained the same.
Lacenaire: "I'm not cruel, I'm logical; I declared war on society a long time ago."
Garance: "And have you killed many people lately, Pierre-Francois?"
*Lacenaire: "No, my sweet, see: no trace of blood; only a few ink stains. But rest
assured, Garance, I'm preparing something extraordinary... When I was young, I
was always more lucid, and more intelligent than the others. They haven't forgiv-
en me for it. What fine youth! And what a prodigious destiny! I have no vanity,
only pride, and I have absolute confidence in myself. Petty thief by necessity, assassin by vocation, my route is well mapped out, my path is straight on, and I shall
walk with my head held high until it falls into the basket! Besides, my father often
said to me: 'Pierre-Francois, you'll end up on the gallows.'"*
Garance: "You're right, Pierre-Francois, you should always listen to your parents."
**In this place which was the brief capital of disturbances, even though it might
have been true that the select company included a certain number of thieves, and
occasionally murderers, the existence of all was mainly characterized by a prodigious inactivity; and it was this which was resented as the most threatening of so
many of the crimes and offences discovered there by the authorities.**
*A thief approaches a valuer's table in the "Robin Redbreast" to have an
object valued: "Is it gold or fake?"*
The valuer turns to his neighbor, a newcomer: "What do you make of it,

Daniel Auteuil in the film *Lacenaire* by Francis Girod

artist? You don't say a word? You're a wise man. You should never say anything."

An informer, who is also a peddler, enters: "Did you dream of cats, or dogs? Did you see troubled waters? Here's the explanation of all your dreams, an illustrated, bound volume." He greets the landlord, and says: "Lacenaire and his band aren't far from here. You've been warned."

Lacenaire and his team enter, with Garance. Drinks are served at his table.

It was the best labyrinth for retaining travellers. Those who lingered there for a few days never left again, or at least as long as it still existed; but the majority saw the end of their none too numerous days there. No-one left these few streets and these few tables where the culminating point of time had been discovered.

Garance: "If I understand it right, whatever you may be, you're philosophers?"
Lacenaire: "And why not?"
Garance: "Oh fine! Philosophy is happy, pretty and special!"

One of Lacenaire's lieutenants suggests they throw someone out who should-n't have been there. Lacenaire agrees. The former gets up to look for the per-son among those dancing. The intruder is grabbed and thrown out through the front window.

They all admired each other for having sustained such a magnificently disastrous challenge; and from this I really believe that not one of those who passed that way ever acquired the slightest honest reputation in the world.

The cafe owner comes along protesting: "What about my windows then?"

Lacenaire answers from his seat, gesturing a knife slitting a throat: "Come off it, can't we enjoy ourselves at the Robin Redbreast anymore?"
The cafe owner: "Oh, Mr. Lacenaire, all I was saying was..."

To digress for a moment on Lacenaire, several books paint a much less flattering portrait of him—the Surrealists loved him, but many others felt he was a dandy who brought persecution on himself. Once Lacenaire had been kicked out of every school and lost every job his father got for him, he purposely succeeded in getting arrested so that he could learn how to be a criminal from the professionals in prison. Most of his crimes were petty thefts, and he ruined his best crimes by needlessly slitting the throats of his victims. Debord had other, more exemplary, heroes than Lacenaire, but the only image he left us with of the occupation was Marcel Carné's Street of Crime in the *Children of Paradise.*

Little Guy was doubtlessly taken by the newsreels of the war, and certainly sided with the Resistance against the Nazi collaborators. And if he would later seem harsh

Parisian women endure public humiliation for taking German lovers during the Occupation

in his breaks with past comrades, it was probably because of this experience of seeing loyalties tested in war where the consequences were severe. It was the Vichy regime that replaced the famous credo "Liberty, Equality, Fraternity" of the French Revolution, with words that would become anathema to Debord: "Work, family, fatherland." The church supported the new regime, which promulgated statutes against Jews and unions. As Germany marched into total war, the Gestapo set up stakes in Paris. Over time the Vichy regime became more fascist, and everyday life was a constant struggle between the militia and the internal resistance movement. Debord gives us the impression that he and his schoolboy chums were familiar with these struggles, and it was this familiarity with war that he would carry over to his revolutionary politics. Meanwhile, the external resistance was organized by General de Gaulle (1890–1970) from London. The American intervention (hostile to de Gaulle) precipitated even more internal resistance, although the Americans formally backed General Giraud (1879–1949) who was sympathetic to the strict policies of the Vichy regime even though he was part of the resistance.

Giraud and de Gaulle were duel presidents of the Committee of National Liberation in Algiers, with de Gaulle soon becoming the only president as the Americans organized an allied military government of their own. The famous landing on the beaches of Normany lead to the liberation of Paris in August. Young Debord saw the newsreels of people standing by in the streets, observing the look of capitulation on the faces of the Germans as they were run out of town. Somewhere between 10,000 and 100,000 Frenchmen were executed for collaborating with the Nazis and many more were deprived of their civic rights. When Debord later called for The Terror of the French Revolution to be visited upon certain people, it was

because he was thirsty for this extreme form of justice that he'd tasted in his youth. After the euphoria of the Liberation died down, nothing pleased young Debord for very long, and everything seemed naked.

Chapter Two

Post-war Paris was a bleak place, rife with unemployment and full of dislocated people. Yet for both social and patriotic reasons workers refused to go back to work without a change in management. Food and other goods were in short supply. Rations, inflation and the incessant outbreak of strikes characterized the immediate post-war period. France accepted American Marshall Plan aide to finance its modernization and to alleviate the immediate suffering of the war-weary populace (with an agreement to keep communists out of the government). The ensuing American-funded, state-led modernization drive spurred industry, particularly the massive car factories on the outskirts of Paris that drew rural men and Algerian immigrants to the capital. The workers in these factories would play a large role in the revolutionary events of '68 and were already viewed as the bellwether of working class sentiments and attitudes. General strikes in 1947 and 1948 proved that workers were capable of unified action—workers wielded considerable power despite the creation of NATO in 1949 and the nomination of Eisenhower (1890–1969) as Supreme Commander in 1950.

Paris was the unquestioned capital of the intellectual world, a place that spawned numerous schools of art and philosophy. Parisian universities struggled to cope with swollen enrollments, often of village boys, after years of closure and bankruptcy. Provincial women flocked to Paris to work in shops and as maids. Vespa mass produced scooters, providing the youth of Europe cheap transportation. The two-piece bikini swimsuit was modeled in Paris days after the U.S. tested an atomic bomb on the island that lent its name to the skimpy new fashion. Hungarian communists, backed by the Red Army, seized power in Budapest while Tide laundry detergent flooded the United States in a storm of advertising. The Iron Curtain was being drawn across Europe—the king of Romania abdicated to the communists as American industries brought their commodities to near-empty French shelves. And by 1947, American films had overrun even the strong French film industry. The American way of life depicted in film (especially its use of cars and appliances) was considered to be a desirable way to live. The high level of American cultural saturation is seen early on by parodies in French films and novels, featuring characters who spoke to each other in the language of advertisements. Today, this language is so pervasive that parody is virtually impossible. As Debord later put it, "Reality rises up in the spectacle, and the spectacle is real."

What the Marshall Plan did for French industry, the Rockefeller Foundation did for social science—production of the 4CV (the "people's car") couldn't keep up with demand; and empirical, quantitative, structuralist studies were financed to contain the Marxists in French academia. In 1946 the Center of Sociological Studies was established in Paris, followed by others for economics and demographic statistics. In 1947, psychology was licensed to be taught in French universities—not the Surrealist use of Freud in all his occult glory to explore the unconscious, but the American use of psychology to codify norms of behavior. And, as Christopher Simpson points out in *The Science of Coercion,* the C.I.A. put WWII psychological warfare techniques to work in French and Italian elections to cast dispersion on communist candidates.

The young Debord, still living with his mother and sister in Cannes, reportedly spent a great deal of time alone—"I had no childhood," he later quipped to one of his teenage friends. Given what would soon be recognized as the "super-intellectuality of Guy," he was probably familiar with the renowned cultural products of his time such as *The Plague* by Albert Camus, Malcom Lowery's *Under the Volcano* and George Orwell's *1984.* Picasso was king of the art world, and Bertold Brecht reigned supreme in the theater, staging his *Mother Courage* shortly after the proclamation of the two separate German republics in 1949. Brecht's "epic theater," that sought to break the passive perspective of the spectator, would be elemental to Debord's theories of anti-aesthetics, but the Surrealists were the biggest influence on Debord when he was in his teens. In 1949, Mao (1893–1976) and his comrades took China, while the seven major oil companies gained control of the ninety percent of world petroleum supplies outside the United States and Soviet bloc. This period was notable for the publication of *The Second Sex* by Simone de Beauvoir and for Simone Weil starving herself to death using Nazi rations. Meanwhile Coca-Cola, Pepsi and new tranquilizers were being marketed around the world. Sociologists were already speaking of the lonely crowd by the time war broke out in Korea in 1950.

What allusions did Debord take from this world filled with commotion and strife? Over the years of his life, the spectacle may have changed, but Debord's eyes always retained the youthful gaze of a battlefield on the immediate horizon. He writes that he supported himself for a time in his late teens at poker, not by cheating, but by virtue of his "strategic talents."

Chapter Three

In May 1950, Debord attended the Cannes Film Festival screening of *Treatise on Slime and Eternity* by Isidore Isou, a collage film that devalued the image and elevated the importance of the soundtrack, largely a melody of "letters." Isou, an anti-poet of Romanian origin, was the leader of a Parisian-based group known as Lettrists. This encounter with Isou was decisive for Debord, who would soon become a Lettrist himself. For this reason, it is important to digress for a moment and take a look at Isou.

Born in 1925, Isou received a classical education that he used to conceive his theory of the evolution of artistic forms—he was only sixteen-years-old. According to this theory, the creator advances step-by-step, creation-by-creation to arrive at a place he called the "center of creation" where every person is God and messiah. In his first book, published in 1946, Isou made a list of

Isidore Isou

works he would create; and testing his theory in the realms of literature, painting, sculpture, cinematography, etc. he dogmatically stuck to the list.

Contrary to the idea of spontaneous genius, Isou examined all the arts and found that they had two phases: a period of *amplitude* when formal experimentation was taken to the limit, followed by a period of *auto-destruction*. In his notorious fits of megalomania he took credit for every aesthetic innovation discovered during his lifetime, and he denounced everyone, eventually including Debord and his "neo-Nazi situationist cinema." Contention was highly contagious at the time, and what now looks like a comical vanguard competition seemed to have been in play as Lettrists disrupted rival scenes, shoplifted and even staged a small riot at an orphanage. A large youth movement came together under the rubric of the Youth Front following the ideas laid out by Isou in his works *Youth Uprising* and *Treatise on the Nuclear Economy.*

In the latter, Isou applied his general theory to economics. He identified the ample phase with the "atomic" economy in the liberal period of Adam Smith (1723–1790) and John Maynard Keynes (1883–1946), both of whom viewed individuals as being driven by personal interest. The following auto-destructive period that Isou called the "molecular" economy was driven by Marxist consciousness of class struggle. Speaking for his fellow youth, Isou noted that even if class warfare somehow disappeared, there would still be social strife due to the fact that kids didn't fit into the economy. Isou created two new class categories: the *interns* who have a place in the circuit of production like spokes on a wheel; and the *externes* who refuse to accept the roles available to them and spend their energy in more glorious ways.

Isou showed how youth were economically exploited, and he was really the first to do so in a way that portrayed their sub-proletariat existence. The externisme movement was essentially reformist, and relied on philanthropy and freeing up credit to youth. While these tendencies were ridiculed by hardened revolutionaries, Isou certainly did discover and identify the latent revolutionary force of young people who didn't fit into the economic system, and whose ranks were growing. Meanwhile, Lettrist "poems" were recited with emphasis on "crescendo-until-howling," and a delirious escalation of verbal slips right in the angst-ridden faces of the existentialists at their opulent cafes. A drunken Lettrist, delighted by every Freudian slip that issued from his mouth, might turn to a woman on the street and ask: "Excuse me miss, may I accomp-annoy you?"

The greatest Lettrist provocation occurred on Easter Sunday, April 9, 1950. With thousands of people in the Notre Dame cathedral, Michel Mourre slipped onto the alter dressed as a Dominican monk and delivered the following sermon written by Lettrist poet Serge Berna:

Today Easter of the Holy Year here under the insignia of the Basilica of Notre Dame de Paris
I accuse
the Universal Catholic Church of the deadly diversion of the force of life in favor of an empty heaven
I accuse
the Catholic Church of a con job
I accuse
the Catholic Church of infecting the world with its mortuary morality of being the chancre sore of the decaying Western World

I tell you the truth: God is dead
We vomit the agonizing tastelessness of your prayers because your prayers are
the greasy smoke of the battlefields of our Europe
Go forth into the tragic and exalted desert of a world where God is dead and
once again till this earth with your bare hands with your PROUD hands
with your unpraying hands

Today Easter of the Holy Year
Here in the Basilica of Notre-Dame de France, we proclaim the death of Jesus
Christ so that at last Man lives.

As Mourre, Berna and a few others made their escape, they had a brief skirmish with the sword-wielding Swiss Guard on duty—one of the iconoclasts was slashed in the face. They escaped the cathedral only to be arrested by the Paris police. This, of course, is the stuff legends are made of.

The next month, Isou and his cohorts were in Cannes for the screening of the *Treatise on Slime and Eternity,* the first auto-destructive film and winner of the Prix d'Avant Garde. Jean Cocteau was there to witness the "scandal," as was the eighteen-year-old Debord. From their meetings with him everyday they were in Cannes, it was evident to the Lettrists that Debord already "had something." His letters to the Lettrists concerning his planned move to Paris were already marked by his now infamous verbal violence. The following letter was sent to Marc O, editor of the Lettrist journal *Ion:*

Serge Berna

September 23, 1950

Dear Marc,

I found your letter late, upon returning from a real voyage to Paris and its environs for slimy* reasons. I couldn't see you Friday morning at the hotel, but I met Isou. I understand the situation. If you come, I will help you show the film. It's the sort of work that wouldn't displease me at all. Those poor fools must accept, and without making us wait. We've seen cinema managers shoot themselves for less in this town abandoned by God and all creators in general. With five friends I disrupted the projection of the film by G.R. Luckily, for the first time in his still brief career, the idiot didn't obtain his customary prize for stupidity. Beyond that, I wrecked the base of support for the cineclub that you wanted and I already kicked its director out the door.

Isou spoke to me about a room for 9,000 francs**. If this room exists, can you reserve it for me for the month of October. Forgive me for importuning about these non-eternal necessities and underscoring their urgent character. I want to (...)***

The forms of courtesy must be revolutionized
Greetings to Pousset and to Isou.

Guy-Ernest

After taking his university entrance exams, Debord moved to Paris—apparently in the autumn of 1951. He told his mother that he was a student, but he never attended a university. Living in an inexpensive hotel on rue Racine, he was much more of a daytime person than his drinking buddies and spent a great deal of time alone. While the celebrities of St. Germain des Pres were at famous watering holes like Deux Maggots and Cafe Flore, Debord would buy two liters of wine—white for him and red for his friend Jean-Michel Mension. After downing these bottles by the river in less than an hour, they would walk over to the dive Chez Moineau for still more wine. Although Debord drank a great deal, notably fifty-fifty mixes of rum and beer, he didn't partake in the hash that was passed around the bar. The place was full of mercenaries, murderers and many petty criminals—it was also where they ate: a plate of vegetables costing only pennies. Around midnight, long before closing, Debord would go home to get up early the next day to plan his overthrow of the world. His young cohorts, including many young (but not pure) correction house girls, were drawn to his magnetic personality, his subtle and powerful will. But like all remarkably creative people, Debord liked to spend a great deal of time alone.

Meanwhile, Isou and Maurice LeMaitre made Lettrist films for screenings at cinema clubs whose origins dated to the Popular Front cultural movement; and they coached the next generation of cinematographers. One protege, Gil Wolman, made a film called *Anticoncept* in 1952. This early ally of Debord, who would join Debord in the formation of the Situationist International, begins his film with a drum roll in the form of cinema history, a lesson that culminates with Isou's discrepant cinema

---

* a reference to Isou's film *Treatise on Slime and Eternity*

** in old francs

***this letter was transcribed and translated from the French radio program *The Situationist International: Wisdom Will Never Return* (1996). The remainder of this phrase is unintelligible.

(a fish swimming in the sea on the screen as the soundtrack broadcasts the voiceover of a love story). Wolman then announces the beginning of a new art form that relies heavily on atonal narration:

I love you I don't love you he loves another
Under the mask she must be beautiful she must be ugly

THEOREM
There's no negation that doesn't affirm itself elsewhere.
Negation is the transitory term to a new period.
Negation of the concept—intrinsic, immutable, a priori—projects this concept outside of the material, reveals it a posteriori to an extrinsic reaction and becomes mutable by so many reactions.

THE ERA OF POETS
IS FINISHED—TODAY I SLEEP

Gil Wolman

The first "screening" on February 11, 1952, at the Avant-Garde Film Club in the Museum of Man in Paris featured the stunt of projecting the film on a large helium balloon. The government censor in attendance banned the work, and eleven Lettrists were arrested for trying to have the movie shown at the Cannes Film Festival. *Anticoncept* would have to wait until the 1980s to find its way, anticlimacticly, to the big screen.

Chapter Four

To hear Debord tell it, his quest for the "geography of real life" began as he drifted around the snow-covered Paris streets in 1951, drinking and reading and engaging in rigorous debates in cafes. Sartre's (1905–1980) concept of "situation" was all the rage at the time (his two volume *Situations I & III* included the major essays "Cartesian Freedom" and "Materialism and Revolution"), but Debord and his cohorts never acknowledged the man who supposedly figured it all out, except as "stupid," "liar," "imbecile," "perishable commodity," "tainted slut," and "nothing" in the *Situationist International* journal that Debord edited. While Debord would agree with Sartre that freedom was only possible in the world, Debord's concept of the "situation" would be at odds with Sartre's recognition of the situation as "facticity" or "the given." For Sartre the key was to choose the meaning of a situation prior to action. But, as Mark Poster points out in *Existential Marxism in Postwar France,* Sartre was unable to overcome the duality of self and world with his concept of the situation. For Debord, as discussed in greater detail below, the situation was what needed to be overturned, and in doing so one became one with the world historic that was one's creation.

Guy Debord as a young man

As for the rest of Debord's proximate cultural landscape, the Surrealist demigods Andre Breton and Paul Valéry were, by then, regarded as relics; yet they did set the example of rebellion outside of party politics, and some of them had the audacity to embrace Marx despite the atrocities taking place in the Soviet empire. Debord admits that he learned from the Surrealists, but his deepest sympathies were with the Dada poet-boxer, Authur "I was a cigar" Craven (1887–1918).

Authur Craven—a nephew of Oscar Wilde born in Laussanne, Switzerland—arrived in Paris in 1909 and became a well-known personality—a party-going poet and world class boxer. His specialty was to throw parties where he would hold court, dancing and talking, with audacious aplomb. In his short-lived anti-art journal *Maintenant,* he wrote: "You have to cram it in your head that art is for the bourgeois, and I mean by bourgeois a man without imagination." When commenting on the Salon des Independants exhibit in 1914, Cravan made the following proto-Dada correspondence: "Painting is walking, running, drinking, eating, sleeping and taking care of one's needs."

Although this onetime European boxing champion certainly preferred fighting to literature and painting, Craven waged a war not to fight in World War I by deserting seventeen countries. Following his instincts, he looked for primitive pleasures in the euphoric free play of his giant body. He was with Duchamp and Picabia in New York in 1917 when they launched an anti-art offensive. Craven's conference on modern art and Futurism resulted in insults against the audience and the beginnings of a strip tease that was only thwarted by the cops. He then went "to Buenos Aires to be unhappy," and to Chile, Peru, etc., travelling on a dubious Russian passport. He disappeared in Mexico in 1920. The Mexican police found two dead men near the Rio Grande—one, dirty blonde and very tall, could've been Cravan. His famous last words? "I'm a man of the extremes of suicide."

Arthur Craven

In 1952, the twenty-year-old Debord was idly drinking in the dives of St. Germain des Pres as Sony introduced the first transistor radios and the contraceptive pill was invented. This was the year a four-day smog wave in London caused the death rate to triple and when Lysenko's tree-planting program in the Soviet Union was finally recognized as a dismal failure. Kellogg's Sugar Frosted Flakes became a national rage in the United States while French forces were bogged down in southeast Asia. The classics were, for the first time, being reprinted in cheap paperbacks—perspectives such as those expressed by Montesquieu's famous quip, "The Spartacus War was the most just war," were synthesized with reappraisals of the anarchist Proudhon (1809–1865) and the utopian socialist Fourier (1772–1837).

Debord was certainly also reading Sade (1740–1814)—texts like *Philosophy in the Bedroom* with its dedication to libertines:

> And you, amiable debauchees, you who since youth have known no limits but those of your desires and who have been governed by your caprices alone, study the cynical Dolmancé, proceed like him and go as far as far as he if you would travel the length of those flowered ways your lechery prepares for you; in Dolmancé's academy be at last convinced it is only by exploring and enlarging the sphere of his tastes and whims, it is only by sacrificing everything to the senses' pleasure that this individual, who never asked to be cast into this universe of woe, that this poor creature who goes under the name of Man, may be able to sow a smattering of roses atop the thorny path of life.

1952 was a decisive year for "Guy-Ernest," as he called himself for many years before eventually dropping the hyphenated "Ernest." This was the year Debord made his first cinematic masterpiece, *Howlings in Favor of Sade*,* and he was already making contemptuous comments about the medium: "The spectacle goes on. Even after drinking, the importance of aesthetics still provides an excellent object for jokes. We have left the cinema." The first version of the film was published in the Lettrist journal *Ion* in April along with his short essay "Prolegomena to All Future Cinema," an essay that foregrounds his ties with this movement: "Lettrist poetry howls for a ruined universe." Yet it's also apparent that Debord was intent on surpassing the Lettrist perspective. In the same essay, he invoked what he called a tridimensional psychology (subject, object, spectator), and made the prophetic remark: "Future arts will be the overthrow of situations, or nothing." And in the film itself, he outlined his Situationist theory: "A science of situations is to be created, which will borrow elements from psychology, statistics, urbanism and ethics. These elements have to coincide in an absolutely new goal: the conscious creation of situations."

In his early version of *Howlings in Favor of Sade,* Debord planned to use nonsense images and nonsense words so as to exceed the howl. The image of a photo on the screen would invade and alter the meaning of a phrase—words on the screen would respond to the spoken words in a dialogue of writing (white letters on a black screen)

---

* This might be more laconically translated as *Howls for Sade,* but I have retained the Richard Parry translation.

Storming the Bastille

and to the spoken words. For example, the following dialogue takes place while a lone Lettrist does a howl improvisation:

> *Subtitle:* "I love you. It must be awful to die. Good-by. You drink too much. What are childhood love affairs? I don't understand you."
> *Voice:* "I knew it. At another time, I regretted it very much."
> *Subtitle:* "Would you like an orange? The beautiful lacerations [dechirements fig. heartbreaks] of volcanic isles. Bygone days."
> *Voice:* "I have nothing more to say to you."
> As telescopic images of the night sky fill the screen, the Lettrist makes his last gasp.

The first version of this film featured numerous "encounters," which he defined as "all the images whereby eroticism isn't tempered, except by the scandalous and hard to believe existence of the police." By the age-specific images and by the text with lines such as "every day the drift of continents distances a girl as beautiful to Gilles de Rais" (a notorious XIXth Century serial killer of young women), we're led to believe that this eroticism involves twelve-year-old girls. To cite another example, the soundtrack contains, "Considerations on sexual relations in France near the end of the Christian era."

Almost all the girls less than fifteen-years-old are off limits to us.

Most perversions are disdained by the public at large.

The Parisian police force is thirty thousand truncheons strong.

There are even more people who neither laugh nor cry at the word morality.

Although there are no references to Sade in the film (a fact that Debord explicitly states in the final version), yet another criminal who was infamous for his violent attacks on young women makes a brief appearance on the soundtrack: "Jack the Ripper was never caught." If this imagery seems to reflect more violence toward women than even the chauvinistic era of the '50s could endure, other lines point to a playful aspect in this sadism:

The first marvel is to come before her without speaking. The female prisoner's hands move no faster than race horses filmed in slow motion. To touch her mouth and breasts, in all innocence, the ropes become water and we roll together towards dawn.

Indeed, Debord seems to be genuinely touched by the suicide of the twelve-year-old radio star Madeleine Reineri, who threw herself into the Isere River near Grenoble: "My little sister, we're not beautiful to look at. The Isere and misery continue. We're powerless." He later adds, "Miss Reineri, in this part of Europe you always have your astonished face and this body, the greatest of promised lands."

Howlings... also pays homage to the Surrealist suicide Jacques Vaché* and Dada "suicide" Arthur Craven (Debord's real hero at that time evidenced by numerous clips of boxing matches planned for the film): "The hurried passage of Jacques Vaché through the clouds of war, that extraordinary driving force inside him, that catastrophic haste which destroyed him; the rude lashing of Arthur Craven, himself swallowed up at that time in the Bay of Mexico..."

By identifying himself with these annihilators of life, Debord seems to be saying to the aesthetic world, and to his fellow Lettrists, "you may be poets, but I'm a warrior" (although not a warrior in the common sense of the term—Debord later repudiated Jacques Vaché as being "conditioned by the military system of the moment," in favor of Cravan's "beautiful testimony of desertion"). In what is undoubtedly the most prophetic line in the film (considering the mysterious circumstances of his own suicide), Debord declares at twenty-one that, "The perfection of suicide is in ambiguity."

---

* Note that Surrealist poets Jacque Rigaut and Rene Crevel, and the Surrealist painters—Oscar Dominguez and Wolfgang Paalen also chose this definitive solution, the later having shot himself in the heart.

The final version of *Howlings in Favor of Sade* retained much of the language of the early version, but it was a substantially different film. The film is only accessible to us in written form, which might be the best way to experience it considering the final twenty-four minutes of darkness and silence. Debord began this, his first film, by writing it into a "Memorandum for a history of cinema." Such hubris was intended to provoke a violent reaction from the film-going public. To ensure this reaction, Debord deployed the anti-spectacular, formal technique of a blank film—no images, simply a screen alternating between black and white. The sound track of dialogue and phrases lifted—and sometimes diverted—from Joyce and newspapers and the civil code, is heard in the white light. The curtain of darkness is sealed in silence, preceded by lines like, "All black, eyes closed to the excess of disaster." The light returns: "His memory always rediscovered it, in a flash, as if burnished by fireworks on contact with water."

The twenty minutes of dialogue and white light are dispersed in fragments across the sixty minutes of silence and darkness on the screen and in the cinema. Wolman opens the film with an improvisation of howls right before the first dialogue, and the film is dedicated to him. The reference to Serge Berna ("Several cathedrals have been erected to the memory of Serge Berna") also highlights the film's ties to the Lettrist movement, as does the reference to "An important Lettrist commando made up of some thirty members" who staged a riotous attack on a notoriously brutal Catholic orphanage that ended in violence and jail time. Indeed, the quotes from the civil code relate to missing persons, insanity, and legal age. The exception is #1793, which was included as a heavy-handed reference to the date of the Terror of the French Revolution.

Three citations by Isou on the soundtrack, a reply to them by Debord and a segment from John Ford's Rio Grande were cut from this early version of the film. Disgarding the fragments that dealt with Isou supported Debord's efforts to go beyond Isou's "discrepant cinema" (films whereby the soundtrack and imagery intentionally fail to coincide) into original territory. This friction between Debord and Isou is evident in the screenplay quotes below.

The inexpressive voices belong to Gil Wolman (voice 1), Guy Debord (voice 2), Serge Berna (voice 3), Barbara Rosenthal (voice 4) Jean-Isidore Isou (voice 5). Knowing who is speaking underscores the conflicts:

Voice 1: Love is only possible in a prerevolutionary period.
Voice 2: None of them love you, you liar. Art begins, grows and disappears because frustrated men bypass the world of official expression and the festivals of its poverty.

Skipping down, a dialogue is presented in which Wolman insults Isou:

Voice 1: Happiness is a new idea in Europe.
Voice 5: "I only know about the actions of men, but in my eyes men are transposed, one for the other. In the final analysis, works alone differentiate us."
Voice 1: And their revolts become conformisms.

Skipping down again, we have Serge Berna's ironic reply to Debord's question:

Voice 2: What's a love that's unique?
Voice 3: I will only answer in the presence of my lawyer.

The last line of the film, *"Nous vivons en enfants perdus nos adventures incompletes,"* (the line that precedes twenty-four minutes of darkness) could be translated literally as "We live as lost children our incomplete adventures."* I would add to this another shade of meaning—the "lost" state of the entire post-war generation of French youth, and their thwarted efforts to live life as an adventure.

The first screening of *Howlings...* took place on June 30, 1952, at the Avant-Garde Cinema Club in the Museum of Man in Paris. It's unclear exactly what happened, but we know that the film was violently interrupted by the public and the management of the club. In *Against Cinema,* his book documenting his first three films, Debord writes that many Lettrists had a falling out over the excesses of the film. The first complete showing of the film was at the Latin Quarter Cinema Club on October 13, where security was ensured by a group of "left Lettrists" and twenty extras from Saint-Germain-des-Pres. In an interview with Greil Marcus (in *Lipstick Traces*), Debord's first wife, Michele Bernstein describes the scene:

> I was there—up in the balcony with Guy, with bags of flour. Below us were all the people we knew—and Isidore Isou, and Marc O, who'd broken with Isou, and who we'd broken with. Before the film Serge Berna came on stage and delivered a wonderful speech on the cinema—pretending to be a professor. This was of course to drop on the people below. And in those days I had a voice—a voice that could break glass. I don't know where it went—if it's smoking or drinking. It wasn't a scream: just a sound I could make. I was

---

* In her translation of Debord's last film *In Girum Imus Nocte et Consumimur Igni,* Lucy Forsyth translates this line as, "We live as the forlorn hope, our unfinished adventures," and she adds a note to the expression enfants perdus: "a select body of troops, sent to ther front to begin an attack as body of skirmishers or a storming party. The Dutch rendering of the phrase verloren hoop (lost troop) conveys the element of risk in the undertaking. Debord's whole sentence wishes to convey this aspect."

to 'howl' when people began to make noise, when they began to complain—I was to make greater noise. And I did. I can't remember if Guy and I even stayed to the finish—you know the last twenty minutes are silence, nothing. But I do know that Serge Berna tried to keep people from leaving. "Don't go!" he said. "At the end there's something really dirty!"

A few months later, the same group who defended that screening prevented *Sadistic Skeleton* from being performed (*Sadistic Skeleton* was a weak joke by people upset with *Howlings...*; really nothing more than a malicious advertisement of a performance by "Rene-Guy Babord" that threatened to turn the lights out in the same hall for fifteen minutes). For its part, *Howlings...* has been compared to Malevitch's white square and Duchamp's transformation of a urinal into readymade art as a challenge to traditional aesthetics, in terms of its impact on the art consumer. According to Jean-Francois Martos' *History of the Situationist International,* Debord was working in the tradition of the early Soviet

Michele Bernstein

cinematographer Dziga Vertov who also considered cinema to be "a spectacle" and a conception of the world that needed to be "negated." With this first masterpiece Debord shows us more than the fact that the cinema screen can be black and that it can be white—he shows us that at times, we have to close our eyes to really see.

Chapter Five

The cracks developing within the Lettrist movement turned into a complete split when Charlie Chaplin came to Paris on his *Limelight* promotion tour. Chaplin had just been branded a subversive by the United States government and barred from returning to American soil. When this world-wide celebrity returned to England, he was received by Queen Elizabeth II at the Court of Saint James; he followed the protocol and bowed before her highness. Paris was even more ecstatic over Chaplin's arrival. The papers were full of stories about him. It was at his final press conference, on October 29, 1952, that the Lettrist International (Debord and Wolman's tendency within the Lettrist movement) had its baptism by fire. As a crowd closed in on the Ritz Hotel, the group caused a minor scandal by breaking through police lines and tossing around their screed.

AN END TO FLAT FEET

Sub-Mack film maker, sub-Max Linder actor, Stavisky of the tears of abandoned child-mothers and the little orphans of Auteuil, you are Chaplin, con artist of sentiments, the master singer of suffering.

The Cinematographer needed his Delly. You gave him your creations and your charity.

Because you say you're weak and oppressed, to attack you is to attack the weak and oppressed. But behind your rattan cane, some already feel the nightstick of a cop.

You're "he-who-turns-the-other-cheek-of-his-butt." But we who are young and beautiful respond "Revolution" as soon as we hear the word "suffering."

Max of Veuzit with flat feet, we don't believe in "absurd persecutions" that make you the victim. In France, the Immigration Service might be called the Advertising Agency. A press conference like yours at Cherbourg could launch any old turnip. You have nothing to fear from the success of *Limelight*.

Go to sleep you fascist slug. Make lots of money, be mundane (top job crawling on your flat stomach before little Elizabeth). Die soon, we'll give you a first-class funeral.

That your last film is really the last.

The fires of the footlights have melted the makeup of the self-proclaimed genius mime exposing a sinister and corrupt old man.

Go home Mister Chaplin

The Lettrist International
Serge BERNA—Jean-L. BRAU—Guy-Ernest DEBORD—Gil J. WOLMAN

The incident was reported in *Combat,* the wartime voice (most notably Camus' voice) of resistance turned national daily, as having been launched by "Lettrists." This prompted the following reply, published in *Combat* on October 11, 1952:

The members of the Lettrist movement are united around new principles of knowledge and each person maintains his independence in regard to how to apply these principles. We all know that Chaplin was a "great creator in the history of cinema" but the baroque and "complete hysteria" around his arrival in France bothered us, as do all expressions of disequilibrium. We're embarrassed that today the world lacks values other than those secondary values of "idolatry" of an "artist." The Lettrists who signed the tract against Chaplin are, by themselves, responsible for the extreme and confused content of their manifesto. As nothing has been resolved in this world, Charlie receives, with applause, the spattering of this non-resolution.

We, the Lettrists, who, from the beginning, were opposed to the tract of our comrades, smile at the inappropriate expression issuing from the gall of youth.

If Charlie must receive mud, it's not for us to throw it at him. There are others (the attorney general for example) who are paid for that.

Thus we distance ourselves from the tract of our friends and associate ourselves with the homage given to Chaplin by the entire populace.

Other Lettrist groups will explain themselves, in their turn, about this affair in their own journals or in the press.

But Charlie and all that is only a simple nuance.

Jean-Isidore ISOU—Maurice LEMAITRE—Gabriel POMERAND

Evidently, Isou had congratulated the participants of the intervention an hour after the event, and then changed his mind. As a group, the Lettrist International (L.I.) responded by using Isou's words against him in an open letter, and then abandoned Isou and his cohorts to "the anonymous and shocked crowd." Debord responded with a tract of his own.

DEATH OF A FELLOW TRAVELLER

During the series of conferences that he made in Europe to promote *Limelight,* Mr. Chaplin was insulted by us at the Ritz Hotel, and denounced as a merchant and cop.

The aging of this man, his indecent obstinacy to display his out-of-date face on our screens, and the poor affection of this poor world that recognizes itself in him, seemed like sufficient reasons to me for this interruption.

Meanwhile, Jean-Isidore Isou, disturbed by the reactions of the admirers of Chaplin—except for the Lettrists, all Frenchmen were admirers of Chaplin—published a disavowal in unacceptable terms.

We were out of the country at the time. When we came back, the explanations that he gave us, and his inappropriate efforts to minimize the whole affair, didn't seem acceptable to us, and in the days that followed we had to give notice that common action would henceforth be impossible.

We have so little passion for literary types and their tactics that the incident is almost forgotten. It's really as if Jean-Isidore Isou was nothing to us, as if he never had his lie and his denial.

Guy-Ernest DEBORD

It should be added that Debord remained true to his words—when Isou, who had been an early supporter of *Howlings in Favor of Sade,* wrote a vitriolic pamphlet *Against Neo-Nazi Situationist Cinema* in 1979 (calling Debord a "sub-ersatz Jean Genet," "pseudo-terrorist," "sub-SS, neo-Nazi," etc.) Debord scarcely acknowledged the attack.

Chapter Six

The first issue of the Internationale Lettriste was inauspicious—it merely reprinted the tracts that play out the polemic with Isou over Chaplin: a hand-typed flyer. The L.I. held its first congress in Aubervilliers on December 7, 1952, and adopted what now appears to be a fairly limited four point platform:

1) Adoption of the principle of majority rule and the utilization of names; 2) Contestation by overstepping culture, which remains to find its pace; 3) Forbid following a regressive morality until the elaboration of precise criteria; 4) Extreme circumspection in the presentation of works that could engage the L.I. and the expulsion ipso facto of whoever publishes a commercial book under his name.

A copy of this platform was signed, sealed in a bottle and thrown into the Aubervilliers canal—the group then repaired to a Spanish bistro to toast their pact. It wasn't until the second issue of the *Lettrist International,* where the group published its manifesto, that we see how radical their intentions were.

lettrist provocation serves to pass the time. revolutionary thought is nowhere else. we pursue our little uproar in the realm of literature. and lacking anything better, naturally it's to manifest ourselves that we write manifestos. offhandedness is a beautiful thing. but our desires were perishable and deceiving. youth is systematic, as they say. weeks multiply in a straight line. our encounters are by chance and our precarious contacts are led astray behind the fragile defense of words. the world turns as if nothing ever was. all said, the human condition doesn't please us. we dismissed isou, who believed in the utility of leaving traces. all that maintains something, contributes to the work of the police. we know that all the ideas and paths that exist are already insufficient. society is divided into lettrists and informers, of whom andre breton is the most notorious. there are no nihilists, there are only weaklings. almost everything is forbidden us. the diversion of minors and the use of drugs are pursued like all our gestures to fill the void. several of our comrades are in prison for theft. we rise up against the pain inflicted on those whose conscience holds that one must absolutely never work. we refuse to discuss it. human relations should be based on passion. if not, the terror.

The document was signed by twelve members of the very fluid membership of the Lettrist International. This manually typed document included a few lines, such as the call for a general strike, by others in the group. But it was Debord who had the first thing to say after the manifesto ("The spectacle is permanent"), and he was the one to get the last word ("new beauty will be THE SITUATION"). Here we find for

Members of the Lettrist International

the first time the expression of the refusal of work that was at the core of their lives. Incidentally, it was in 1953 that Debord made his celebrated NEVER WORK inscription in chalk on a wall on Rue de Seine. A photographer stopped to get a shot for a humorous postcard, but Debord wasn't kidding, and later called it, "the most important trace ever revealed on the site of Saint-Germain-des-Pres, as testimony of a particular lifestyle that attempted to affirm itself there." Indeed, contemporary practitioners of the refusal of work have found considerable inspiration in the expression Debord and his circle gave to this cause.

The reference in the L.I. manifesto to the Terror of 1793 echoes phrases found elsewhere, such as "Happiness is a new idea in Europe," that are traced to the icy tone and caustic wit of Saint Just (1767–1794), the youngest giant of the French Revolution. Debord was obviously influenced by Saint Just's style, and given Debord's reputation as prose stylist, it's interesting to examine who Saint Just was. After getting a first-rate education, little Louis Antoine stole his mother's silver and

Saint Just

ran away to Paris. While in prison for this crime, he wrote a libertine poem of sex (mostly rape), that rejected all received values with as much wit as a nineteen-year-old could muster. There are many forms of conscience in this world, and Saint Just's was, in part, composed of a strange sense of virtue taken from his classical education. This is the man on whose conscience historians have traced the report that began the great trials of the Terror: "the government of France is revolutionary until the peace." For some, Saint Just embodies beauty and youth in revolution; for others, he's the archangel—the portrait that comes down to us is of a cold and somewhat androgynous little devil. He distrusted the embryonic industrial capitalism of his time and advocated price controls to stop inflation. Although he was basically a social democrat, he's best remembered for his work on the notorious Committee of Public Safety. His conscience, like Debord's, felt free to judge.

Chapter Seven

The year 1953 began with devastating floods in the Netherlands. It was also the year Stalin died, succeeded first by Malenkov, then (after Minister of Internal Affairs Beria was shot as a traitor) by Khrushchev as first secretary of the Communist

Party. In what was perhaps the biggest foreign policy disaster of the century, the United States used its C.I.A. to restore the Shah to power in Iran. As a precursor of future trends, *Playboy* began publishing, Watson and Crick discovered DNA and the Church of Scientology was founded in Washington, DC. This was also the year that Parisians first encountered television broadcasts.

Issue number three of the *Lettrist International,* August 1953, was typeset in newsprint columns. It featured photographs and was professionally printed. The lead article calls for all revolutionaries to recommence the civil war in Franco's Spain: "The churches that our friends burned in that country that have been rebuilt. The Middle Ages begins at the border, and our silence affirms it." There are reports on two projects that Debord doesn't appear to have realized. The first is a film called *La Belle Jeunesse* (Beautiful Youth). The second is a "three dimensional novel" made out of photos and fragments from journals glued on bottles of rum, "leaving it up to the reader to follow the ideas, the lost thread of a labyrinth of simultaneous anecdotes." But the most striking thing to appear in this issue is Debord's highly characteristic article:

TO PUT AN END TO NIHILISTIC COMFORT
We know that all the new realities are themselves provisional, and too little for us to suffer. We defend them because we don't know anything better to do; and because, in the end, it's our job.

But indifference isn't permitted in the face of the suffocating values of the present when they're guaranteed by a society of prisons and when we live before the doors of prisons.

At no price do we want to participate, to accept keeping quiet, to accept.

It's not out of arrogance that it displeases us to resemble everyone else.

Red wine and negation in cafes, the first truths of despair won't be the end of these lives that are so difficult to defend against the sins of silence, the hundred ways to FALL IN STEP.

Aside from this constantly felt lack, aside from the inevitable and inexcusable loss of everything that we loved, the game is still played. Every form of propaganda will be good.

We promote an insurrection that's important to us, in accordance with our revindications.

We are witness to a certain idea of happiness even if we know it by losing—this idea on which every revolutionary program should be aligned.

"We will not go on crusade," was Michele Bernstein's response in her novel *La Nuit* to Debord's posturing when the Bossuet (1627–1704) side of Debord's Janus face appeared before her. Jacques-Benigne Bossuet was a bishop from Meaux known for his

Lettrist International #3

frequently adopted universal history, astute maxims ("The real goal in politics is to make life easy and people happy") and tributes to the dead. The history that Bossuet created to educate Louis XIVth's son is interesting because of the highly moralistic way Bossuet made comparative portraits of the great figures of history. According to Michele Bernstein, Debord's favorite was Bossuet's *Panegyric of Saint Bernard**:

> Bernard, Bernard, this green youth won't last forever: the fatal hour will come that cuts all false hopes by an irrevocable judgment; life leaves us like a false friend in the

---

* Like Debord, Saint Bernard (1090–1153) wrote some of the most polished prose of his day, and he strived to live an authentic and original life: "What does philosophy matter to me? My masters are the apostles; they didn't teach me to read Plato or untwine the subtleties of Aristotle, they taught me how to live. And, believe me, that is no little knowledge." In 1113, Bernard led thirty of his companions to the gates of Citeaux to live the apostolic life. Like Debord, Bernard is known for his stormy friendships and involvement in the controversies of his time. Bernard was opposed to the radical ideas that flourished in the XIIth Century, and the disastrous Second Crusade he launched was a failed attempt to reverse the radical trends.

midst of our enterprises. The rich of this Earth, who enjoy an agreeable life and imagine themselves to have great advantages, will be astonished to find empty hands.

While Debord and the rest of the L.I. groped for a pure way to live, they in no way shared the Cistercian's asceticism. The L.I. drank in seedy Chez Moineau around the corner from Saint-Germain-des-Pres, a bar which was captured at that time in Ed van der Elsken's photo book *Parijs!* and in his photo-novel *Love on the Left Bank*.

Perhaps the best portrait of the group emerges in the letter from Gil Wolman to Jean-Louis Brau.* The letter, dated July 20, 1953, was sent to Brau in the Sahara:

Jacques-Benigne Bousuet

… just returned! For my part nothing happened in regard to the editor in Algeria. Where was everything when you left? Joel has been out, provisionally, for a while now.

Freedom likewise for Jean-Michel and Fred (car theft—drunk, of course). Eliane, the little one, got out of jail last week after a dramatic arrest in a maid's quarters near Vincennes with Joel and Jean-Michel (must I tell you that they were drunk) refusing to open for the police who came back in force. In the process they lost the L.I. seal. Linda hasn't been sentenced yet—Sarah is still inside but her sister, sixteen and a half, took her place. There were other arrests for drugs, for who knows what, but it's tedious. Then there's G.E. who spent ten days in a sanatorium where they sent him (his parents) after a failed attempt to asphyxiate himself. The day before yesterday I copiously threw up at Moineau's. The latest amusement in the quartier is to spend the night in the catacombs (another discovery by Joel)...

The G.E. was Guy-Ernest Debord. After many months of experiments with various scandals, at twenty-one years of age, Debord attempted suicide by asphyxiation. "Around me, I saw a great many individuals who died young, and not always by suicide,

---

* Brau's Run Comrade, the *Old World is Behind You!* is indispensable for the history of the L.I.

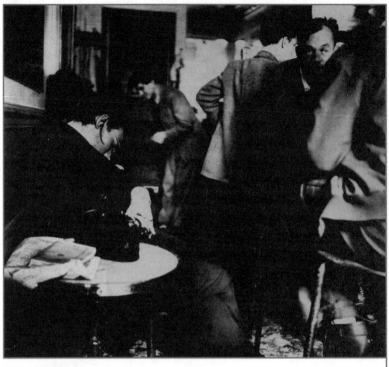

Chez Moineau

as frequent as that was," as Debord later recalled in his *Panegyric*. It's not fair to speculate on this attempted suicide. All we know is that he survived his passions, but he didn't give them up; and as we will see, he continued to pursue them insatiably.

Chapter Eight

In October 1953, Ivan Chtcheglov, aka Gilles Ivain, presented his "Formulary for a New Urbanism" to his fellow members of the Lettrist International. It's hard to underestimate the importance of this essay on Debord and his circle. In *In Girum Imus Nocte et Consumimur Igni* Debord spoke of Chtcheglov in these words:

> But can I ever forget he who I see everywhere in the greatest moments of our adventures; he who, in those uncertain days opened up a new road and hastened there so quickly, choosing those who could come—for no-one else was his equal that year? It had been said that merely by looking at towns and at life, they were transformed. He discovered in one year subject matter for demands for a whole century; the depths and mysteries of urban space were his conquests.

Half-poetry, the remainder a mix of art, architecture and city planning critique, Chtcheglov's essay would inspire the Dutch Situationist Constant and others to try to create a "unitary urbanism." Unitary urbanism was defined as, "The theory of the combined use of arts and techniques for the integral construction of a milieu in dynamic relation with experiments in behavior." More than any other Situationist, Chtcheglov and his short essay continue to inspire people to drift* through city streets. Although he didn't come up with the term "psycho-geography,"** Chtcheglov's name is associated with the earliest legends of this strategy. I'll explain why below, but first, a taste of the essay that ultimately led the author to the sanitarium.

Formulary for a New Urbanism
Sire, I'm from the other country
We're bored in the city. There's no longer a Temple of the Sun. Between the legs of the women walking by, the Dadaists imagined a monkey wrench and the Surrealists a crystal cup. That's lost. We know how to read every promise in faces— the latest stage of morphology. The poetry of the billboards lasted twenty years. We're bored in the city. We really have to strain to still discover mysteries on the sidewalk billboards. The latest state of humor and poetry:

    Show-bath of the Patriarches
    Meat Cutting Machines
    Notre-Dame Zoo
    Sports Pharmacy
    Translucent Concrete
    Golden Touch Sawmill
    Center for Functional Recuperation
    Sainte-Anne Ambulance

---

*   *dérive,* in French, "a mode of experimental behavior linked to the conditions of urban society: a technique of transient passage through varied ambiances."

** "the study of the specific effects of the geographical environment, consciously organized or not, on the emotions and behavior of individuals."

Cafe Fifth Avenue
Prolonged Volunteers Street
Family Boarding House in the Garden
Hotel of Strangers
Wild Street

And the swimming pool on the Street of Little Girls. And the police station on Rendezvous Street. The medical-surgical clinic and the free placement center on the Quai des Orfevres. The artificial flowers on Sun Street. The Castle Cellars Hotel, the Ocean Bar and the Coming and Going Cafe. The Hotel of the Epoch.

And the strange statue of Dr. Philippe Pinel, benefactor of the insane, in the last evenings of summer. To explore Paris.

Pinel, it should be pointed out, wanted to release all those held in insane asylums. I wonder if the last lines weren't added by Debord when the essay was finally published in the *Situationist International* journal in 1957, because, as Debord said in his film *In Girum...* (a film that made use of footage originally intended for a film on Chtcheglov): "The finest player of us all was lost in the forests of madness." Debord added, "There is no greater madness than the present organization of life." Depicting Chtcheglov as Prince Valiant and King Ludwig II (the Bavarian castle builder who inspired the Disney castle), Debord states: "The powers that be, with their paltry falsified information—which misleads them almost as much as it numbs those under their administration—have not yet been able to calculate what the rapid passage of this man has cost them. But what does it matter? Shipwreckers have their name writ only in water."

Chtcheglov was a wildman, a transplanted Russian who was once arrested with dynamite, threatening to blow up the Eiffel Tower because a light on it kept him awake. He drifted for months on end, filtering his visions of Paris through Chirico paintings and eclectic mythologies. He was eventually excluded from the L.I. in a purge of the "old guard." The reasons given for Chtcheglov's exclusion were "mythomania, delirium and lack of revolutionary consciousness," but he was made a founding member of the Situationist International "from afar." Michele Bernstein described it to Greil Marcus:

He went mad. But he was not mad. He had been excluded—he was convinced the Dalai Lama was controlling what was happening to us. And then, one day, he had a fight with his wife. He broke up a cafe, smashed everything. His wife—who was a filthy swine—called the police. She called an ambulance. Because she was his wife, she was able to commit him. He was taken away to an institution, and given insulin shock. And electroshock. After that, he was mad. Guy and I went to visit him: he was eating with his hands, with saliva dripping from his mouth. He was mad—the way you know when someone is mad. The letters he wrote to us were babble. And he is still there, if he isn't dead. He was very shortly sent to a halfway house, where he had freedom, where he could come and go. But he'd developed the disease where he couldn't live outside the asylum.

Chtcheglov's seminal "Formulary For A New Urbanism" follows this call to "explore Paris" by expressing the desperation and hazards of this sort of adventure:

… stranded in the Red Cellars of Pali-Kao, without music, without geography, no longer setting off for the hacienda where the roots think of the child and where the wine is finished off with fables from an old almanac. Now that's finished. You'll never see the hacienda. It doesn't exist. The hacienda must be built.

As a testament to the power of these words, a "Hacienda" was built as a nightclub in Manchester, England by punk/pop impresario Tony Wilson.

Evoking the phenomenon that geographers now call "sequence occupance" (one thing taking the place of another in a given space), Chtcheglov describes the way residues and ghosts of the past alter the perspective of the city. He found fragments of this past in the strange places he discovered on his drifts, and in these fragments he imagined a symbolic urbanism that corresponded to the labyrinth in the Jardin des Plantes, "at the entry to which is written (height of absurdity, Ariadne unemployed): *Games are forbidden in the labyrinth.*"

No enemy of technology per se, Chtcheglov wanted to integrate science and mythology as part of a drive to create a new, mobile civilization that would supersede the "mechanical civilizations and frigid architecture." He proposed a wild architecture that modulated reality and engendered dreams, "producing influences in accordance with the eternal spectrum of human desires." Modify your surroundings in reality and in your dreams, Chtcheglov tells us, and you can modify your life. He envisioned these modifications to be continuous, based on the way relativity operates in the modern mind. Many of the lines in his essay are priceless:

Dancers at The Hacienda nightclub in 1996

A mental disease has swept the planet: banalization. [...]

Presented with the alternative of love or a garbage disposal unit, young people of all countries have chosen the garbage disposal unit. It has become essential to bring about a complete spiritual transformation by bringing to light forgotten desires and by creating new ones. And by carrying out an intensive propaganda in favor of these desires.

Whereas Chtcheglov was more critical of Chirico when he was writing from the asylum, he made it clear in his now legendary "formulary" that he borrowed Chirico's method of using psychological obsessions to give a strange perspective to painting the

Chirico

streets and plazas of Italian cities. Chtcheglov had surely read Chirico's novel *Hebdomeros,* which traces the artist's psychological adventure with absences and presences in time and space. Chtcheglov wanted to take Chirico off the museum walls and inflict these "blueprints" on the masses so, as Chtcheglov wrote in another one of his often-quoted lines, "Everyone will live in his own personal 'cathedral'..." We find traces of Fourier's "harmony of the passions" and Huizinga's championing of play in this new city that would have Bizarre, Happy, Tragic, Historical, Useful and Sinister districts. "Perhaps also a Death Quarter, not for dying in, but so as to have somewhere to *live in peace,* and I'm

thinking here of Mexico and of a principle of cruelty in innocence that appeals to me more every day."

Chapter Nine

The crucial 1952–1953 period of Debord's life is best presented in *Memoires,* a work that was not published until 1959. What are *Memoires?* They are pages comprised of plates of phrases, photos, drawings and cartoons that Debord cut out of other works, and then pasted up in a randomly suggestive manner. Debord then had his comrade and friend, the Danish artist Asger Jorn (1914–1973), taint these "prefabricated elements" with paint. The colors suggest possible readings of the phrases or simply lend a mood to the images. These plates were then bound in sandpaper to destroy any other books it came into contact with—Debord calls them an anti-book.

Debord's relationship with Jorn will be discussed in greater detail below. Here, it's important to note that the book was published at Jorn's expense and given away as a sumptuous gift to friends. In 1993, the book was reprinted by Éditions Les Belles Lettres—Debord added the following attestation: "The rare works of my youth were specialized. One must admit that a taste for generalized negation unified them. It was in great harmony with the life that we lived." Readers of French will certainly experience something of a dreamlike sensation, like the memory of a memory, when they spend an hour or so absorbing the book. The phrases reproduced below are in order, but abridged to provide a concise, but hopefully still evocative, reading of the book:

JUNE 1952
"Let the dead bury the dead, and pity them... Our kind will be the first to enter into a new life while still alive." Marx Letter to Ruge

A memory of you? Yes, I want

This curious system of narrative

It's about a subject deeply impregnated with alcohol

Of course, I'll agitate events and express considerations

But the originality of man, until now, was his possession of a rapid access memory

What are you thinking about?

I found the breasts of Barbara

She was sixteen

The erotic frenzy mined the bases of the established order

The wine of life is poured, and only the dregs remain in this pompous cellar

Extraordinarily correct tone for speaking about this life

All the elements of an American detective novel were found there—violence, sexuality, cruelty, but the scene

Who has made, in so few images, a more beautiful poem of solitude?

DECEMBER 1952
"Every era aspires to a more beautiful world. The more the present is somber and confused, the deeper this desire. During the decline of the Middle Ages, life was full of a somber melancholy..." Huizinga, *The Waning of the Middle Ages*

At the time I'm speaking

It's too late

She smiled at me and next to hers was the smile of Colgate toothpaste

Everyone's a genius at twenty

There's some wine left

The night and the snow

The deserted quais

Not drunk at the moment

Drinking

SEPTEMBER 1953
"How bad! and who can one trust? Dare I say ardor, good will and good disposition were on our side. But in half an hour, the maneouvers of the Prussian king made the cavalry and infantry yield; all were taken back without running away, but without ever looking back..." Soubise Letter to Choiseul

In the streets of Paris a new power was formed that didn't exist the previous century

The apparition of drifters

The freedom of movement of groups that formed and disbanded and therefore couldn't follow another itinerary

In an adventure of such a span it would be ridiculous to fix any priorities

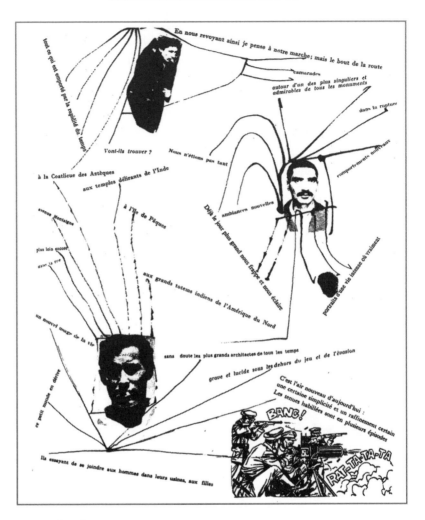

Help to create a situation

A new use of life

The art of parties

The history of the North-West Passage. A long march

We lived very quickly

On condition of not letting oneself be duped by the illusory understanding that memory gives us, this quest can't be in vain

Naturally one has understood that these ambiguites don't owe anything to psychology, they're born in the interferences of situations

A floating city

It's a game of life and place

An opinion expressed on the walls of Paris annonces the ephemeral passage

Spectacle without any well-defined specialty other than scandals

A new current takes us a little to the left

The situation of this castle is charming

The double game of comedy and drama, of drama and entertainment, all that Nothing stops for us. It's the natural state for us, and at the same time, the most against our inclination. We burn with desire to find

The mysterious castle

It's not enough to want to create new cities so that, suddenly, all problems are resolved

In the day-to-day struggle

The stirring accidents

I didn't give all the details because, after all, who can tell everything without suffering mortal boredom

We get back to shore

It seems that important progress was made towards the realization of these dreams

We all seem like travelers who have crossed a very big country

The tide went out

Where will we find ourselves tommorow?

Debord ends the book with the line "I wanted to speak the beautiful language of my century," to which he adds, in his 1993 preface, "I didn't perform so much to be listened to." None of the phrases were written by Debord, a decidedly Dadaist strategy. The whole, however, is distinctly his. Many of the motifs—the drinking, the young girls, the drifting, and above all, the refusal to forget his personal history—reappear in later works. It's doubtful that the spirit of adventure of *Memoires* comes across in the reassembled phrases above, but it's that spirit that really animates this early work.

The eyes drift across the page—drawn to splashes of color, images and typefaces—and a feeling of discovery stirs the mind. It's a network of ideas in which lines cross in every direction and give off colors. Turning the page is like turning a blind corner of a desolate, dimly-lit street. Shadows move across the wall, the shadows of Debord's memories. These are the memories of moments that he gave representation to with great pleasure, just knowing that the moment he did so, these fugitive moments would be repeated forever. The style reflects an adventurous mind that knew how to explore the immediate terrain in previously unforseen ways. This offhand style also gives the impression that discoveries come entirely by chance. To experience *Memories* is to feel the spark that suddenly zapped Debord in his youth and burned his entire life.

Chapter Ten

In the summer of 1954, the L.I. reappeared after a hiatus with a new publication, *Potlatch*. The name "potlatch" refers to the practice of ruinous gift-giving by northwest Native Americans. This practice was heralded by sociologist Marcel Mauss in *The Gift*, and then by Georges Bataille (1897–1962), the dissident Surrealist whose theories of excess (*The Accursed Share: Essay On General Economy*) and derision of poetry and work were certainly met with the silent praise by the L.I. partisans. In his time, Marx (1818–1863) had stressed the point that the world was rich, and Bataille was certainly indebted to Marx, but Bataille significantly recast the conception of wealth by focusing on the degree to which consumption and waste correspond to life. The textual evidence tying Bataille to the L.I. isn't very explicit, but I think that it is safe to say that the L.I., and later the S.I., would have had a hard time conceiving of a non-market means of exchange if not for the ground-breaking works of Georges Bataille. The only citation of Bataille in the Situationist International was in a quote from an article on the S.I., but thesis 198 of *Society of the Spectacle* clearly evokes Bataille: "Those who denounce the absurdity or the perils of incitement to waste in the society of economic abundance do not understand the purpose of waste..."

Any discussion of Bataille's possible influence on Debord must look into the Hegel revival in France during the Thirties. It seems that Debord took more from the early commentator and Hegel translator, Jean Hyppolite despite Debord's denunciation of Hyppolite after attending a lecture. Hyppolite's reading of Hegel posited freedom as the reconciliation of man with his destiny in history—life as the "voyage of discovery." For Bataille, the lectures given by Alexandre Kojève (1902–1968) on Hegel at the *Ecole Pratique des Hautes Etudes* were of supreme importance. Although Kojève was a Marxist-Existentialist who read into Hegel the progression from the master-slave dialectic to free workers, Kojève didn't distance himself from Hegel's "satisfaction" (with Napoleon as the ideal of self-conscious Man) enough for Bataille's taste. For Bataille, the fundamental point of departure was "dissatisfaction," which made Bataille a dissident Kojèvian, but a Kojèvian nonetheless. Without going into too much detail, Bataille's basic anthropology was indebted to Kojève's reading of Hegel that equated every action with negation—without it Bataille would not have been able to reverse the common perspective on waste, a reversal of perspective that equates life with consumption in his influential *The Accursed Share.*

The accursed share is the waste that is given off by every gesture, by every act of negation, such as eating. By eating, life is destroyed, but life is also affirmed because what is consumed engenders life in the form of the growth of new cells. Once excrement is factored into this equation, it becomes clear that the sum of energy produced by an organism is always more than that needed to maintain the life of the organism. In other words, there exists a superabundance of energy in the world that is wasted in superfluous ways. Plants wouldn't grow if they didn't have more energy than they needed. All claims of scarcity are refuted by the superabundance of life and energy on the planet. In Bataille's schema, the role of humans is to consume more of the excess energy from the sun that hits the planet than other animals. Extravagant gifts, death, festivals, wars and revolutions are some of the majestic and glorious ways this excess energy can be squandered. As I will show below, Debord drew on other Hegelian interpretations to develop his own reading of Hegel. But it is unlikely Debord and his cohorts would've been able to conceive of their post-workerist Marxism, or "consumer communism" without Bataille's study. Without explicitly acknowledging Bataille, Debord clearly applied non-scarcity economics to the theories of the French New Left and Hungarian Marxists.

It's best to resist any attempt to make a correlation between Bataille's groups, the Acephale (a semi-secret avant-garde bent on human sacrifice) and the College of Sociology (public readings of scholarly speeches), and Debord's L.I. and S.I. The prevalence of mysticism and "the sacred" in Bataille's groups engendered the type of thinking eschewed by Debord, and the exclusion of the likes of Chtcheglov and Berna demonstrates this very conclusively. The *internationale* of the L.I. and the S.I. attests to their links with the anarcho-communist worker groups of the past, but Marx's one time Jewishness, and Bakunin's relationship with the Masons meant little to the L.I. and S.I. It must be stated here that Debord was very conscious of the historical antecedents of the quest of a millenarian utopia, such as the heretical sects of the middle ages, and while he may have mimicked aspects of their efforts to punch a hole in history with a social revolution, he took great pains to highlight the mystical flaws of these movements. Yet unlike those who would only comment on communities, such as the cloistered academics of the Frankfurt School, both Bataille and Debord had actual experience with the freedoms and

Georges Bataille

forms of soveriegnty found in these closed communities.

The strongest link between Bataille and Debord is Isidore Ducasse, aka Comte de Lautreamont (1846–1870), the author of the infamous *Maldoror and Poems*. Heralded as one of the first Surrealist books, *Maldoror* has been called an "oceanic text," a "frenetic monologue," infantile, brilliant, a work of genius and above all EVIL. In his preface to *Literature and Evil,* Georges Bataille gives the following interpretation of the genre:

> Literature is either the essential or nothing. I believe that Evil—an acute form of Evil—which it expresses, has a sovereign value for us. But this concept does not exclude morality: on the contrary, it demands a 'hypermorality.'
>
> Literature is communication. Communication requires loyalty. A rigorous morality results from complicity in the knowledge of Evil, which is the basis of intense communication.

Literature is not innocent. It is guilty and should admit it. Action alone has its rights, its prerogatives. I wanted to prove that literature is a return to childhood. But does the childhood that governs literature have a truth of its own? Kafka's honesty, which abrogates no rights for itself. Whatever the lesson contained in Genet's books, Sartre's defense is inadmissible. Literature had to plead guilty.[1]

NOTES

1. I have omitted from this collection a study on *Les Chants de Maldoror* which stood so well on its own that it seemed superfluous. There is hardly any point in my saying that Lautreamont's poetry corresponds to my theories. Are his poems not literature pleading guilty? They baffle us, but if they can be understood it is surely in the light of my interpretation.

Like the Surrealists before him, the young Debord was drawn to this supreme practitioner of the literature of evil and adopted his method of plagiarism. In the incomparable Comte de Lautréamont's own words: "Words expressing evil are destined to take on a more positive meaning. Ideas improve. The meaning of words takes part in this process. *Plagiarism is necessary. Progress implies it."* Debord rediscovered and amplified Lautreamont's method of *détournement* (diverting an existing phrase by changing or adding a few choice words), using texts by Hegel, Freud, the civil code, science fiction novels as well as comics and films. The astonishing hubris of these appropriations elicited charges of megalomania, which Debord and his cohorts shamelessly accepted with equal arrogance. The opening line of *Society of the Spectacle,* for example, diverts the opening lines of Marx's *Capital:* "All life in societies under the reign of modern conditions of production displays itself as an immense accumulation of *spectacles."*

Debord states that the most beautiful thing he ever saw was a close-cutting bolt of lightning; in the realm of the arts, Lautreamont's collection of *Poems* was the only thing that even came close to lightning. Debord's affinity with the enigmatic author of *Maldoror* and *Poems* (and the grandfather of *détournement*) is evoked in this telling quote from *Panegyric:* "I would've had few illnesses if alcohol hadn't eventually brought me some: from insomnia to vertigo by way of gout. 'Beautiful, like the trembling of hands in alcoholism,' said Lautréamont. There are mornings that are stirring, but difficult."

Chapter Eleven

The rules of engagement of *Potlatch,* "the most engaged publication in the world," were:

If you believe you have
GENIUS
or if you think you have only
A BRILLIANT INTELLIGENCE
write the Lettrist International

Potlatch was the L.I.'s way of "breaking the circuit" of normative thought "when and where it wanted." These street sheets were passed out around L.I. haunts, such as place de la Contrescarpe, a zone that Chtcheglov had psychogeographically transformed into "Continent Contrescarpe" in January of 1954 (a zone encompassing much of the 5th district of Paris). The L.I. also sent *Potlatch* to people chosen arbitrarily out of the phone book and to people they thought would least want to receive it. This cultural work for the creation of a new civilization was facilitated by the now notorious Anti-Copyright: "All texts published in *Potlatch* can be reproduced, adapted or quoted without any mention of the source."

As *Potlatch* picked up steam in 1954, the editors came up with a column called "The Best News of the Week," which reported what was of interest in the daily newspapers, ironic and otherwise, to the members of the Lettrist International. As would be expected, there were notices of strikes in Tokyo and West Germany, and the uprising in Tunisia. After the Vietnamese Spring Offensive in Dien Bien Phu, the *Potlatch* staff was amused when Vice President Nixon conceded that "a bowl full of rice" won't stop people from becoming communists. The only "Best News of the Month" column was on a collective, and violent, "riot to laugh" in Stockholm.

Perhaps the strangest correspondence made in "The Best News of the Week" was the declaration that "The Cathars Were Right" when reprinting an article on American scientists' discovery of the anti-proton. This ironic affirmation of the Cathars' heretical theology of the coexistence of a good god and a bad god (the Demiurge), was a joke. But it was a serious joke that confirmed the L.I.'s use of negation as their moving principle. While the L.I. by no means shared the absolute asceticism of the Cathars, the L.I. shared the "The Cathar desire for the annihilation of the earth that expressed a refusal of life degraded to mere survival, a refusal that the Cathar religiosity condemned to self-destruction," as Raoul Vaneigem put it in *The Movement of the Free Spirit*. And while the Cathars practiced suicide by starvation as a theological imperative to deprive this degraded life of its substance, Debord and the L.I. were more likely to starve because they were the anti-matter of productive society. In reality, the L.I. were more like Vaneigem's beloved Brethren of the Free Spirit, a movement that Norman Cohn labeled "an elite of amoral supermen" in his widely read *The Pursuit of the Millennium*. Both the Free Spirit and the L.I. were bands of revolutionary antinomian marginals who trusted their senses and didn't refuse the pleasures of the world. It should be noted that Cohn's brandishing of peasants who participated in these neo-Manichaen sects as "proto-Nazis" is as erroneous as those who would smear Debord and the Situationists with the jeer "neo-Nazi." Mani was a IIIrd Century Persian magician who, when he converted to Christianity, sought to synthesize it with the dualism of his native Zoroastrianism. The Manichaean doctrine of illumination and suffering eventually spread to Europe via the Balkan Bogomil sect to southern Gaul. Pope Innocent III (1160–1216) was so concerned with neo-Manichaean groups like the Cathars, Humiliati and Albigensians that he sponsored the Franciscan order to lure away their recruits. Then, in very Nazi-like fashion, the Pope launched a crusade (1209) that eliminated the heretical sects. While Debord's thought can be considered Manichaean in the black and white duality of spectacle and life, Debord explicitly eschewed any "obscene declarations of mysticism and Christianity" and he insulted people for being "deist," or "crypto-Catholic," or "a messmate of God," or again "a Christian astronaut."

Debord agreed with Marx when he wrote,

> The criticism of religion is the prerequisite of all criticism. Where he sought a superman in the fantastic reality of heaven, man only found the reflection of himself and he is no longer satisfied to find the mere appearance of himself... This state and this society produce religion, which is an inverted consciousness of the world... The call for the abolition of religion's illusory happiness is the demand for real happiness. To call on the people to give up their illusions about their condition is to call on them to give up a condition that requires illusions. The criticism of religion is, in embryo, the criticism of the valley of tears that has religion as its halo.

In "Waiting for the Closure of Churches," the L.I. protested the pyschogeographic effects of using the word "saint" and other religious names on streets. But in agreement with the Cathars, the L.I. was against "The Minimum for Life." Taking the ultra-left stance against unions, Debord and the L.I. protested that unions never took the totality of workers lives into account, that workers experienced few joys and never knew the pleasure of taking up arms to break their chains. The minimum to maintain life was demanding much too little:

> Don't talk about possible understandings, but unacceptable realities. Ask the Algerian workers of Regie Renault where's their leisure, their country, their women? Ask them what they can hope for? The social struggle can't be bureaucratic, only passionate. To judge the disastrous results of professional unions, it suffices to analyze the spontaneous strikes of August 1953; the resolution of the base of workers; the sabotage by the cowards of the centralized organization; abandoned

Continental Contrescarpe

by the C.G.T. [trade union federation] that didn't know how to provoke a central strike, nor utilize it victoriously when it came into being. On the contrary, one must be conscious of a few facts that can impassion the debate: the fact, for example, that our friends exist everywhere in the world, and that we will recognize each other in combat. The fact that life goes on, and that we aren't waiting to be compensated outside of what we create for ourselves. It's simply a question of courage.

These were strong words for what was a very reactionary year (1954): the year of a C.I.A.-led coup in Guatemala, the McCarthy hearings: the world's first nuclear power plant began operation in Obninsk while McDonald's began the proliferation that would make it the world's largest food-service chain. French troops were routed in Vietnam in the Dien Bien Phu, and increased their presence in Algeria from 60,000 to 500,000 after the beginning of the insurrection. Mendes-France (1907–1982) came to power to deal with the Algerian crisis, drawing support from the American funded and stylized magazine *L'Express* (where Mauriac and Camus wrote and a Mendes-France promotion was targeted at youth—a "passively fascist" journal according to Michele Bernstein, despite its pretensions of being on the left). By all appearances, the publication of Simone de Beauvoir's *The Mandarins,* marked the apogee of the Sartre legend and notions of "the people" and "praxis" that had been given wide circulation in *Les temps moderns.* But the era of the man in the gray flannel suit, who had made his peace with imperialism and modernization, wouldn't last for long. Debord, for his part, wrote, "Naturally, we don't have a minute to waste reading the novels and romances of this little year 1954. [...] The fear of real questions and a complacency that permeates their intellectual methods, group together all the professional writers, whether they want to be edifying or rebels like Camus. What these men lack is The Terror."

What were the real questions? Leisure. Work. Adventure, and the construction of situations in a permanent free play of passion. The L.I. pursued their quest for this Grail by drifting around Paris, building castles of adventure in their minds and recording their thoughts for *Potlatch.* In the summer of '54, the role of chief editor of the journal went from Andre-Frank Concord (excluded for "neo-boudhism, evangelism, spiritism," he would make a Stalinesque "auto-critique" in issue 12) to Mohamed Dahou at 32 rue de la Montagne Genevieve, a seedy hotel above a bar called the The Golden Cask. In a three-issues-in-one vacation special, the L.I. reported that an empty car barreled down a hill and crashed into the interior of the bar at a high rate of speed: By a "happy chance," no Lettrists were there. Was it a rival gang? An L.I. prank? A police attack? Whatever the case, that address would serve as the headquarters for L.I. and S.I. for many years to come.

With little psychogeographic reports such as "You Take the First Road" by Gil Wolman, or Michele Bernstein's agreement with the idea that all cars other than taxis be banned from the city, it's clear that the group continued to play its psychogeographic games. And in the journal they railed against Corbusier's new white cathedral, Notre Dame du Haut at Ronchamp in insulting terms that defy translation. Naturally, the L.I. despised Corbusier for working on a church, and in a more general sense the group detested the sterility of Corbusier's urbanism. Debord and Jacques Fillon felt, in their "Résumé 1954," that the entire year could be described vis-a-vis drifting: "The big cities are favorable for the diversion that we call *drifting.* *Drifting* is a technique of displacement without end. It's founded on the influence of the decor. All houses are beautiful. Architecture should become *passionate.* [...] Putting a value on leisure isn't a joke. We recall that it's about inventing new games."

No description of Debord's activity in 1954 would be complete, if it didn't include an account of the polemic between the Surrealists and the L.I. It seems that the Surrealists were upset by an incompetent editing job of a special edition of the journal *Drunken Boat* for the centenary of Arthur Rimbaud. They wrote a tract ironically entitled "It Begins Well!" to ridicule the editor's attribution of the first poem in the bulletin to Rimbaud when it was actually a well-known sonnet by someone else. The Surrealists then contacted the Lettrist

International regarding a joint intervention during a centenary ceremony of Rimbaud in Charleville.

Despite their "serious reservations" about these lackeys of the Surrealist movement, the L.I. accepted. Debord and a Surrealist named Legrand wrote a tract together that would appear on the flip side of "It Begins Well!" to be used during the action against the ceremony, which, most repugnantly, was to be held after Sunday mass. A few weeks later, the Surrealists came back, complaining that they couldn't support the following phrase: "in a society founded on class struggle, there can't be any 'impartial' literary criticism. All criticism uses, in one way or another, successive esthetic shakeups to defend the ideology of the dominant class."

The Surrealists didn't like the Marxist tone of the phrase and didn't want to get caught up in a protest that seemed political. This was reported by the L.I. on the flip side of "It Begins Well!" under the title "And It Ends Badly." The L.I. tract also reported that one of the Surrealists claimed that the Marxism in the phrase was dubious. When told that the word "science" had been replaced by "literary criticism" in an article by Lenin, the Surrealists claimed that Lenin wasn't an authority on Marxism.

The L.I. had the good humor to laugh this off, adding that the Surrealists were probably authorities on Surrealism.

Yet another Surrealist doubted the Marxist credentials of the phrase, and Legrand, who wasn't a Marxist, couldn't very well explain how he'd collaborated in writing a Marxist text. The L.I. went on to belittle the way Surrealists lived and to insult his majesty, the king of Surrealism, Andre Breton. Breton responded with a tract that was clandestinely distributed. The L.I. finally caught up with a Surrealist who'd signed the tract. In a little scuffle on the street, the L.I. took a copy and published it in *Potlatch* #14. The Surrealists lamented that the L.I. hooligans were more concerned with their publicity than with the legacy of Rimbaud, and that they weren't loyal to ideas like good Russian revolutionaries. The L.I. was all too happy to print this denunciation of them made by the Surrealists. The ferocity of the L.I. critique of the Surrealists stems from the anxiety of influence; an influence that is seen in their collective existence, internationalism, group proclamations, group photos, manifestos, hatred of work, practice of the drift, anti-bourgeois revolutionary stance, etc. Above all, it was from the Surrealists that Debord learned the lesson of the dangers of having one's works co-opted by bourgeois society.

Chapter Twelve

Members of the L.I. created collages, or *metagraphies* as they were called in Lettrist parlance, such as Debord's "Time Passes, and In Effect, We Pass With It." This work evoked the Spanish Civil War against a background of contemporary events. The title of the work highlights Debord's predilection for works dealing with substantial issues (content over form) and his identification of human life with time. Despite their production of cultural artifacts, Debord went to great pains to remind the readers of *Potlatch* that the L.I. was no mere literary exercise or school of modern art. The L.I. was an experimental form of collective existence that valued its use of time above all else.*

At one point in 1955, the L.I. were to exhibit their collages at galleries in Brussels and Liege as they had in Paris the previous year (not much is written about this exhibit, although Debord sounded fairly Leninist on the flyer: "Nothing is of even momentary interest to us except for its utility in revolutionary *provocation:* what's in play is the seizing of power"). But the Belgian project was rejected when the gallery

---

* The group funded itself by episodically accepting a long list of jobs: "translator, hairdresser, telephone operator, statistician, knitter, receptionist, boxer, free-lance writer, real estate agent, dishwasher, salesperson, letter carrier, African game hunter, typist, cinematographer, tutor, unskilled laborer, secretary, butcher, bartender, sardine packer."

owner wouldn't grant the L.I.'s wish to print another typically outrageous text on the invitations. The correspondence between the Lettrists and the gallery owner ended up with Debord calling him "stupid" and "snotty"; this prompted the gallery owner to run to the French embassy over the broken contract.

For the most part, Debord and the L.I. "intensively pursued their psychogeographic research" in the streets. Their "Project for Rational Embellishments of the City of Paris" (diverting the Surrealists' "irrational embellishments") called for opening the metro all night and connecting the rooftops with bridges and opening them for strolls. Regarding the treatment of churches, Debord was for "the total destruction of religious buildings of all faiths." The group was against cemeteries and all traces of cadavers. They didn't care much for museums—the artistic masterpieces could just as well be hung in bars. They thought it would be a good idea to have free access to prisons, so that tourists could visit them. And the L.I. wanted all the monuments and dirty street names removed from the city. In the middle of what is sometimes referred to as the second French Revolution (the inundation of washing machines, the doubling of electric use, the explosion of cheap suburban housing, etc.) these Lettrist embellishments were rational attacks on the past and present—imbued with revolutionary passion.

Over the course of 1955, Debord turned his attention to theory in a series of essays—"The Big Sleep and its Clients," "Architecture and Play," "The Last Days of Pompei" (with Mohamed Dahou), "Why Lettrism?" (with Gil Wolman); and the unsigned L.I. collaboration "Intelligent Panorama of the Avant-Garde at the End of 1955." All of these essays appeared in *Potlatch*. In a rare collaboration, members of the L.I. contributed to the Belgian Surrealist journal *Naked Lips*—that year Debord chipped in "Introduction to a Critique of Urban Geography." He also scripted and produced a cassette recording for radio entitled *The Value of Education* in which four voices exchanged a dialogue composed of diverted phrases.*

In "The Big Sleep and its Clients," Debord displays dissatisfaction with the artistic products of the isolated intellectuals who wanted to be experimental. Dada had served its purpose, in its time, but the repetition of Dada gestures was now simply the repetition of a form of art that attracted university kids and granted a little celebrity to the perpetrators. Debord pointed out that most insults directed at art entailed contradictions, such as aesthetic values against ugliness or economic class solidarity:

---

* These phrases originally appeared in the following works: *Panegyric for Bernard of Clairvaux* by Bossuet, *General Geography* by Demangeon and Meynier, *France-Soir* of November 5, 1954, The Books of Jeremiah, Psalms and Samuel, *The Communist Manifesto* by Marx and Engles and *Reports and Speeches at the Convention* by Saint-Just.

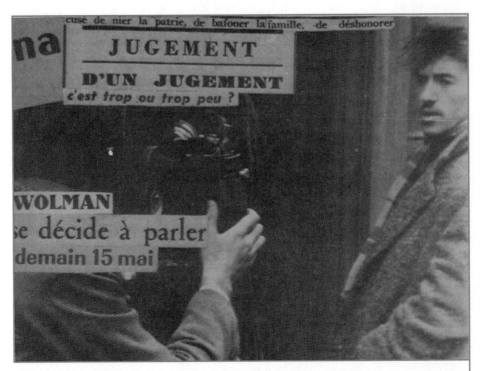

Portrait of Gil Wolman by G.E. Debord, February 1954

The generation of Freud and the Dada movement contributed to the entrench-
ment of a psychology and morality that are condemned by the contradictions of
the moment. This generation didn't leave anything behind other than the styles
that some would like to believe are definitive.

Debord was holding out for new states of being, for the discovery of "superior
desires" that would be so attractive as to devalue the realization of other works of art
and necessarily lead to the conscious realization of situations.

On the face of it, this invention of new desires seems a little out of step with what
was happening around the world. The Warsaw Pact was formed in 1955. Mao's rapid
collectivization of Chinese agriculture resulted in the liquidation of the peasants who
resisted, peasants who had been the backbone of the revolution. France deployed
troops in the civil war in Vietnam—the Republic of South Vietnam was proclaimed
and the country divided along the 17th parallel. The Sultan of Morocco returned home
and moves were made for independence from France as a huge national debate erupted over France's "pacification" policy in Algeria. All this repression and imperialism
going on, and Guy wants to discover new desires (albeit on a revolutionary scale).

Although Debord would later take great pride in being out of step with his times, there is an uncanny coincidence between the publication of his essay "Architecture and Play" that discussed the famous castles of a deranged Bavarian king and the opening of Disneyland in Anaheim, California. Indeed, the essay is illustrated by a photo of Debord's comrade Jacques Fillon in the Ideal Palace. For Debord, however, the best coincidence (and no mere question of chance) was the existence of a bar named The End of the World near rue Mouffetard: "Beautiful adventures, as they say, can only find their origin and framework in beautiful districts." According to Debord, Lettrist International theories on architecture and drifting were based on the passion for play; and he ends his essay (after evoking Huizinga's famous essay on play) by stating that the rules of the game should progress from being arbitrary, to a *moral* foundation.

Another *Potlatch* essay of 1955, "The Last Days of Pompei" is an attack on an article dealing with the exposition of Gaulic money at the Pedagogic Museum. Debord and Dahou aren't content with any school of art (primitive, modern, classical, socialist realist, traditionalist, irrealist) or any bourgeoise critique, left or right. They recall that the last time they went into the Pedagogic Museum was in 1952 to interrupt the Congress of Youth Poetry, "the last such exhibition in Paris, as far as we

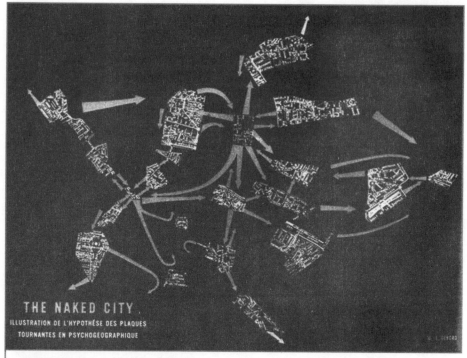

THE NAKED CITY,
ILLUSTRATION DE L'HYPOTHÉSE DES PLAQUES
TOURNANTES EN PSYCHOGÉOGRAPHIQUE

Debord's *The Naked City*, reversed out after the cover of the *S.I. Anthology* by Ken Knabb

know, and several police cars were called in the direction of the museum to defend the Youth Poetry against our critique." Perhaps Debord felt compelled to recall this incident because in 1955, beat poet Allen Ginsberg read his *Howl* to widespread underground acclaim. As Debord wrote elsewhere, "The watchdogs are united in howling to death."

"Why Lettrism?" is as much a long look back as "Intelligent Panorama of the Avant-Garde at the End of 1955" is a sweeping survey of the present. The two essays give the L.I. a definitive sense of what was, and what is (so as to anticipate what would be and therefore live up to their avant-garde claims). Needless to say, capital-

Guy Debord

ist literature and the false avant-garde of formalism (abstract painting at that time) revealed a petite-bourgeois mentality to Debord and Wolman, which provides a partial answer to the question "Why Lettrism?" They also answer this question with another question: "Baseball or automatic writing—why do it?" And in answering this question, the authors make it clear that all success must be measured against something that makes the earth shake, like revolution. Anything less is a failure.

Debord and Wolman took pride in having taken a measure of control over their lives—they no longer practiced bad habits like poetry, or hung out with Surrealists. After citing charges made against them (a tactic Debord would continually deploy), namely that they were "theoreticians animated by the virus of 'supersession,' always for purely verbal effects," the authors replied: "By interdicting the diverse pigs who approach us, and making the confusionist attempt at a 'common action' finish badly (completely lacking indulgence), we prove to these same individuals the necessary existence of the virus in question. But if we're sick, our detractors are dead." As for the exclusions in the L.I.: "It's better to change friends than ideas."

The "Intelligent Panorama of the Avant-Garde at the End of 1955" treats (however briefly, dismissively or provocatively) urbanism, poetry, exploration, cinema, philosophy, plastic arts, politics, propaganda, literature, etc. Undoubtedly, the most interesting aspect of the essay fell under the rubric "Educational Games," namely ideological boxing—two contestants square off over a theme like Zen or the New Left and have at it. Although extra points are given for insults, an umpire makes sure that one contestant doesn't interrupt the other and a clock signals the end of a round.

During a break, fans bring their contestant booze or coffee or, "in certain cases," drugs. A "K.O." is proclaimed by the judge when one of the contestants is so disconcerted by the violence of the game that he or she can't follow the discussion. If there's no K.O., the winner is decided on points.

"Introduction to a Critique of Urban Geography," which appeared in *Naked Lips* #6, is one of Debord's more elegant early essays. As the title suggests, Debord points to the synthesizing science of geography as a research framework for a new lifestyle. He begins by pointing out that geography deals with the material conditions that sustain life, be they the composition of soil or climate, etc., and their relationship with the economic structure of a given society. Psychogeography (a term coined by an illiterate Algerian in 1953), is the study of "the exact laws and precise effects of a geographic milieu, consciously arranged or not, acting directly on the behavior of individuals." The adjective "psychogeographic" pertains to the application of these studies and their results on human emotions, and to any situation that "reveals the same spirit of discovery." By way of example, Debord writes that if monotheism is a desert, the Continental Contrescarpe (the area in the 5th district of Paris around place de la Contrescarpe) is more inclined to "atheism, forgetting and the disorientation of habitual reflexes." He also mentions other entrenched zones of psychic climates—happy and sad districts that might not have anything to do with rich and poor sectors of a city.

Debord scoffs at the idea that creative urban planning entails moving more cars more quickly through the city. He would, to his dismay, live to see this goal pursued to such a degree that the previously luxurious 6th district was reduced to omnipresent parade of cars billowing out their nauseating smoke. Yet it was already apparent to Debord that cars and Coca-Cola were very meager symbols of privilege, and he said so. His stated goal was to systematically refine his provocations (provocations in the form of propositions), so as to turn life into a passionate game. These propositions would challenge people to use the wealth of the world to surpass the decaying social organization. He valued what could be diverted into the creation of ambiances that supported this end, and he called for the depreciation of everything else. The difficulty, as he foresaw it, wasn't one of sufficient abundance to transform the world, but to bring enough "serious seduction" to bear in his apparently delirious propositions. To satisfy this quantitative need, he called for using all means of communications to "throw a mass of desires on the market," and also to use "a sort of boisterous abstention" to expose "the radical deception of the amateurs who use these same means of communication." This, he calculated, would promote an "uneasy atmosphere favorable to the introduction of a few new notions of pleasure."

What did he mean by "a few new notions of pleasure"? The example he gave was a bad joke from the first *Potlatch:*

Choose a country, city and street. Build a house, furnish and decorate it. Choose the season and time. Bring some people together with alcohol and music. The lighting and conversation should be circumstantial, like the climate outside or your memories. If our calculations are correct, you should be satisfied with the results.

After evoking Chtcheglov's beloved Chirico and other artists who created a visual transformation of the cityscape, Debord argues that "new beauty can only be the beauty of situations." Psychogeographic maps (see *Naked City* above) were how Debord chose to represent these possibilities, "to clarify certain non-gratuitous displacements to promote a perfect lack of submission to habitual solicitations—the solicitations of this series being catalogued under the term of tourism, the popular drug that is as repugnant as sports or buying on credit." Debord didn't think much of a friend of his using a map of London to lose his way in Hartz, Germany even though this did correspond somewhat to the sort of displacement Debord had in mind. He was much more in favor of the idea proposed by the editor of *Naked Lips* to take all the equestrian statues and put them on a desert plane. This was intended to recreate a cavalry charge dedicated to the big massacres in history, and to educate the young.

Debord begins to wind up "Critique of Urban Geography" with a quote: "'The imaginary is that which tends to become real,' an author wrote, who, because of his notorious misconduct, I've since forgotten his name." Readers familiar with the events of May '68 might recognize the kernels of slogans such as "The Imagination To Power," or "I take my desires for reality because I believe in the reality of my desires" in the phrase Debord quotes. This might be reaching, and I'm not saying that Debord penned the later phrases, but there's no disputing the fact that Debord's propositions would have great influence on the realities of '68, if not on the realities of the mid-50s when the horrors of French imperialism and the sterility of modernization that left nothing to the imagination. Debord concluded:

No year goes by when people we liked, not understanding the present possibilities, succumb to some gaudy capitulation. But they don't reinforce the enemy camp that already includes millions of imbeciles, and where one is objectively condemned to be an imbecile. The first moral deficiency remains indulgence in all its forms.

Chapter Thirteen

During the Autumn of 1955, Alexander Trocchi (1925–1984) resigned as the editor of the Paris-based, English language journal *Merlin* to join the Lettrist International. Trocchi was six years older than Debord, and had spent a few years of WWII as a seaman, eventually becoming an officer, escorting arctic convoys to

Murmansk. He was tall, striking—often described as being imposing with his big nose and sunken eyes. Women reportedly loved Trocchi and he'd already married and abandoned his wife and daughters when he joined the L.I. One of Trocchi's poet friends in Paris said that he had, "a face comparable to Burt Lancaster's, a man full of worldly confidence." Debord may have seen something of his Dada boxer-poet hero Arthur Craven in Trocchi. As he edited the influential avant-garde journal *Merlin,* Trocchi cultivated a coterie of English, American, Canadian and South African poets with his trademark charm, guile and bluster. His friends included Henry Miller, Samuel Beckett, Robert Creeley, Eugene Ionesco, George Plimpton, John P. Marquand Jr. and Pablo Neruda. Debord knew that it took all types of people to change the world, and Trocchi was just the sort of shameless adventurer Debord wanted. But Debord had one very severe condition—Trocchi had to break with all his former colleagues and friends to join the L.I.

Alexander Trocchi

As the editor of *Merlin,* Trocchi had befriended Sartre and received permission to reprint anything he wanted from *Les Temps Modern.* His editorial perspective is summed up as follows:

> Some ways of talking about literature are more useful than other ways of talking about literature. All ways of talking involve the use of distinctions. That is alright so long as those distinctions are not allowed to harden, that is to say, if we abandon them as soon as they cease to be useful. Most of the traditional categories are merely distinctions, hallowed by antiquity, which have been allowed to harden, and which, in the hands of unscience, have become an inquisitorial rack to which the flesh of contemporary writing is to be twisted. James Joyce's *Ulysses* broke one rack for the intelligent; they saw that it did not amount to much to say that it was not a novel, the significant point being that it was obviously a great work of genius... Since then there have been other instances of rack-breaking; instances, but the principle does not appear to have been grasped, even by the intelligent reading public. That principle may be stated simply: all categories are utilitarian; when they cease to be recognized as such, they become obnoxious.

Trocchi, of course, took his own stabs at breaking the rack. He is perhaps best known for his junkie journal *Cain's Book* (Grove, 1960), which he wrote while tending a barge in New York. The book made him something of an underground cult figure. His grisly first novel, *Young Adam* (another tale set on a barge), and his Olympia Press porn novels *Thongs, White Thighs, Helen & Desire, The Carnal Days of Helen Seferis, School for Sin,* and his ghost-written Volume V of Frank Harris' *My Life and Loves* have been put out in the United States in inexpensive editions by Masquerade Books. His *Sappho of Lesbos* is much harder to find, but the collection *Writers in Revolt,* that he edited with Terry Southern, and his translation (with R.E. Wyngaard) of *I, Jan Cremer* can be found in the bargain bins of many used book stores. His affinity with Debord is seen in the title of his poetry collection: *Man at Leisure.*

Debord may also have been impressed with the "experimental" behavior Trocchi had been engaged in as the raw material for his porn novels. As Andrew Murray Scott reports in *Alexander Trocchi: The Making of the Monster,* Trocchi was infamous for having sex with a prostitute in front of his female companion, and bedding the wife of a friend and then the young clerk of the English Bookshop. Trocchi actually trained groups of married women on the finer points of sex, correcting their technique with a ruler. Scott describes the incredible scene that developed at the Bal de Quat'zarts of French art students:

A traditional feature was 'le spectacle' for which each of the students' studios competed for a prize, awarded to the most spectacular. The first 'spectacle' in 1954 consisted of a spread-eagled naked girl, painted entirely blue, suspended apparently effortlessly in mid-air. But the studio which had invited the *Merlin* group had nothing prepared for their 'spectacle' and it looked as though the spotlight, when it moved in their direction, would illuminate an empty balcony. On discovering this embarrassing situation, with about ten minutes in hand, Alex announced that his group would put on a spectacle on their behalf, and one which would probably win the prize. This came as news to his friends. His idea was that Jane and he would engage in the act of sexual intercourse—naked—on the balcony while the others, like harem eunuches, fanned the lovers with sheafs of straw. This was an outrageous idea, and daring, but carried away by the loud music and the atmosphere of the event, the others readily agreed. Jane sped up the narrow stairs to the balcony. Alex took a preparatory swig from a wine bottle and prepared to join her. Unfortunately, in his haste, he knocked his head against the underside of the balcony and tumbled back down the stairs. He was out cold. Meanwhile, Jane, in the balcony was ready and was calling for him. The spotlight was just veering in their direction... The tableau it revealed was an enigma which puzzled the audience; the rear-view of a naked woman looking away in expectation, while a single blue figure (Plimpton) languidly fanned her with a single sheaf of straw. No-one could quite comprehend the symbolism. The spotlight lingered, then moved on. When he came round, Alex was furious: 'Why didn't one of you take my place?' he demanded.

According to Scott's biography, Trocchi came into contact with Debord in early 1955, and by Autumn, he would write to his brother: "I reject the entire system... the answer is *revolution*. Not in the objective, idealistic sense, but there in the heart of every man... a new attitude... the Revolution has already taken place in me. I am outside your world and am no longer governed by your laws..." Trocchi had already been shooting heroin on occasion, and began spending most of his time reading in a small rented room, only going out to play pinball and "distract" himself with a woman.

If one reads Trocchi's novel *Cain's Book* for autobiographical details, it seems likely that Trocchi traveled around Europe with Debord's comrade Mohammed Dahou, perhaps dealing hash—this is the portrait that Trocchi painted of the otherwise very obscure figure Dahou:

"Have you heard from that Arab friend of yours?...what was his name?..."

"Midhou," I said. We had taken Alan by bus to Aubervilliers where we knew a Spanish place. It was hidden away in the Spanish slum of Paris near a canal. It was to this district that those who were not poets came over the Pyrenees after the Spanish Civil War.

Midhou was a great smoker of hashish, a troubadour, an Algerian in Paris who ate with his hands. Seated cross-legged on the floor, the snarl of his lips emphasized by his Mexican moustache, he made his hands upwards into claws and spoke of flesh. The heavy brow, the receding forehead, the small, pointed ears, the black eyes of a bird of prey, the foreign words spat from clenched teeth, the claw becoming a fist, becoming a knife, becoming a hand.

"Yeah, I heard he went to Algeria," Alan said.

"I got one postcard," I said. "But I heard indirectly he lost half his face driving a truck into a brick wall in Algiers. There was a police road block. I don't know whether he was carrying guns or hashish."

"Poor guy," Alan said. "Is he all right now?"

"I heard he was. I heard he was back in Paris for a while and was the same as ever. Do you remember his guitar?"

It's hard to say if Debord knew about Trocchi's use of hard drugs when he was an "active, founding member of the Situationist International," because Trocchi was just beginning to use. Although Debord supported Trocchi in his subsequent scraps with the law on drug charges, Debord was later emphatic in his denunciation of *stupefiants,* as they're called in French.

In 1956, Debord traveled to London with Trocchi to show *Howlings in Favor of Sade* at the Institute of Contemporary Arts. Asger Jorn's biographer describes the screening:

> During the final silence of twenty-four minutes, when the only sound in the room was the turning of the reel, a member of the audience got up, thanked Mrs. Morland for an interesting evening and apologized for having to leave early. Everyone else stayed to the end, hoping that a sensational tidbit might still be coming. When the lights went up there was an immediate babble of protest. People stood around and made angry speeches. One man threatened to resign from the I.C.A. unless the money for his ticket was refunded. Another complained that he and his wife had come all the way from Wimbledon and had paid for a baby-sitter, because neither of them wanted to miss the film. These protests were so odd that it was as if Guy Debord himself were present, in his role of Mephistopheles, hypnotizing these ordinary English people into making fools of themselves in public.
>
> The noise from the lecture room was so loud that it reached the next audience, queueing on the stairs for the second house. Those who had just seen the film came out of the auditorium and tried to persuade their friends on the stairs to go home, instead of wasting their time and money. But the atmosphere was so charged with excitement that this well-intentioned advice had the opposite effect. The newcomers became all the more anxious to see the film, since nobody imagined that the show would be a complete blank!
>
> Afterwards one realized that Debord's use of emptiness and silence had played on the nerves of the spectators, finally causing them to let out "howls in favor of Sade."

After Debord traveled with Trocchi to London, Trocchi "hesitated" in emigrating to New York, perhaps because he was leaving Europe and Debord behind. "I remember long, wonderful psychogeographical walks in London with Guy," Trocchi told Greil Marcus in *Lipstick Traces.* "He took me to places in London I didn't know, that he didn't know, that he sensed, that I'd never have been to if I hadn't been with him. He was a man who could discover a city." Trocchi would "resign" from the S.I. in 1964, but this was after Debord published Trocchi's *Sigma manifesto* in 1963 with the note that it was "no longer as a member of the S.I." due, no doubt, to Trocchi's association with "mystical cretins" such as Colin Wilson and Allen Ginsberg. Again, from the Marcus' *Lipstick Traces* interview:

> Guy thought the world was going to collapse on its own, and we were going to take over. I wanted to do that—to take over the world. But you can't take over the

world by excluding people from it! Guy wouldn't even mention the names of the people I was involved with—Timothy Leary, Ronnie Laing. I remember the last letter he sent me: 'Your name sticks in the minds of decent men.' He was like Lenin; he was an absolutist, constantly kicking people out—until he was the only one left. And exclusions were total. It meant ostracism, cutting people. Ultimately, it leads to shooting people—that's where it would have led if Guy had ever 'taken over.' And I couldn't shoot anyone. [...] It wasn't a question of loyalty. Guy has my loyalty. I loved the man. [...] Guy, Guy. WHAT IS IT? I'm talking to you now, even if you will never speak to me! [...] There was a magical quality to Guy. Distances didn't seem to matter to the man. Walking in London, in the daytime, at night, he'd bring me to a spot he'd found, and the place would begin to live. Some old, forgotten part of London. Then he'd reach back for a story, for a piece of history, as if he'd been born there. He'd quote from Marx, or Treasure Island, or de Quincey—do you know de Quincey?

Marcus follows this interview with a telling passage from de Quincey's diary of his opium-driven drifts through London, and then paints a somewhat disparaging portrait of Trocchi in his London apartment in 1983, a year before his death.*

Chapter Fourteen

In a rather short, unattributed article at the end of *Potlatch* #26, the Cardinal de Retz (1613–1679) is held up as "The Good Example." The article aims all the characteristic scorn of Debord's pen at an author of a book on Retz: "without resisting the most conventional morality in regard to his character, [the author] gives jus-

---

* This is some of the most highly recommended reading in *Lipstick Traces*. I do, however, take exception to Marcus' foreword to *Cain's Book*—not to his characterization of the book as "art in spite of itself," but his advice to let go of Trocchi's personal legends. His life may have been beside the point, but as Trocchi wrote in *Cain's Book*: "What's not beside the point is false." Some of the legends are simply incredible, such as using a false collar and portable pulpit to escape drug raids, shooting up on television, and the All Points Bulletin for him in the U.S. on drug charges, which he avoided by stealing two of Plimpton's suits to disguise his escape to England. Readers of Scott's biography are certain to be entertained by these legends. But the legend of Trocchi as a source of artistic inspiration to many young people involved in the Venice Beach beat scene (among them Jim Morrison) is more important. Trocchi's life, however pathetic it seemed to Marcus, continues to inspire. And as we've seen, Trocchi had first been inspired by Debord.

tice to the ridiculous assertion that he was motivated by ambition." In the French revolution known as the Fronde (1648–1652) Retz, or "Gondi" as he is referred to by the L.I., suffered one glorious defeat after another. But the anonymous author of the *Potlatch* article claims that "The extraordinarily playful value of the life of Gondi, and of this Fronde of which he was the most remarkable inventor, remains to be analyzed from a truly modern perspective."

This isn't the place for such an analysis, *but an understanding of the Fronde and Gondi's role in it* are important because Debord would later call himself "Gondi."*

The word fronde means sling or slingshot—Orest Ranum explains the full connotation of the word in his work on *The Fronde*: "Picked up by street singers and writers of doggerel, the word *fronde* became a shorthand way to evoke the congeries of disorderly, illegal, and violent activities. Allusions to the *fronde* often center on the idea of a collective prank or an adolescent game that could turn sour, become violent, and even take the lives of some of the participants." After 1648 the word *fronde* denoted the revolts in Paris and the provinces that constituted the last real threat to the reign of Louis XIV (much the same way the events of May 1968 are often referred to as the last significant challenge to consumer capitalism). In his *Memoires,* Retz gives his idiosyncratic account of the term:

> Bachoumont once said, in jest, that the Parliament acted like the schoolboys in the Paris ditches, who fling stones and run away when they see the police, only to meet again as soon as he turns his back. That was thought a very pretty comparison. It came to be a subject for ballads, and upon the peace between the King and Parliament, it was revived and applied to those who were not agreed with the Court; and we studied to give it all possible currency, because we observed that it excited the wrath of the people. We therefore resolved that night to wear hat bands made in the form of a slingshot, and had a great number of them made ready to be distributed among a parcel of rough fellows, and we wore them our selves (last of all, for it would have looked much like affectation and spoilt all had we been the first in the mode). It is inexpressible what influence this trifle had upon the people—their bread, hats, gloves, handkerchiefs, fans, ornaments were all a la mode de la Fronde, and we ourselves were more in the fashion by this trifle than in reality. And the truth is we had need of all our shifts to support us against the whole Royal Family.

What began with delinquents slinging mud at the passing carriages of nobles and

---

* See "A Brief History of the Fronde and Gondi's Role In It," in the au's *The Neo-Catiline Conspiracy and Other Essays.*

breaking carriage house windows with slingshots progressed to a judges strike—they completely stopped prosecuting cases and addressed protests to the crown instead. Eventually other royal officials, such as the treasurers, and some princes and their clients got into the act. Taxes had tripled in the years prior to 1648, and people just couldn't and didn't pay the snakes who had purchased the right to be tax collectors. Priests like Cardinal Retz, passed out alms to the poor and published inflammatory pamphlets to put a spin on events. The lesson that Ranum draws from this is that revolutions can be effected by those who already have power. The author of *The Fronde* mentions the historical imagination of Retz that Debord no doubt cultivated in himself:

Cardinal de Retz, or "Gondi"

In periods of social and political upheaval, there are always individuals who have a sense of what will happen next, because they have a historical imagination and can draw inferences from past human experience and apply them to the conditions of their day. In the events of 1648, a great number of Frenchmen went from day to day, with no clear idea of what was going to happen next, while others saw apocalyptic visions of a revolution that meant the end of the world. Educated Frenchmen busily applied Roman history to the current situation; others, notably Omer Talon and Cardinal Retz, became obsessed by the possibility that the French were experiencing events akin to the civil wars of the late sixteenth century. Parisians doing guard duty or drinking in cabarets would remember the pillaging of cities by rampaging troops, the rapes of women, the desecration of churches, the blockade of Paris, and the hysteria triggered by food shortages. The fears that prompted the building of barricades in 1648 were based every bit as much on an authentic and comprehensive history of the social and military dynamics that the city faced as on the fears of learned judges who always seemed to find an appropriate Latin quotation to explain or to understand their times. The diversity of historical imaginations may have held a greater place in the minds of Parisians of 1648 than it does in the minds of peoples in Western societies today.

What made Gondi "The Good Example" for Debord? First and foremost would be Retz' recognition that people with little property were most willing to risk what they had for revolution. He made it his business to "to know all the poor of Paris." As a psychogeographer, Debord would certainly agree with Retz' assessment that popular revolution "would have an admirable effect in the city." Then there was Gondi's ability to stage events to take the high ground. In a sublime example of political theater Gondi staged an attack on a lesser magistrate using prearranged gunfire. The latter cut himself to get his allies to come to his assistance against Mazarin's henchmen who were said to be "murdering the frondeurs." Retz was the best example of the sense of drama and insolence that animated the baroque world. Debord undoubtedly also admired Gondi's political-cultural consciousness that treated his enemies with elegant scorn:

> Cardinal de Richelieu managed the kingdom as mountebanks do their patients, with violent remedies which put strength into it, but it was only a convulsive strength which exhausted its vital organs. Cardinal Mazarin, like a very unskillful physician, did not observe that the vital organs were decayed, nor had he the skill to support them by the chemical preparations of his predecessor; but his only remedy was to let blood, which he drew so plentifully that the patient fell into a lethargy, and our medicaster was yet so stupid as to mistake this lethargy for a real state of health.

But above all Debord admired Gondi's knowledge of how and when to seize the critical moment, the heroic judgment that Gondi speaks of here: "I am of opinion there are greater qualities necessary to make a good head of a party than to make an emperor who is to govern the whole world, and that resolution ought to run parallel with judgment—heroic judgment, which is able to discern the extraordinary from what we call the impossible."

Chapter Fifteen

Whereas Greil Marcus' Janus-faced portrait of Debord had the head of Saint-Just on one side of the coin and Bossuet on the other, another image emerges from the traces Debord left behind. Perhaps it's because the Fronde is much more obscure than the great French Revolution that Marcus chose to accent Saint-Just over Gondi despite the fact that Debord chose to sometimes call himself "Gondi" after the events of May 1968.* However much Debord may have appreciated the maxims, universal history and elegies to the dead of Bossuet, it appears that by 1956 he pre-

---

* Mentioned on the back cover of the Champ Libre edition of *Society of the Spectacle.*

ferred to parody a devil like Lenin than a religious figure such as Bossuet who was in servitude to his king, and whom Debord probably brought with him from his schoolboy days. Bossuet's history is clearly flawed vis-a-vis Debord's mature interpretation of history because Bossuet posits an eternity external to the lived events of history. Marcus, consciously writing for an American audience, scarcely mentions the way Debord made left-handed compliments to Lenin by plagiarizing him and diverting his phrases. Rather than Saint-Just and Bossuet, I think that Debord modeled himself on Gondi while very self-consciously doing a bad boy parody of Lenin.

In their 1956 *Naked Lips* article "*Détournement:* How to Use" Debord and Wolman went so far as to subvert a socialist realist drawing of Lenin by cutting and pasting a bare-chested women on his forehead as if it were a thought bubble. They also suggested that the title of "Heroic Symphony" be changed to "Lenin Symphony." According to Debord and Wolman, appropriations of the classics for their educative value, such as those effected by Brecht in his *Mother Courage,* didn't go far enough. The L.I. called for correcting the classics, or integrating fragments into a new work in a way that changed the meaning of these fragments. The stage of "serious-parody" in diversions was attained when the diverted elements weren't simply comic, but sublime in the way the original was emptied of meaning and forgotten. Like Lenin, Debord felt that the only justification he needed for his extreme diversions (of the entire heritage of literature and art) for partisan propaganda was that it gave him access to history.

After making the obligatory reference to the grandfather of these diversions of pre-existing poetry and philosophy, the incomparable Lautreamont, Debord and Wolman remark that the advertising industry is now most ripe for diversions; although they're quick to point out that anything, such as a phrase or photograph cut out of the newspaper (a minor diversion), or a slogan by Saint-Just or a film sequence by Eisenstein (a major diversion), could be used. Debord refers to his collage on the Spanish Civil War to point out the manner in which a diverted element that's furthest from the subject can have the biggest impact—here the use of a clipped lipstick ad brings home the revolutionary sentiment: "Pretty lips are painted red."

The authors called for extreme simplification in the use of diversions for immediate recognition and effect on memory. However, the diverted phrase shouldn't just be a rational response to an existing slogan, as with Lautreamont, because this approach can be confused with a banal repartee. It's more powerful, the authors advise, to transform the pre-existing element by a reversal of values effected by the quick addition of a new title (or interchanging titles) or, for example, by holding a black mass in a famous church. This was the "real means of proletarian artistic teaching, the first outline of literary communism."

To finish, we must briefly cite a few aspects of what we call ultra-diversion; that is, types of diversions applied to everyday social life. Gestures and words can be charged with another meaning, and have been throughout history for practical reasons. The secret societies of ancient China possessed great refinement in recognizing each other, encompassing most mundane attitudes (how to use cups; to drink; to cut citations of poems at agreed upon points). The need for a secret language, passwords, is inseparable from a tendency to play. The idea is that any sign, any word is prone to being converted into something else, even its opposite.

Debord and Wolman foresaw their diversions eventually including the situations they constructed; perhaps on the scale of and in the way the appellation Red Army was used by the royalists of the Vendee (after the symbolism of the heart of Jesus

"The universe turns on the tips of tits"

Hungarian workers, 1956

Christ), only to be used later by the Soviet army. As will be shown later, the ability to know when and how to turn one event into another (such as turning a student protest into a general strike) was what Debord was teaching himself. Yet it may have just looked as though he was making a parody of Lenin. To express his "heroic judgment" as Gondi put it (i.e., between the extraordinary and the impossible), Debord would clip one of Lenin's most famous phrases and use it as the title of a *Potlatch* article "One Step Back."

But before getting to this important little essay, it should be noted that by 1956 (the year of the classic brinkmanship over the Suez Canal), unsigned articles such as the auto-critique "Contradictions in the Activity of the Lettrist International" described the "obligatorily precarious" aspect of their position: "It's much too late to make art; a little too early to concretely make situations of some amplitude; the need to act isn't in doubt." Although a taste for play was what animated the group, the artists were under fire, even when they maintained an anti-art stance. Another element in the L.I., motivated by "a taste for the unknown and mystery at any price," was drawn to occult and theosophical traditions. According to the author of the essay, most likely Debord, this group profited from the political freedom of their "vaguely anarchistic" revolutionary association to make "the worst theoretical errors, against materialist psychogeography in particular, and against all rational situationist attitudes."

According to the author, every effort to liquidate one tendency reinforced the other or promoted intellectual immobility: "Intellectuals, embarrassed by the situation, talk about becoming masons or butchers, or they effectively do it for a few weeks, simply making a transfer (corresponding to the level of conscience they imagine they have) like "the most repugnant religious conversion." These were harsh words to be writing on the heels of Khrushchev's denunciation of Stalin at the XXth Communist Party Conference in 1956, the year the Soviets cracked down on the Polish and Hungarian worker council protests. And if this wasn't bad enough timing for Debord to come off sounding like Lenin in a bad mood, this was also when Hollingsworth came out with his *The Organization Man* (that warned about the dangers of "belongingness" in a bureaucratic culture). Debord sounded like the chairman of the corporate board as he warned *Potlatch* readers that not many people had what it took to belong to the Lettrist International: "Don't be surprised if the radical changes in needs and perspectives entails here (as in any branch of the economy), rather large losses of specialized personnel." Those who didn't have the intelligence or the moral fortitude to break with their friends, family, work and leisure could count on being purged, demonstrating that Debord was as much *of* his times as going against them.

In his "Theory of the Drift," published in *Naked Lips,* Debord specified what this research entailed. To drift isn't to stroll or take a trip, but "a technique of transient passage through varied ambiances." The idea is to open oneself up to the urban terrain and to new encounters while observing the currents and fixed points of the city that might constitute entrance and exit points of specific zones. Debord and his fellow drifters drifted through the microclimates of Paris—the administrative zones, the tourist zones, etc.—always looking for the limitations and possibilities they presented him. Debord felt that chance was more important than psychogeographic observation, but warns that chance needs new conditions to really work—otherwise chance is a conservative force that leads to repetition of old habits. In other words, chance encounters can become routine.

Debord found that the best drift was composed of several small groups of two or three psychogeographers with a common orientation who would meet after the drift to formulate objective conclusions from the experience. If four or five people participate, the quality of the drift declines, although if ten or more people participate, the drift tends to naturally turn back into multiple drifts of smaller groups. These drifts can last a few hours, a few days or even a few months. The L.I. would specify the area of their drifts, although some drifts were intentionally vague. A drift could encompass a city, a district or just a train station.

In the "Theory of the Drift," Debord goes on to explain that he and the L.I. hitch-hiked non-stop all over Paris during a transport strike "under the pretext of driving anywhere just to provoke more confusion."

The general goal of these drifts was to explore and reveal the effects of the labyrinth of the modern city on human behavior. The L.I. developed their knowledge of the components and spacial situation of the "ambient units" of the city, looking for the principal passageways and possible defenses. These ambient units were grouped together on "continental plates" using old maps, aerial photos and experimental drifts. The idea wasn't to fix these continents in stone, rather to find their margins and propose ways to change the architecture so that these frontiers disappear, like the coming together of continental plates in Unitary Urbanism. This Unitary Urbanism, or UU, was later defined as: "The theory of the combined use of arts and techniques for the integral construction of a milieu in dynamic relation with experiments in behavior." And at the end of his essay, Debord flatly states, "The difficulties of the drift, are those of freedom," adding: "One day we'll build cities for drifting."

Despite the requirements of this rigorous activity and the harsh words about artists, Debord and the L.I. befriended the already very well-established Danish painter Asger Jorn in 1955. By 1956, Jorn appeared in the pages of *Potlatch* with the suggestion that French theaters stage the classics with actors on drugs to accelerate the process of cultural decay. Jorn had been one of, if not perhaps the biggest, mover and shaker of the post-war European art scene. Jorn was certainly more than a painter (he was a theoretician, organizer, adventurer, prankster, socialist, sculptor, etc.), but he was primarily a painter, and Debord rarely masked his contempt for painters regardless how socially engaged they were. To make matters even worse in Debord's eyes, Jorn had a fascination for magic and the occult, as reflected in the title of his 1957 painting, *The Sorcerers of Pozzo Garitta II.*

Asger Jorn

Although Debord was the primary force of the Situationist International—from the beginning to the end—the group would have been much more limited in scope had it not been for Jorn's recruitment of an international coterie of avant-garde artists from his COBRA (acronym for the art group with bases in COpenhagen, BRussells, Amsterdam) days (1948–1951), and his funding of the S.I. journal. Jorn had progressed from his youthful woodcut illustrations via the influence of Miro to a style reminiscent of Dubuffet and de Kooning, only much more brutal and anti-aesthetic. Jorn was extraordinarily gestural and spontaneous; his bold use of color and technique were robust and markedly physical, like Jorn himself. Many of Jorn's canvases are aggressive and evoke challenge and struggle, such as his '57 canvas *Animal Without Prey*. But Jorn paintings are almost always playful, as if he sought to capture the game of life at decisive moments with his spontaneous use of impasto. What makes Jorn so appealing is that he shares the drama and heavy sense of fate of someone who was involved in the resistance in the war, but he slips in his Danish sense of humor or maliciously smothers the entire canvas with his very insouciant satire.

Jorn and the other COBRA artists had charged themselves with changing postwar culture by creating art that would relate to revolutionary changes in society. They were opposed to both the functionalism of Bauhaus that ignored the effects of the architectural ambiance on the psychology of humans and to the sort of Surrealism that turned the human body into a chest of drawers. Jorn was highly critical of the idealism inherent in Breton's idea of pure psychic expression: "Surrealists like Breton want to exteriorize. What do they want to exteriorize? *Pure* thought. [...] The metaphysical world isn't capable of surpassing the material world that produces it." As an experimental group, the COBRA artists placed supreme importance on a spontaneity that was free of Bauhaus rationalism and Surrealist idealism.

Jorn called COBRA art "abstraction that didn't believe in abstraction" in his theoretical book *Pour la forme* published by the Situationist International in 1958, adding that there was symbolic content to all abstractions. For Jorn in his COBRA days, desires and morals were valued over reason and aesthetics. The Dutch artist Constant, a future Situationist, was one of most radical COBRA members; and his manifesto gives you an idea where their heads were: "... individualist culture, which is condemned with the society that made it, offers no possibility for imagination and desire, and impedes the vital expression of man..." Indeed, bringing together the Belgian group Revolutionary Surrealism, the Dutch Reflex crew, and the Danes of Host into the COBRA collective was just the sort of difficult task that Jorn wanted to recreate with the Situationist International.

In early September 1957, Jorn convened a conference of his International Movement for an Imaginist Bauhaus in the Italian town of Alba with the idea of bringing together avant-garde artists from across Europe. The best account of Jorn's Imaginist Bauhaus project are in his own words in 1957:

Notes on the Formation of an Imaginist Bauhaus
What was the Bauhaus?
The Bauhaus was an answer to the question: What 'education' do artists need in order to take their place in the machine age?

How was the Bauhaus idea realized?

It was realized with a 'school' in Germany; first at Weimar, then at Dessau; founded by the architect Walter Gropius in 1919—destroyed by the Nazis in 1933.

What is the International Movement for an Imaginist Bauhaus?
It is the answer to the question where and how to find a justified place for artists in the machine age. This answer demonstrates that the education carried out by the old Bauhaus is false.

How has the idea of an International Movement for an Imaginist Bauhaus been realized?
The Movement was founded in Switzerland in 1953 as a tendency for the forming of a united organization capable of promoting an integral revolutionary cultural attitude. In 1954 the experience of the Albissola gathering demonstrated that experimental artists must get hold of industrial means and subject them to their own nonutilitarian ends. In 1955 an imaginist laboratory was founded at Alba. Conclusion of the Albissola experience: complete inflationary devaluation of modern values of decoration (cf. ceramics produced by children). In 1957 the Movement promulgates the watchword of psychogeograpical action.

What we want.
We want the same economic and practical means and possibilities that are already at the disposal of scientific research, of whose great results everyone is aware.

Artistic research is identical to 'human science,' which for us means 'concerned' science, not purely historical science. This research should be carried out by artists with the assistance of scientists.

The first institute ever formed for this purpose is the experimental laboratory for free artistic research founded September 29, 1955, at Alba. Such a laboratory is not an instructional institution; it simply offers new possibilities for artistic experimentation.

The leaders of the old Bauhaus were great masters with exceptional talents, but they were bad teachers. The pupils' works were only pious imitations of their masters. The real influence of the latter was indirect, by force of example: Ruskin on Van de Velde, Van de Velde on Gropius.

This is not at all a critique, it is simply a statement of fact from which the following conclusions may be drawn. The direct transfer of artistic gifts is impossible, artistic adaptation takes place through a series of contradictory phases: Stupefaction—Wonder—Imitation—Rejection—Experience—Possession.

None of these phases can be avoided, although they need not all be gone through by any one individual.

Our practical conclusion is the following: we are abandoning all efforts at pedagogical action and moving toward experimental activity.

For most art connoisseurs, it's easy to forget the educational aspect of the original Bauhaus and focus on the works that continue to occupy so much of the art world. Jorn was particularly conscious of this "pedagogical action" because he had attended a teachers' college in his youth.

At the Alba Congress, Jorn was made a member of the directorship committee of the Lettrist International; and the L.I. delegate, Gil Wolman, brought up a couple of the points that found their way into the final resolution of the congress.

▼ Necessity of an integral framework of life by means of unitary urbanism using a combination of all modern arts and technologies.

▼ Acknowledgment of the essential interdependence between unitary urbanism and a future lifestyle.

... The Alba Congress probably marks one of the difficult stages in the struggle for a new sensibility and a new culture, a struggle which is itself part of the general revolutionary resurgence characterizing the year 1956, visible in the upsurge of the masses in the USSR, Poland and Hungary (although in the latter case we see the dangerously confusing revival of rotten old watchwords of clerical nationalism resulting from the fatal error of the prohibition of any Marxist opposition), in the successes of the Algerian insurrection and in the major strikes in Spain. These developments allow us the greatest hopes for the near future. *(Potlatch #27,* November, 1956)

The following Spring (May, 1957), on the eve of the founding of the Situationist International, Debord published his "One Step Back" in *Potlatch* right behind the lead editorial that left no doubt about the para-Dada, Marxist orientation of the L.I. In "One Step Back," Debord acknowledged that in order to grow and become an authentically international organization, the L.I. would have to change its tactics: "We must seize modern culture and use it for our ends, and no longer mount an outside oppositional campaign founded exclusively on the future development of our problems." Debord called for the formulation of theses that could be applied to this end, but in a step back, acknowledged that the L.I. would have to accept a minority position in the new organization in order for unification to go through.

It's clear that one of the main reasons for this "one step back" was a lack of funds. The L.I., we're told, could create new sentiments easier than it could create new professions. Debord warned of the dangers of serving "the last fragments of modern esthetics" and worried about all the painters suddenly in their midst. "We have to run the risk of a regression," Debord admitted as if he were Lenin discussing his New Economic Policy. After taking a couple of quick shots at art galleries and poetry books, Debord again acknowledged that they have to come to grips with the existing framework of the world and the need for forces and resources other than those at the immediate disposition of the L.I.

Part II

The Situationist Years 1957–1972

Guy Debord on the right

Chapter Sixteen

Despite this willingness to take "one step back" in order create the Situationist International, Debord cleared the ranks of the L.I. in his typically implacable terms. The *Potlatch* report on the exclusion of Gil Wolman, for example, reads like an obituary: "Wolman played an important part in 1952 in the organization of the Lettrist left and in the founding of the L.I. He was the author of 'megapneumatique' poems, a theory of 'cinematochrone' and a film; he was the Lettrist delegate to the congress in Alba, September 1956. He was twenty-seven years old." Although Debord never retracted his exclusions, the next year he would write that these purges,

continually moved toward a sort of absolutist rigor leading to an equally absolute isolation and ineffectuality, and ultimately to a certain immobility, a degeneration of the spirit of critique and discovery. We must definitively supersede this sectarian conduct in favor of real actions. This should be the sole criterion on which we join or separate from comrades. Naturally this does not mean that we should renounce breaks, as everyone urges us to do. We think, on the contrary, that it is necessary to go still further in breaking with habits and persons.

The unification of Jorn's Imaginist Bauhaus (including Giuseppe Pinot-Gallizio), Debord's Lettrist International (including Mohamed Dahou), and Ralph Rumney's London Psychogeographical Association into the Situationist International took place July 28, 1957 in Cosio d'Arroscia. Debord's *Report on the Construction of Situations and on the Conditions for Organization and Action of the Situationist International Tendency*, which circulated as an internal S.I. document, promulgated the group's principles. This report may seem heavy on Marxist rhetoric ("the bourgeoisie in its phase of liquidation"), but patient readers will find an excellent critique of the avant-garde and very cogent expression of the S.I.'s blueprint for changing the world.

Debord notes that the bourgeoise's control of commerce enables them to divert artistic innovation away from any "comprehensive contestation" toward utilitarian disciplines or innocuous, fragmentary works that are open to interpretation. As he traces the development of the early avant-garde, Debord concludes that none of these groups had the necessary political backbone to unify their art with the workers movement. Futurism "collapsed, going from nationalism to fascism without ever attaining a more complete theoretical vision of its time." Although the "dissolution of Dadaism was a result of its purely negative definition," Debord asserts that "the Dadaist spirit has influenced all the movements that have come after it."

A Dadaist-type negation must be present in any later constructive position as long as the social conditions that impose the repetition of rotten superstructures—conditions that have already been condemned quite definitively—have not been wiped out by force.

Debord devotes several paragraphs to Surrealism, admiring the Surrealists prior to 1930 for their internal discipline and dialectical materialism; as well as their use of desire and surprise. But ultimately, his critique is ruthless:

> The error that is at the root of Surrealism is the idea of the infinite richness of the unconscious imagination. The cause of the ideological failure of Surrealism was its belief that the unconscious was finally discovered as the ultimate force of life. Having revised the history of ideas accordingly, it stopped there. We now know that the unconscious imagination is poor, that automatic writing is monotonous, and that the whole genre of ostentatious Surrealist "weirdness" has ceased to be very surprising. The formal fidelity to this style of imagination ultimately leads back to the antipodes of the modern conditions of imagination: back to traditional occultism. The extent to which Surrealism has remained in dependence on its hypothesis regarding the unconscious can be seen in the work of theoretical investigation attempted by second-generation Surrealists: Calas and Mabille relate everything to the two successive aspects of the Surrealist practice of the unconscious—the one to psychoanalysis, the other to cosmic influences. In fact, the discovery of the role of the unconscious was a surprise, an innovation, not a law of future surprises and innovations. Freud had also ended up discovering this when he wrote, "Everything conscious wears out. What is unconscious remains unaltered. But once it is set loose, does it not fall into ruins in its turn?"

Debord goes on to point out the folly of opposing an irrational society with irrational means, adding that Surrealism was ultimately absorbed into everyday commerce. According to Debord, it's necessary to rationalize the world beyond its superficially logical values as a condition for impassioning the world. The Surrealists were theoretically incompetent and unwilling to align themselves with the workers, hence they "joined the camp of mystical idealism." The U.S. avant-garde was labeled "insipidly conformist," and Debord was particularly harsh in regard to the role "exotic" cultural products imported from third world countries played in developed countries: "exoticism which does, however, serve the primary purpose of exoticism: escape from the real conditions of life and creation." Debord rejected wholesale the Socialist Realism of the Eastern Bloc, with the exception of Brecht who put the spectacle in question with his epic theater. To his credit, Debord doesn't spare Jorn's COBRA friends from accusations of a "lack of ideological rigor," nor does he obscure the "sharp struggles among different tendencies" within the Lettrist International. On

Founding members of the Situationists International

the eve of the founding of the S.I., however, Debord was willing to put these conflicts in the past.

The "Toward a Situationist International" section of Debord's *Report* reads like a manifesto. In order to construct situations, both the material environment and human behavior need to be transformed and supercharged by playing games that quantitatively increase human life. Debord envisioned the creation of a "Situationist city" by diverting existing architecture, urban planning, cinema, etc. For the first time he mentions the distribution of "different varieties of food and drink" as an aspect of unitary urbanism. The acoustic and atmospheric environment would continually be put to experimental use as Situationists playfully intervene in their urban milieu. Those who would want to take up situationistic struggles should note that while these games were, and still are, radical in regard to societal norms, Debord explicitly makes the point that they entail a highly moralistic revolution in mores.

"The Situationist game is not distinct from a moral choice, the taking of one's stand in favor of what will ensure the future reign of freedom and play," he writes, adding below that, *nonintervention* is the "very principle of the spectacle." Debord's morality is the morality of life and happiness: "... this will to playful creation must be extended to all known forms of human relationships, so as to influence, for example, the historical evolution of sentiments like friendship and love."

In the last public issue of *Potlatch,* Debord addressed the article "Still More Effort if You Want to Be Situationists" to Mohamed Dahou who must've been up to the task because he made the cut. At this time, Debord was concerned with cultural "decomposition." This term was later defined as,

The process in which the traditional cultural forms have destroyed themselves as a result of the emergence of superior means of dominating nature which enable and require superior cultural constructions. We can distinguish between an active phase of the decomposition and effective demolition of the old superstructures— which came to an end around 1930—and a phase of repetition which has prevailed since then. The delay in the transition from decomposition to new construction is linked to the delay in the revolutionary liquidation of capitalism.

In his *Potlatch* essay to Dahou, Debord adds a few new touches to the idea of con-structing situations—he now calls for taking the "decorcomportement dialectic" (of unitary urbanism and psychogeographic drifting) to a new theater of operations, for a disabused critique of existing conditions and their "*integration* in a unitary spacio-temporal construction (the situation: dynamic system of a milieu and of playful comportment) that realizes a superior *accord of form and content.*" To underscore his megalomanic ambitions, Debord states that the existing decay was only of interest insofar as it marked the end of one civilization and the beginning of another— arguably a Nietzschian perspective based on the style of civilizations.

Citing the infamous monkey paintings that rivaled honest tashiste painting, Debord scoffs at the way passive consumers admire this cultural decay. In this light he mentions how well his film *Howlings in Favor of Sade* was received at the London Institute of Contemporary Art, adding that people tend to prefer works that mask this decay a little. Debord added to the decay taking place in the year 1957 in a work that was conceived and executed during a weekend visit to Jorn's studio in Copenhagen. *Fin de Copenhague* is Jorn and Debord's first attempt at collaborative collage along the lines of the more substantial *Memoires* (1958) described above. *The Architectural Review's* well-informed treatment of *Fin de Copenhague* describes the booklet perfectly:

> The old Futurist and Dadaist techniques of insult, abuse and satire die hard, if only because the Modern Movement that grew out of them has developed almost as many pomposities, inhumanities and hypocrisies as the attitudes it has replaced. Among the most salutary recent eruptions of the grand old method is Asger Jorn's *Fin de Copenhague,* an editon-de-luxe limited to 200 copies and bound in flong, that uses the combined techniques of collage and action-painting to satirize gemutlich Europe in general, the author's native Copenhagen in par-ticular, and Le Corbusier in passing. Thus, much of the 'text' has been clipped from steamy newspaper serials and confronted with clippings from the ultimate guardian of middle-class morality, the agony column of Elle; noisy slogans (*APPELS, Voter Vie Transformee, Le Probleme est Resolu*) have been culled from

Fin de Copenhague

many sources, but all recall the propaganda for la Ville Radieuse; and Copenhagen is satirized not only as the seat of ancestral boredoms, and in other standard terms, but also for being a 'well-planned city,' in the sense of making a pretty pattern of black and green in the planner's report—only in this case the pretty pattern is produced by applying place-names to patches of mechanical tint superimposed on (apparently) an action painting that has 'run,' 5. The result has the elegance, and the lack of meaning, of a zoning diagram, and the paper-planners pretensions are cut down to size by the accurately backhanded caption '*Un splendide paysage que Bernard Buffet a souvent peint.*'

The whole of this urbanistic cold douche was realized—one understands—in a single afternoon of inspired exasperation, and is a remarkable piece of improvisation among the techniques of graphic reproduction. All the collage material for the text and pictorial illustrations was the product of a lunchtime excursion to a single news-stand and—when pasted-up—provided the plates for the second, black and white, printing on the pages. The first run through the press, for the colorwork, however, resulted in what are virtually monotypes, the color being applied by Jorn himself, and somewhat different on every sheet. The whole cavalier attitude to the sacred rituals of printing may be taken as a fair example of the frame of mind that prompts Jorn to refer to himself and his colleagues as the Bauhaus Imaginiste or even the Bauhaus Imaginaire. The scope of the original Bauhaus ran from typography to town planning as well, and one hopes that Jorn may be inspired or exasperated enough in the near future to demolish some of the middle sections of this spectrum—the home and furniture magazines should provide a wealth of over-ripe material.

At a time when Algerian F.L.N. "terrorists" were disrupting France, Mao was launching his Great Leap Forward and the Soviets did the same with their first Sputnik satellite, Debord and Jorn were co-opting the images and language of their enemy—these spectacular advertisements were thus deflated in value, and recoded in a context that suggested Situationist themes. As Debord said: "Ultimately, any sign or word is susceptible to being converted into something else, even its opposite."

Chapter Seventeen

Young Boys, Young Girls
Some aptitude for supersession and play.
Without special knowledge.
If intelligent or beautiful,
You can enter into the meaning of History
WITH THE SITUATIONISTS
Don't telephone. Write or show up:
32 rue de la Montagne-Genevieve, Paris 5th

As the first issue of the *Situationist International* journal was about to go to press in the Spring of 1958, French colonial forces bombed the Tunisian village of Sakhiet Sidi Youssef, killing school children and other innocent civilians. The upshot was so great that French troops were forced to evacuate the country with the help of British and American forces. A military-led government of public safety was declared in Algeria to try to come to grips with the sharp conflict between France and the *fellagahs*—the IVth French Republic, associated with the torturous colonial polices and brutal modernization, was shaken to its foundation as hundreds of thousands protested in the streets of Paris. De Gaulle exploited the crisis by using the mass media to appear to be the only person capable of resolving the situation. The political parties and parliamentarians were hostile to de Gaulle, but increasingly looked to him and the military as a solution. After the French conquest of Corsica, de Gaulle was invested with full powers and authorized to write a new constitution.

In an unsigned article on the back of the first issue of *Situationist International,* titled "A Civil War in France," the author(s) flatly blamed the communist party and the major trade union alliance, the C.G.T., for not launching an unlimited general strike after the big protest marches on May 28. The author, quite probably Debord as Editor-in-Chief (although Dahou and Bernstein were also likely to have weighed in on the matter), wrote that de Gaulle appealed to schoolboy notions of the grandeur of

de Gaulle in Algeria

France under Louis XIV, adding that the goal of the ascension of the general-president was the "liquidation of democracy in this country, the triumph of fascist authority." From its first public proclamation, the S.I. declared war on de Gaulle.

"This isn't Catilina at our doors, it's death" was the quote that adorned the article—it was from the grandfather of anarchy P.-J. Proudhon, taken from a letter to Herzen in 1849. Although Marx (particularly works from the 1842–1847 period such as *Economic and Philosophical Manuscripts, Theses on Feuerback* and *The Poverty of Philosophy)* was the point of departure for the group, by the choice of this quote, the author of "A Civil War in France" sought to evoke a little anarchistic urgency and wildness to the situation. A good part of this chapter deals with Debord's take on Marx and his disciples, so it's worth noting that Debord wasn't an uncritical follower. In *Society of the Spectacle,* Debord would criticize Marx's identification of proletarian revolution with the seizure of state power, although he was quick to point out that authentic anarchism, the "ideology of pure liberty," suffered from many historical and practical illusions. But what is most striking about the quote at the top of this paragraph is the reference to Catilina, or the Catiline Conspiracy.

Debord's grasp of universal history, gleaned from Bossuet and Hegel, took him back to Rome in 63 BC I'm tempted to tell you to forget everything that's been written above about Saint-Just or Lenin being Debord's historical analog—none come as close as to what the historian Sallust (86–34 BC) tells us about Catiline: "From his youth he had delighted in civil war, bloodshed, robbery, and political strife, and it was in such occupations that he spent his early manhood." Sallust might as well have been writing about Debord as he describes how Catiline mustered his forces to attempt revolution by the cancellation of debt:

> Amid the corruption of the great city Catiline could easily surround himself, as with a bodyguard, with gangs of profligates and criminals. Debauchees, adulterers, and gamblers, who had squandered their inheritances in gaming-dens, pot-houses, and brothels; anyone who had bankrupted himself to buy impunity for his infamous or criminal acts; men convicted anywhere of murder or sacrilege, or living in fear of conviction; cut-throats and perjurers, too, who made a trade as false witnesses or shedding the blood of fellow citizens; in short, all who were in disgrace or afflicted by poverty or consciousness of guilt, were Catiline's intimate associates. And if anyone as yet innocent happened to become friendly with him, the temptations to which daily intercourse with Catiline exposed him soon made him as evil a ruffian as the rest.

In Debord's only signed article in the first issue of *Situationist International,* he made it clear that, like Catiline, Situationists were "professional revolutionaries." This is of interest because Debord would later deride the adjective "professional," adding that he had himself been a very good professional, but that it was a mystery to most people exactly what sort of professional he was. "Theses on Cultural Revolution" calls for passionate participation in life as opposed to making past elements of life felt in a work of art—Debord knew that sensations far superior to those produced by a work of art could be created. Situationist activity sought to free humans from their commodity status in the labor market through the extension of leisure and the disappearance of the division of labor, "beginning with the division of artistic labor." Leisure time is only free time, Debord tells us, *if* humans have all the modern materials and instruments at their disposal to make revolutionary art for the experimental construction of everyday life. This catch phrase "everyday life," which would become the axis of virtually all Situationist analysis, reflects the influence of Marxist philosopher Henri Lefebvre (1905–1991).

Henri Lefebvre was perhaps the most influential Marxists philosopher in post-war France, and certainly the most significant thinker associated with the journal *Arguments*. Founded in 1956 by former P.C.F. (French Communist Party) members, *Arguments* was a focal point of those who were seduced by the romanticism of the Resistance struggle to join the communist cause. They were all disillusioned by Stalin's excesses, and a few of the *Arguments* group had visited the Polish councils during the '56 upheavals. Most of the group, like Lefebvre, looked for ways to understand the current situation by reading the young Marx of the *Economic and Philosophical Manuscripts* of 1844 who spoke to problems of alienation and objectification.

Whereas Debord acknowledges Lefebvre's identification of the discord between the decay of old superstructures and the need for communist revolution in his "Theses," he disputes Lefebvre's hyphenated construct—the "romantic-revolutionary." Revolutionaries had to effect actual cultural modifications. There was nothing romantic about this, as is seen in one of Debord's often quoted phrases: "Victory will go to those who know how to make disorder without liking it." In his editorial in *Situationist International* #3 Debord was very critical of Lefebvre's poetry and other efforts to express sentiments about bygone moments of life, especially exceptional moments and moments fraught with contradictions, that produce profound sensations—according to Debord, modern art had already explored these contradictions to the point where expression itself had been destroyed. Debord wanted to create and banalize these exceptional moments, and he made it very clear that his concept of the situation was not a work of art. To clarify what he had in mind, he quoted Marx: "to act on exterior nature and transform it... transforms at the same time his own nature."

Debord also disagreed in part with Lucien Goldman (the French translator and interpreter of Georg Lukacs' influential *History and Class Consciousness*). Goldman argued that the only alternative to art united (not separated) with life was romanticism. Romanticism was the only exception to the rule that artistic expression was reification—in other words, art (like other reifications) inverts the world so that what is live becomes dead and vice versa. Debord agreed with Goldman's assertion that art as a separate sphere of life would disappear, along with law, religion, etc., as these specialized activities dissolve into a classless society. But for Debord, romanticism was no exception to the rule that art was the alienating reflection of real life.

Debord's denunciation of romanticism is interesting because romantic traits have long been associated with revolutionaries—the romantic as the noble outlaw, the giant rebel, the calm hero. Yet it is difficult not to notice something of the romantic in Debord; something of the world-weary, egoistic and skeptical romantic who longs for commitment to absolutes outside the self, while refusing ordinary standards and demanding the moral freedom of the superior individual. Rousseau, Chateaubriand, Byron, Baudelaire, Musset, "walking naked in this masquerade called life." You know the type: they drown the despair of their nostalgic egos in pleasure and debauchery and bare their souls with brutal honesty. The only romantics to engender the Situationist's sympathy were the Bousingots who, after the French revolution of 1830, showed that poetry could exist without the poem by their scandals in the streets and extreme fashions. But it was Drieu La Rochelle, the romantic heavy drinker and suicide (1945), who wrote words that could well apply to Debord: "Suicide is the resource of men whose strength had been corroded by rust, the rust of everyday life."

For Hegel (1770–1831), one of Debord's guiding lights, romanticism was the apogee and the end of art. In his *Introductory Remarks on Aesthetics,* Hegel modified Schiller's *Letters on the Aesthetic Education of Mankind* so as to prove the point that

Georg Hegel

art and religion rely on "picture thinking" and are hence inferior to philosophy. Here Hegel echoes Plato's progression towards the pure apprehension of ideas; the progression from the sensations of art, to the mental imagery of religion, to the imageless conceptions of philosophy. Philosophy somehow no longer relies on sensuous expression and is purely conceptual. As art develops from animal symbols to approximate the divine, to humans as the measure of the divine in Greek sculpture and then to romantic art, art develops into poetry—the highest art form. Hegel grounds this judgment on the questionable assertion that the content of poetry is more detached from its medium (language) than other arts—for Hegel, language is a vehicle of thought, not constitutive of it. As art develops into the poetry of Hegel's time, art loses its internal unity. The depths of human subjectivity are now too complex for sensual forms. The reflexive, open-ended works of Friedrich Schlegel and Novalis reduced the process itself into the product. Hence for Hegel, romantic irony marked the end of art. In Hegel's schema, art is a rational need that compels a person to be conscious of the internal and external world, and to make the world an object in which the person recognizes him or herself. Art reveals the truth of the world to consciousness through the senses; and through its content art is on the same plane as religion and philosophy. Art unites with religion in philosophy, which are forms of, and superseded by, Absolute Mind.

While I realize that this digression insults the intelligence of some readers, it's necessary because Hegel is so central to Debord's thought.

Absolute Mind discounts any opposition or contradiction between knowledge and its object, or between law and impulse—when Hegel's Absolute Mind manifests itself in a individual, there is no validity to Kant's famous opposition between freedom and necessity. In other words, nature's externality loses its absolute opposition to human freedom when viewed from this theoretical perspective. Rather than posing perpetual obstacles to satisfaction, natural contingencies lead to self-knowledge and provide the conditions by which freedom and reason are manifest—that is, once freedom is (theoretically) realized in Absolute Mind. For Hegel, all events and accidents of history follow the logic of freedom—history is the unfolding of Mind and Freedom in stages:

1. Oriental World: China, India, Persia (the ruler is free)
2. Antiquity: Greece vs. Rome (some, but not slaves, are free)
3. Germanic World (from Christ on, the realization that all humans should be free)

Freedom becomes a practical proposition when history arrives at the French Revolution. Hegel was in his late teens when the French Revolution took place and was an enthusiastic supporter of it. He even established risky contacts with secret Jacobin societies in Germany, although he was opposed to the excesses of the Terror on the grounds that it was the abstract assertion of freedom unrelated to the moral and institutional context. Hegel was overwhelmed when he saw Napoleon (1769–1821, the "World Soul") during the latter's attack on Jena in 1803—Napoleon would, according to Hegel, give the French Revolution a positive legacy. Working with Kant's use of the categories of the *subject* of knowledge (the knower) and *object* of knowledge (the known) Hegel developed his system (using elements from Spinoza and Fitche) as Napoleon advanced on Prussia and the last remnants of the Holy Roman Empire.

For Hegel, the subject-object duality was resolved in process; the historical *process* that goes beyond things and concepts of things to the unity of subject and object in the total man. With this historical backdrop, Hegel concluded that the essence of humanity is the experience of consciousness as a journey that always contains in it the faint outline of the history of the world's culture; an awareness of history as a journey of intellectual reflection and self-discovery. Using the fragments left behind, history became humanity's struggle to seize the totality of its past by conceiving of the self-realization of humanity as a whole. This awareness, and the awareness of it, or self-consciousness, is always a highly subjective consciousness that is aware of the object that it lacks. Desire gives birth to Freedom, to the awareness of unity and purpose. But consciousness is also aware of its isolation and separation from other consciousness. The self-conscious conduct of history requires that individual consciousness be related by, say, the Desire for Freedom.

Hegel's logic isn't based on logical identities, as with Aristotle's syllogisms, rather on the "totality," which for Hegel is the developmental process of "moments" (not stages or phases) overcoming each other and serving as elements in a structure. Whereas Aristotle's logic deals with separate identities in a deductive way, Hegel's logic is concerned with the dynamic movement of totality; be it in the overcoming, supersession (or sublation, *aufhebung*) that preserves what is overcome; or again, the power of negation that can reveal contradictions in any identity or category, and is thus able to dissolve static thought into fluid thoughts that aim towards the totality. The schizophrenia suffered by Hegel's sister and his poet friend Holderlin are what compelled Hegel to recognize this principle of negation or self-division/contradiction. For Hegel, negation means the difference or opposition or reflection that reveals the insufficiency or incoherence of a category. For Debord and his cohorts, negation entailed the destruction of contemporary civilization so as to build anew. Negation is the vital aspect of Hegel's dialectic now expressed in the famous formula "thesis, antithesis, synthesis" that always implies the negation of negation.

Absolute Mind is the complete self-consciousness and self-possession that comes at the end of the thinking process. Hegel, particularly the young Hegel that Marxists such as Debord consider as a basic point of departure, sought the "realization of freedom in the external world," and world history was the process that effected this realization. But for Hegel nothing that was genuinely external could create freedom (one could argue against Hegel, especially not the history of the world that one doesn't participate in creating). Hegel believed that this Absolute Mind is what makes history and that it is the philosopher's consciousness that manifests Absolute Mind. Marx and Engels were highly critical of this proposition because Hegel's history was only created in the speculative imagination, and they sought to solve the "riddle of history" by the *genuine* resolution of oppositions, such as freedom and necessity, in communism.

For Hegel, once Absolute Mind is attained, art is no longer necessary. When historical time invades the artistic sphere, historical time introduces the principle of the necessary dissolution of art. At this stage art loses its place in life as a means to authentic truth, and is no longer satisfying. Real needs and interests displace art in the sphere of representation because in order to satisfy these needs and interests, an individual's reflective capacity is full of thoughts and abstract representations far removed from art. Nonetheless, Hegel approved of romantic art's ability to appropriate the world, warts and all. In the romantic world, everything becomes an artistic object that manifests the internal subjectivity of the artist, but when this subjectivity "acquires primordial importance," Hegel wrote in his *Aesthetics,* "the negation implied in death becomes the negation of this subjectivity, that which renders it terrifying." In other words, when extreme subjectivity, such as anxiousness over death, begins to effect the romantic artist, romantic art loses its unity and beauty. Art dies in *appearance,* in the same ideal way that Absolute Mind makes history.

August von Ciezkowski (1814–1894), a well-travelled Pole who studied and worked in Germany, was the first to formulate the left Hegelian demand for the realization of philosophy in his *Prolegomena zur Historizosophie* (1838). Ciezkowski insisted that the external conditions of social life, not the conceptual problems that Hegel uncovered, represented the real obstacles to the realization of philosophy. For example, Hegel's schema of history miraculously found freedom in the Prussian state. For Ciezkowski, this stage was not a complete reconciliation of oppositions, rather a set of conditions that would make philosophic reconciliation possible. Ciezkowski collapsed Hegel's first three epochs, the Oriental, Greek and Roman worlds, into the stage of beauty (characterized by "being"); and made the Germano-Christian era the second stage of truth (characterized by "thought"). Ciezkowski's third stage of "the Good," the epoch of "praxis," would reconcile thought with being in action. Hegel would have dismissed this as prophecy. In a formulation that comes very close to Situationist theory's call for the creation of a new civilization, Ciezkowski's age of praxis would negate and transcend limitations in the objective realization of subjectivity. This age of action would realize beauty and truth in a society where, "being and thought must disappear in action, art and philosophy in social life." Debord quotes Ciezkowski on a board in his film version of *Society of the Spectacle:*

> After the direct practice of art has ceased to be the most distinguished thing; and this sermon devolves onto theory (such as it is), art detaches itself from theory in so far as a synthetic post-theoretical practice is formed, which has as its primary goal the foundation and truth of art as philosophy.

Bakunin and Herzen acknowledged their debt to Ciezkowski, and although Marx claimed that he never read Ciezkowski, this claim is probably as spurious as Nietzsche's claim that he never read Max Stirner's (1806–1856) line: "God is dead." For Marx, art was a compensation for a real life that is alienated in the separated economy. As with Hegel and Ciezkowski, the supersession of art would occur at a historical stage. Simplifying greatly, we see that for Marx, private property is the material expression of alienation because it appropriates human life, and art is only one particular mode of production that corresponds to the general laws of production. The suppression of private property coincides with the suppression of all alienating forces, such as art, and the simultaneous realization of art by free humans in a classless society. Marx didn't say exactly how art would be realized, and because of his economic, and more pointedly "workerist," perspective, Marx couldn't envision the suppression and realization of art as being creativity applied to the art of living. Debord applied Marx's statement "one can't realize philosophy with suppressing it" to art so that the formula called for the suppression and realization of art for the supersession of art (supersession—*anfhebung*—in Hegel and Marx means both to abolish and transcend, as with Marx's "critique" that tears away the veil of mystifications of philosophy while preserving some of its moments). As Jean-Francois Martos, author of *History of the Situationist International* put it, Marx envisioned the simultaneous suppression of the proletariat and realization of philosophy: Situationist theory called for the "simultaneous suppression of the proletariat and the realization of art after the auto-negation of art and the last international attack of the proletariat against the merchant world."

A great deal of Debord's effort in 1958 went toward the suppression of art. The lead editorial in the first issue of *Situationist International*, "The Bitter Victory of Surrealism" slammed a love letter written by a poor robot at the University of Manchester because it read like automatic writing. The use of tape recorders for sleep learning was one of the more repugnant uses of the subversive techniques of Surrealism. But nothing was worse than the use of brainstorming by managers in the United States as a cure for the virus of revolution. On November 18, Debord participated in a seminar on the topic "Is Surrealism Alive or Dead?" on the condition, accepted by those presenting the seminar, that official Surrealists be invited. The Surrealists who showed up objected to the use of tape recorded speeches, and their scandal was limited to throwing a burning newspaper into the hall on their way out. Debord's recorded speech was accompanied by guitar:

[...] The real question is: what is the role of Surrealism today?

From its origins, Surrealism is comparable with romanticism in its antagonism between attempts to affirm a new use of life, and a reactionary escape from reality.

[...] Surrealism today is perfectly boring and reactionary... Surrealist dreams correspond to bourgeois weakness, to artistic nostalgia, and to the refusal to envision the emancipatory use of the superior technical means of our time. By seizing these means, collective concrete experimentation on new environments and behaviors correspond to the beginning of a cultural revolution, outside of which, there is no authentic revolutionary culture.

In reporting on the event, Debord managed to get in a few kicks against Isou. And, just as Isou had constituted the retrograde element of Lettrism when Debord and Wolman created the Lettrist International, Debord railed against those who would prolong the life of the artistic spectacle and try to remake COBRA within the Situationist movement. These artists were branded the "right wing" of the S.I. In the *Situationist International,* literature got a periodic whipping, most often Robbe-Grillet. Poetry needed to be replaced and accomplished by revolutionary games. Music, painting, cinema—nothing was spared. It wasn't surprising that the S.I. celebrated the actions of an Italian painter who damaged a Rafael painting, and that Situationists in Belgium perpetrated a scandal against the Assembly of International Art Critics in Brussels.

Instead of creating works of art, the S.I. wanted to discover new desires and create the ambiances for their realization. Play was the primary modality in this realization of desires, but not play as was commonly understood at the time. Organized sports and intellectual exercises, such as chess, focused on competition, which was completely eliminated in Situationist games. The Situationist conception of play involves the communal creation of a playful ambiance, and the extension of these ambiances to the point that games invade all of life. One person might be the director of a given game, but this was only a "momentary subordination." The "livers" of a situation might effect interventions or bring strangers into the action to augment the power of play and provoke conditions favorable for direct living. Situationist games were to lead to living in accordance with desires, and to the struggle to discover new desires once certain commonplace desires had been realized. Not much thought was given to creating a harmony of desires; the S.I. seemed to take it for granted that desire depended on will, and life was a clash of wills.

While Debord opposed the shabby remains of modern art with Situationist games, the same theory and praxis of revolutionary play was used to oppose revolutionary intellectuals. The group *Socialisme or Barbarie,* with whom Debord would later collaborate, was berated for conceiving of the proletariat as "a sort of Hidden God of history" (a position akin to one Debord eventually adopted!). On this front, the S.I. lashed out at those who opposed general strikes and civil war. A member of the *Arguments* group that Lefebvre belonged to was chastised for belatedly discovering that politics was the only art, because he failed to realize that the goal of revolutionaries was to suppress politics. Without mentioning Lefebvre by name, the S.I. (and we can never forget that Debord was the dominant force in the movement) called for a critique of daily life and a new idea of happiness that entailed profound personal change.

Given the primary influence of Lefebvre on Debord's theory (the result of direct contact and collaboration), we might take a little diversion and see what roads Lefebvre took to get to *Arguments*. After attaining his doctorate in philosophy from the Sorbonne at eighteen, Lefebvre ran in bohemian circles that toyed with spiritualist and metaphysical ideas. Eventually he joined the P.C.F. and got down to the business of a serious Marxist analysis of society and revolution. He was first referred to Hegel by Breton, whose understanding of Hegel was limited, but this reference was crucial for Lefebvre's Hegelian interpretation of Marx. Lefebvre was associated with the first real Marxist theoretical journal to appear in France, *La Revue Marxiste*, first published in 1929. The journal was crushed by the P.C.F. (French Communist Party) in a notorious way that only added to Lefebvre's prestige.

Then, as Arthur Hirsh tells it in *The French Left*:

Lefebvre's first major study of Marxist philosophy, "Dialectical Materialism," was published in 1939. It immediately established him as the Party's leading philosopher. In this work he examined the differences between formal logic and dialectical logic, arguing in favor of the Hegelian dialectic. Following in Marx's footsteps he then criticized the idealist edifice of Hegel's system, while retaining his dialectical method as developed in the Phenomonology. Feurbacian materialism was given its due as an important state of transition from Hegel's idealism to Marx's dialectical materialism. The latter was presented as a philosophical method for analyzing the totality of knowledge and reality. Even while advocating the orthodox assertion of the dialectic of nature, Lefebvre laid stress on praxis as the core of Marx's thought. He also carefully avoided the dogmatic constriction of Marxism to nothing more than a positivist theory of political economy. He presented dialectical materialism as a totality, and quoting freely from Marx's *1844 Manuscripts*, he introduced the concepts of alienation and "total man." Through revolutionary praxis, the alienated individual could overcome self-fragmentation and emerge as a total human being, completely reconciled with self and the totality of Nature and human being.

Over the course of the next decade and a half, Lefebvre sparred with Breton, Sartre and others, as well as the Communist party itself. His stormy relationship with the party led to his eventual exclusion. Debord and the Situationists were certainly acquainted with all of Lefebvre's work both as a popularizer of Marxism, and as a profound theoretician, philosopher and literary critic, but it was *Critique of Everyday Life* that sparked the most interest within the S.I. In this work, Lefebvre argues that *new forms of alienation were spreading,* but that any consciousness of this alienation was short-circuited by the ideologies of marketing and consumption. Other ideologies were masked as science, and lent their support to the science of alienation—alienation itself being the only thing that unified the otherwise fragmented society. As a thorough-going Marxist, Lefebvre argued that the only way to overcome this alienation was revolution. Michel Trebitsch gives succinct expression to this in his preface to *Critique of Everyday Life:*

"Man must be everyday, or he will not be at all": in the first pages of *Critique of Everyday Life* Lefebvre uses this aphorism to show that from its starting point in everyday life the critique of everyday life can lead to the revolution of everyday life. "Everyday man" is the man of praxis, and praxis alone will enable him to free himself from alienation and attain the concrete totality of the "total man," at one and the same time the subject and the object of his becoming, a theme which was to become central to Lefebvre from *Dialectical Materialism* onwards. In other words, the only means of acceding to totality was via revolution. This quest for totality, which was to lead Lefebvre from "philosophical revolution" to Marxism, is none other than the quest for a theoretical method capable of reconciling thought and life, of changing life completely, of producing one's life as one creates a work.

Debord and Lefebvre carried on a dialogue from 1958 to 1963; and because of the obvious influence on Debord of *Critique of Everyday Life* we need to look at it in greater detail. Lefebvre was concerned with how people lived—where they spent their time, what their work routine was like, what sorts of pressures a person was under, etc. For Lefebvre, Marxism provides the critical knowledge of everyday life, and he hoped that applying this critical knowledge to the actual conditions would make a contribution to the art of living, i.e. the end of alienation. Entire books have been written on this topic, and Lefebvre's contribution warrants a lengthy essay that goes beyond the scope of this book on Debord. However, a brief outline of the essential points of the "Marxism as Critical Knowledge" section of the book, with illustrative quotes, will illuminate his trajectory and its influence on Situationist theory:

1. CRITIQUE OF INDIVIDUALITY

CENTRAL THEME: PRIVATE CONSCIOUSNESS

"We must supersede private 'consciousness'"

2. CRITIQUE OF MYSTIFICATIONS

CENTRAL THEME: "MYSTIFIED CONSCIOUSNESS"

"Bourgeois individualism implies the dreary, ludicrous repetition of individuals who are curiously similar in their way of being themselves and of keeping themselves to themselves, in their speech, their gestures, their everyday habits (meal times, rest times, entertainments, fashions, ideas, expressions)."

3. CRITIQUE OF MONEY

CENTRAL THEME: FETISHISM AND ECONOMIC ALIENATION

"Although deprivation and alienation are different for the proletarian and non-proletarian, one thing unites them: money, the alienated essence of the human being. This alienation is constant, i.e. practical and everyday."

4. CRITIQUE OF NEEDS

CENTRAL THEME: PSYCHOLOGICAL AND MORAL ALIENATION

"The more needs a human being has, the more he exists. The more powers and aptitudes he is able to exercise, the more he is free."

5. CRITIQUE OF WORK

CENTRAL THEME: THE ALIENATION OF THE WORKER AND OF MAN

"The human being—ceasing to be human—is turned into a tool to be used by other tools (the means of production), a thing to be used by another thing (money), and an object to be used by a class, a mass of individuals who are themselves 'deprived' of reality and truth (the capitalists). And his labor, which ought to humanize him, becomes something done under duress instead of being a vital and human need, since it is itself nothing more than a means (of 'earning a living') rather than a contribution to man's essence, freely imparted."

6. CRITIQUE OF FREEDOM

CENTRAL THEME: MAN'S POWER OVER NATURE AND OVER HIS OWN NATURE

"It is a complex dialectic: needs are becoming more extensive, more numerous, but because the productive forces are broadening, the extension of needs may imply their humanization, a reduction in the number of hours worked to satisfy immediate needs, a reduction of the time spent at work generally, a universalization both of wealth and of leisure. If, in a sense, the realm of natural necessity is growing more extensive, since the needs of modern man are tending towards greater complexity than those of primitive man, then the realm of freedom will only become greater and more profoundly rooted in nature as a result."

In the fifth section of *Critique of Everyday Life*, "written one Sunday in the French Countryside" Lefebvre visits the festivals of Greece, Rome and rural France. He gets a little carried away with the internal coherence of these peasant societies that lent an aura of mystery to trivial events, until he regains his Marxist bearings that condemns these festivals when they were accompanied with religious symbolism. All the moral imperatives of religion that tell people how to react to birth, death and every other aspect of life destroy "superior moments," such as the purely bacchanalian festival. This destruction then weighs on every aspect of daily life. But Lefevbre sees possibilities for a full life in these festive moments, lamenting only the fact that "life is lagging behind what is possible." Lefevbre called for comparing modern life with the past and the possible, contrasting moments such as everyday life and festival, critiquing the trivial by the exceptional and vice versa; confronting human reality with morality, psychology, philosophy, religion, literature, etc. The goal is a humanistic one: "the realization of total man" in a sexually-charged cultural revolution taking place in a creatively revitalized modern city.

Surprisingly, Lefevbre got little credit for this recipe for revolution, even though he was a professor at Nanterre where the events of May '68 were sparked. Baudrillard, then a Maoist, was Lefevbre's assistant. The Situationist's allies at Nanterre, the *Enragés* (who took their name from the proto-anarchists led by Jacques Roux during the French Revolution) took Lefevbre's classes. At the time, much of the credit for the '68 events went (erroneously) to Herbert Marcuse and other members of the Frankfurt School even though Lefevbre himself suggested slogans such as, "Let everyday life become a work of art!" To be sure, Lefevbre wasn't without his German influences; he acknowledged his debt to Heidegger (the philosopher of "being-there" in "average-everydayness") whom Debord called a "poor Nazi." Debord would have been able to find everything that Lefevbre took from *Being and Time* in Luckacs' *History and Class Consciousness*, which had a huge influence on Heidegger.

In a much earlier work, unknown to Lefebvre, Lukacs had established the opposition between the mechanical, dreary repetition of everyday life of "trivial life" and "authentic life," when a being creates or becomes a work of art. In his major work, *History and Class Consciousness*, Lukacs discarded this formulation in favor of locating consciousness in historicity and finding alienation in "reification of consciousness." Michele Bernstein, in her first-person novel *Tous les chevaux du roi* (dedicated to "Guy") plays with this concept by having the "other woman" ask Debord's character Gilles about his profession.

Carol: "What do you do?"

"Reification," answered Gilles.

"It's a serious study," I added.

"Yes," he said.

"I see," observed Carole with admiration. "It's very serious work with big books and lots of papers on a large table."

"No," Gilles said, "I drift. Principally, I drift."

What, then, is meant by reification? The definition in a modern American dictionary of sociology refers to reification as the fallacy of regarding an abstraction such as an "authoritarian personality" as a real phenomenon. But for the Hungarian Georg Lukacs, the founding father of Western Marxism, reification has a different meaning in his 1923 work *History and Class Consciousness*. This celebrated work is generally considered to be a romantic, anti-scientific, humanist recasting of Marx reminiscent of Marx's *Economic and Philosophical Manuscripts,* which wouldn't be discovered for another decade.

History and Class Consciousness is a collection of eight essays, most of which were "attempts, arising out of actual work for the party, to clarify the theoretical problems of the revolutionary movement in the mind of the author and his readers." Of the two exceptions to this rule, the chapter "Reification and the Consciousness of the Proletariat" (the major essay in the book) was the most inspiring to Debord. The other exception offers numerous false justifications for the success of the Bolshevik revolution and the "magnificent" development of the Russian Party under Lenin, reversing Lukacs' respect for Rosa Luxemburg in the early essays of *History of and Class Consciousness* when Lukacs still favored a blend of councils and vanguard parties. Despite Lukacs' reverence for Lenin, the book was denounced by Soviet authorities at the Vth World Congress of the Comintern. Lukacs was forced to make a self-repudiation, and he went so far as to attack Rosa Luxemburg's "illusion of an 'organic,' *purely proletarian* revolution," which is a striking contradiction given Lukacs' call for the proletarian to become the universal subject of history: "The proletariat seen as the identical subject-object of the real history of mankind." As a proletarian theorist, Debord insisted on the later formulation and wanted nothing if not for the rabble to live a history of their own making. This problem of the historical subject has important implications for Lukacs' reification, but first we need to look at how Lukacs used Marx to develop his theory of reification. The following is Lukacs' citation of Marx (from *Capital*) that illustrates, in part, what Lukacs means by reification:

A commodity is therefore a mysterious thing, simply because in it the social character of men's labor appears to them as an objective character stamped upon the product of that labor. The relation of the producer to the sum total of their own labor is presented to them as a social relation, existing not between themselves, but between the products of their labor. This is the reason why the products of labor become commodities, social things whose qualities are at the same time perceptible and imperceptible by the senses... It is only a definite social relation between men that assumes, in their eyes, the fantastic form of a relation between things.

Reification is therefore a distinct form of objectification where social relations between people are transformed into relations between things. Things take on a personification—commodities speak to each other in a language all their own as they move on the market. By the 1920s, the commodity had become the "universal category" of society for Lukacs, and this reification had squeezed humans into functions that a thing such as a robot could perform, to serve other things. People become things and relate to each other with things that they worship like the fetishistic objects of "primitive" peoples (rather than religious trinkets, money and commodities are the objects invested with occult power). But because Lukacs hadn't read Marx's *Economic and Philosophical Manuscripts* he had conflated the processes of objectification and reification.*

Rosa Luxemburg

Rather than being the strictly pejorative term it is today, "objectification" was, for Marx, the natural way humans project themselves in the world through their productive activity. Objectification can either be good (free people contemplating themselves in the world of their own making), or bad (alienation). What Lukacs had theorized was the objectification of human subjectivity, ignoring Marx's key concept of praxis whereby humans form themselves and nature by producing objects with their labor. Marx used praxis to analyze human history as it formed itself through its social and economic activity. Lukacs took a more idealistic approach to praxis by equating it with the objectification of subjectivity in class consciousness. Given Debord's contempt for labor, it's not sur-

---

*   In his 1967 preface to *History and Class Consciousness,* having read the young Marx, Lukacs wrote: "'I can still remember even today the overwhelming effect produced in me by Marx's statement that objectification was the primary material attribute of all things and relations.' This links up with the idea already mentioned that objectification is a natural means by which man masters the world and as such it can be either a positive or negative fact. By contrast, alienation is a special variant of that activity that becomes operative in definite social conditions. This completely shattered the theoretical foundations of what had been the particular achievement of *History and Class Consciousness.*"

prising that he would not insist on a purely Marxist interpretation of praxis that privileged labor as forming the social world. Debord wanted the historical praxis of revolution, not work, to transform the world.

Lukacs developed Marx's concept of fetishism with psychology and history into reification in large part by positing the proletariat as the subject-object of history. To understand what is meant by this identification of the proletariat as both the agent of history and object, I invoke the Neapolitan philosopher Giambattista Vico (1688–1744), and his famous humanist critique of Descartes' scientism subsumed in the verum-factum principle, i.e., you can only know what you make and make what you know. In other words, understanding is a function of participation rather than spectatorship. For Vico man must be concieved in a historical way, as part of a process of anthropogenesis. The unity of the subject and object is thus achieved by reversing the process of knowing, and mirroring the process of genesis—human history, for Vico, corresponds to the stages of human life:

1. Infancy: the state of barbarism and patriarchy of man the hunter, governed by magic.
2. Adolescence: the state of feudalism with a minority of lords and a majority of slaves.
3. Adulthood: the "new" state, the adulthood of humanity.

According to Lukacs, the bourgeoisie couldn't attain a total, unifed world view such as this because its thought was bogged down in Kantian categories, such as phenomenal vs. noumenal knowledge or descriptive vs. normative knowledge. And because of its class status, the bourgeoisie could never know a world that it didn't create. Although the proletariat could know the world that it created, it was prevented from doing so by the imposition of fragmentary, reifying mystification on the world by means of scientistic explanations. This fragmented worldview is at odds with the Marxist notion of the essence of humans as "the aggregate of social relations," and creates individuals who are alienated from their essential nature in the social process—individuals detached from the community. The bourgeoisie thus lost the ability to both understand and put the historical process in motion. The living flux of history was transformed into a dead naturalism comprised of Marx's fetishism of commodities and Max Weber's bureaucratic rationalization of the world. The only way to dereify bourgeois institutions was by proletarian revolution in which the subject of history, the proletariat, would become identical with the social world it creates. For Lukacs, and Debord after him, it is the Marxist perspective on human history that defines authentic proletarian consciousness as *the ability to explain the contemporary world and guide a revolution.* Lukacs:

To say that class consciousness has no psychological reality does not imply that it is a mere fiction. Its reality is vouched for by its ability to explain the infinitely painful path of the proletarian revolution, with its many reverses, its constant return to its starting point, and the incessant self-criticism of which Marx speaks in the celebrated passage of *The Eighteenth Brumaire*. Only the consciousness of the proletariat can point to the way that leads out of the impasse of capitalism… And if the proletariat finds the economic inhumanity to which it is subjected easier to understand than the political, and the political easier to understand than the cultural, then all these separations point to the extent of the still unconquered power of capitalist forms of life in the proletariat itself.

In terms of this discussion of Debord, it should be noted that Lefebvre never really developed Marx's notion of reification to the extent that Lukacs did; and that Karl Korsch (1889–1961), another Western Marxist influence on Debord, held that fetishism sufficed to describe reification. Noting that Marx never used the term, Korsch contended that there was no need for another conceptual term like reification. Korsch's *Marxism and Philosophy* was published at the same time as Lukacs *History and Class Consciousness,* and Korsch's name was associated with Lukacs for many years before he, and then others, highlighted the differences in their thinking. The son of a German banker, Korsch studied law before going to England where he was attracted to the Fabian socialists' practical attempts to implement socialism. Radicalized by WWI, Korsch's first Marxist works were concrete plans for the realization of socialism (against the professors of the Second International who had no "practical future-oriented thoughts"), and at the empirical verification of Marxist theory—Debord would call for similar projects during the 1970 Orientation Debate of the S.I. Korsch's most active moment in politics was as the Communist Minister of Justice in the First United Front government of Thuringe in 1923.

In *Marxism and Philosophy,* Korsch is at his most Hegelian, quoting Hegel when he held that philosophy is "its own epoch comprehended in thought." Korsch sought to explain Marxist theory historically, as the development of proletarian practice rather than the other way around. This insistence on theory following practice and conceiving the workers' movement historically go to the core of Debord's *Society of the Spectacle*. Korsch was pro-Bolshevik, but following Zinoviev's denunciation of him (in the same breath as Lukacs) he insisted on the validity of his book and headed west. While Lukacs was in exile in the USSR and pro-Stalin, Korsch called Stalin a Nazi counter-revolutionary. Even more than Rosa Luxemburg, Korsh advocated the supremacy of councils over the party and was skeptical of any Jacobin seizure of State power. A friend and teacher of Marxism to Brecht, Korsh would become a major source of inspiration for the New Left with his anti-authoritarian, activist tendencies. Debord seems to follow Korsch when the latter equates the historical action of the proletariat with the historical process—the history of the revolutionary process being one of proletarian praxis. Debord did, however, refuse all scientific readings of Marx, which is where Korsch's research turned in his later years when he denounced Hegel as a "German mystic."

Marx, Hegel, Lukacs, Korsch and Lefebvre formed the basis of Debord's thought, and Debord would apply the concepts of reification and fetishism to the exploding consumer culture under the influence of these thinkers. The influence of Lefebvre on the S.I. is transparently evident in Debord's essays "Theses on Cultural Revolution" (S.I. #1), "The Declaration of Amsterdam" (with Constant in S.I. #2), "Situationist Positions on Circulation" in (S.I. #3), and "Perspectives for Conscious Alterations in Daily Life" (cassette recording played at Lefebvre's conference of the Group for Research on Everyday Life and published in S.I. #6). It was probably just a coincidence that the major schism in the S.I. between the hard core revolutionaries and the artists in 1962 (anticipated by Debord as far back as his *Potlatch* article "One Step Back") was followed the next year by Debord's break with Lefebvre. But it is an interesting coincidence. Although Lefebvre was not an artist, his concerns were more relevant to the Situationists concept of unitary urbanism (favored by the artists in the group) than, say, Lukacs call for social revolution. While his break with Lefebvre was not over a theoretical disagreement (indeed, Lefebvre agreed, point for point, word for word with the Debord-Kotanyi-Vaneigem collaboration "Theses on the Paris Commune" and claimed them as his own in his book on the Paris Commune), Debord was developing lines of attack more in keeping with Lukacs than Lefebvre. In 1958, for example, Constant and Debord were able to agree on eleven points relating to unitary urbanism, Debord authoring the first and last points. The last of which would figure in their future split: "A constructed situation is the means to approach unitary urbanism, and unitary urbanism is the base of development of the construction of situations, as play and as what is serious about a freer society." At the IIIrd Situationist conference in 1959, the goal of integrating experimental culture in everyday life was suspended due to the necessity of creating a freer society through social revolution. Unitary urbanism was seen as a just first step on the path to a greater upheaval. Given Constant's preoccupation with experimental models of New Babylon (a name offered by Debord), Constant insisted on the central position of unitary urbanism and on collective activity in this realm as an alternative to making art, adding "uniting with a non-existent social revolution is utopian." Debord fired back, calling the notion of mistaking unitary urbanism for totality, "dogmatic idealism." Constant resigned from the S.I. in 1960. By this time "Negation and Consumption in the Cultural Sphere" as Debord called it in the penultimate chapter of *Society of the Spectacle* had become second nature to him and his closest associates.

The last chapter of Debord's major theoretical work is much more of an extension of Lukacs and Korsch than Lefebvre. Here, the invocation of Mannheim (who,
as a member of the Hungaro-Marxism school was working in the Lucakian tradition)
provided Debord with the means to make the accusation of history-blindness and
society-blindness in the charge of "false consciousness." The problems inherent in
the concept of "false consciousness" that exempts Marxism from the charge of "ideology" will be discussed in the context of a synopsis of *Society of the Spectacle*.

Here it's important to note that Debord was predisposed to the use of ideology
not just as the total ideology found in the Great Consensus of the spectacle, but also
in ways that legitimizes the egocentric-manichean trend of committed political
thought—he knew how to create an enemy and effect exclusions for crimes such as
"reactionary and idealist theses." As Michele Bernstein, author of the essay "No
Useless Leniency," that set an equally severe tone, put it in *Tous les chevaux du roi:*
"It's true that Gilles put an end to relations for frivolous reasons. I saw him be deliberately mean. But for a small number of people whose ways he liked, his friendship
was solid; his kindness proved it." Readers of *Situationist International* prone to
schadenfreud can take pleasure in the way the "Venetian jungle" overpowered and
closed in on Ralph Rumney (he failed to complete his psychogeography report on
Venice in time due to personal problems, and was excluded), or the way two Dutch
architects were excluded the instant they agreed to design a church.

Chapter Eighteen

Georges Pompidou

De Gaulle's Vth French Republic was
approved by referendum in 1958, and by
1959 the regime had legalized press censorship of
newspapers that disagreed with Gaullist positions. This was an auspicious time to launch a
revolutionary organization and journal—suspect
publications were impounded until March,
1965. Pompidou was appointed to run the government with strict, pro-industrial policies, such
as allowing the work week to climb from 44
hours per week at the time of the liberation, to 46
hours in 1966. The rural exodus would continue
so that by 1961, the population of the metropoli-
tan area of Paris would swell to 7.7 million. Along with the strides in French industry
that enabled the country to join the European Common Market, inequality had risen
sharply; and although French society prided itself on innovation, modernization,

adaptability, etc. the central fact of life was bureaucratic authority and consumption.

Meanwhile, strange things were happening around the world. In 1959, Castro's "humanistic" revolution swept Cuba, and the following year, the crisis in the Belgian Congo put every colonial power's legitimacy in question. De Gaulle entered into self-determination talks with Algeria and promised a referendum on the issue, much to the consternation of the French in Algeria and to the military. Elements of the military formed the notorious secret organization known as the O.A.S. that engaged the Algerian F.L.N. on every front. Strikers risked heavy government and O.A.S. reprisals during the '58–'62 period (the Evian Accords granted Algerian Independence in 1962). Stateside, Eisenhower warned of the omnipotence of the military-industrial-complex. And when Patrice Lumumba (a source of inspiration for the Situationists) was killed in the Congo in 1961, reportedly by the C.I.A., it must've seemed highly risky to Debord to be taking such extreme, ultra-left positions. The same year, these troubled waters began to boil in the Bay of Pigs (Cuban forces repelling the C.I.A.-led invasion), and the South Korean military junta overthrew the democratically elected government.

Debord, writing about himself in the third person in *Situationist International,* wants the world to know that he's fearless: "Interrogated on November 21, 1960, by the judicial police for his participation in the Declaration of the 121 against French

militarism in Algeria, Debord responded that he signed it as soon as it was communicated to him," which was right after the publication of the ordinances banning it. Debord went on to say that the only reason he didn't help write and distribute the declaration was because he wasn't given the chance, but he told the cops that he took full responsibility for having done so. This was around the same time as Trocchi's narrow escape from his APB in the United States for drug charges. And in 1958, Jorn refused to answer questions regarding his affiliation with a communist organization on his visa application, which effectively barred him from the United States. These were people of conviction who specialized in scandals and preferred danger to fear.

Throughout the following years, people from twenty countries met in order to enter into this obscure conspiracy of limitless demands. How many hasty journeys! How many long disputes! How many clandestine meetings in all the ports of Europe! Thus was mapped out the best-made program for felling with a single suspicion the whole of social life: classes, specialisms, work and entertainment, commodity and urbanism, ideology and State—we showed that it should all be thrown out. (from Debord's cinematic memoir *In Girum Imus Nocte et Consumimur Igni*)

In April 1959, the IIIrd S.I. conference took place in Munich and the IVth in London in 1960. Divergences in theory over unitary urbanism and social revolution (largely between Debord and Constant) were first exposed to the general assembly in Munich—a clear sign of a future split. The London conference abandoned the federative organization of the S.I. along national lines in favor of a Central Council— the members to be named at each conference. At the meeting, held at a "secret address" (the British Sailors Society), Debord proposed a questionnaire asking: 1) What forces the S.I. could count on in society; and 2) In what conditions. The responses led to an all night discussion. The S.I. "Manifesto," which had been written in May 1960, was unanimously adopted: "The revolutionary players of all countries can unite in the S.I. to begin to exit the prehistory of everyday life."

Jorn's biographer, Guy Atkins, describes "The Situationists in London" in humorous remarks that illuminate Debord:

They had been advertised to start at 8:15 p.m. but shortly before 9 o'clock the group of Situationists who occupied the anteroom and bar of the I.C.A. were still wrangling over the English translation of their 'declaration.' At this point Mrs. Dorothy Morland, the director of the I.C.A., asked me to tell Guy Debord (who doesn't speak English), that she would cancel the meeting if he was not ready to begin by 9 o'clock. I thought that such an ultimatum would be counterproductive, so I reversed the message. I told Guy Debord that the directrice was most anxious that the text of the statement should be as authentic as possible and that the audience was quite willing to wait as long as necessary. At this Debord immediately gathered up his papers and the group filed into the auditorium.

Atkins went on to explain that the first (and only) question, a general question about "Situationism" received the following response: "Guy Debord stood up and said in French 'We're not here to answer cuntish questions'. At this he and the other Situationists walked out. One of the interesting features of the evening had been the remarkable consistency of the play-acting by the Situationist audience in an unrehearsed situation."

Another perspective on these events is offered by Jacqueline de Jong whose first encounter with the Situationists as a group was in London. She noted that the task of explaining Situationist theory fell to the Belgian Maurice Wyckaert, but his drunken

Jacqueline de Jong

monologue—rich in jargon—was lost on the I.C.A. audience: what the audience did comprehend (his call to turn the I.C.A. into a Situationist center) staggered them. According to de Jong, it wasn't play acting that the Situationists were engaged in—Jorn preferred to dine with his New York agent, Debord didn't want to be seen in public and there were very real language problems. In the end, the only significant thing produced at the conference was a tract calling for Trocchi's release from prison.

De Jong describes Debord as being funny, intelligent, arrogant, strict, impossible and "superior," although she concedes that this attitude wasn't unjustified. She went from her native Holland to Paris and spent some time with Debord wandering around Les Halles and environs ("his universe"). She recalls the way they explored buildings in the process of demolition to examine how they had been constructed. She makes the interesting point that Debord wasn't writing much at that time, he was "creating ideas."

The Central Council would meet in Brussels (where the Bureau of Unitary Urbanism had set up shop after Constant's resignation), Paris (where it worked out

plans for a micro-city on an Italian island), and Munich (where it accepted the resignation of Jorn), before the Vth conference in Goteborg, Sweden, in 1961. When one of the conference participants allowed that he didn't really comprehend Situationist theory, Debord enigmatically responded: "No one said that Mayakovsky was intelligent because he didn't understand math or French; but anyone could confirm his intelligence given the proof that he didn't understand anything about Futurism." By the end of the session there was reportedly some howling of insults taking place between theorists and artists:

"Your theory is going to fly right back in your faces!"

"Cultural pimps!"

Jorn's resignation "to combat his glory" didn't prevent his collaboration with the S.I., for about a year, under the pseudonym George Keller. In his 1969 work *At the Foot of the Wall,* Jorn would comment, "It's my duty to underline the decisive role for me played by the Situationist movement, and in particular, my friend Guy Debord." Rumor has it that Jorn continued to finance the S.I. journal by giving Debord paintings, but his lack of direct involvement must have put financial pressure on the group. Guy Atkins' describes the part played by Jorn in the movement:

> Jorn's role in the Situationist movement (as in COBRA) was that of a catalyst and team leader. Guy Debord on his own lacked the personal warmth and persuasiveness to draw people of different nationalities and talents into an active working partnership. As a prototype Marxist intellectual Debord needed an ally who could patch up the difficult human relationships and who could rise about the petty egoisms and squabbles of the members. Their quarrels came into the open the moment Jorn's leadership was withdrawn in 1961.
>
> Jorn's contribution to the S.I. literature consisted of five articles printed in the official magazine. These were designed (to use Jorn's phrase in another context) to

strike a balance between the serious and the fatuous (*IS,* I, p.23). He regarded absurdity and fatuity as important social values. Games, in his view, are absurdities conducted under a system of rules. In one of his articles, Pataphysics: a religion in the making (*IS,* VI, p.23), he quotes the anarchist slogan "to each man his own absurdities." This article (printed after his resignation from the movement) earned him a footnote from Guy Debord, who vented his dislike for pataphysical humor by calling such humor "static and non-creative." Better static humor, one feels, than none at all.

It was with Jorn's technical skill, artistic ability and funds that Debord was able to create and publish, in 1959, the *Memoires* book discussed in chapter 9. This commemorative looking back and *programmatic glance forward* would mark much of Debord's artistic propaganda, and was echoed in his "The Role of *Potlatch,* Then and Now" in a special "one shot" of *Potlatch* as an internal S.I. document (the plan to produce a new series of *Potlatch* in Holland was never carried out beyond this one issue). Reportedly Jorn was looking for ways to waste the vast amount of money he made on his paintings, and started the Dansk-Fransk Experimental-filmskompagni to underwrite two Debord films.

Debord's *On the Passage of a Few People Through a Rather Brief Unit of Time* is a twenty minute, black and white film that can be considered as "notes on the origins of the Situationist movement; notes that, by this fact, evidently contain a reflection on their own language." In addition to recordings of the French and German debates of the IIIrd S.I. Conference in Munich, the soundtrack included commentary in an announcer's voice (Jean Harnois), a sad voice (Guy Debord) and a young girl's voice (Claude Brabant). The commentary was mostly composed of diverted phrases from "classic thinkers, a science fiction novel, or the worst sociologist then in style." In order to avoid a spectacular viewpoint, every time the camera panned close to a monument, the point of view was reversed, giving the view from the monument. Debord had some rather extravagant plans to divert popular films (the Russian general in *For Whom the Bell Tolls* answering the phone and remarking that it's too late, the offensive had been launched and would fail like the others to illustrate the failure and intentions of revolutionaries in the 1950s). But he couldn't get the rights for most of the films he had chosen. A publicity film was used, along with film of Andre Mrugalski's photographs in a diverted sequence of a "documentary on art."

The film opens in Paris circa 1952 and evokes the bohemian slumming of the Lettrist days—St. Germain des Pres, the coming and going of police vans and the outside walls of prisons. The underage girls, the labyrinth, remarks on "the ambience of play"—these and other familiar motifs make an appearance in the documentary film that, above all, posed questions about the nature of cinematic enterprises.

Debord makes use of the blank screen to underscore the spoken word, but the images range from Paris to Japan to the Algeria of May 1958 when the "parachutists" took over. Interestingly, it is the announcer and not Debord who accounts for the origins of the Situationist movement:

> This neighborhood was made for wretched occupations and intellectual tourism. The sedentary population of the upper floors was sheltered from the influences of the street. This neighborhood has remained the same. It was the strange setting for our story. Here, a systematic questioning of all the diversions and works of a society, a total critique of its idea of happiness was expressed in acts. These people also scorned "subjective profundity." They were interested in nothing but an adequate and concrete expression of themselves.

Debord's voice, sad as it is, is nonetheless forward-looking, concerned with missed opportunities, but also with what is to be done. Perhaps the best explanation for Debord adopting this melancholic tone is in Michele Bernstein's 1960 novel *Tous les chevaux du roi*— Gilles, the character modeled on Debord,

Still from *On the Passage...*

has an interesting exchange on being sad with a young woman:

> "We've found a way to remain adolescents, or like them. We won't grow old except in the last extreme. We'll let you in on the plot."
> "Good," Carol smiled, "I'll never be sad."
> "Ah, yes," he said, "one must be sad. Enormously. Otherwise you'll grow old right away."
> She joked: "You're sad alot."
> "Me? Awfully," Gilles said.
> "What a strange way to be sad," she said to him.
> "The best."

The following passage from the film, in Debord's voice, represents another angle on what is essentially the same dissatisfaction, recast in terms of courage:

> The appearance of events that we didn't make, that others made against us, obliges us from now on to be aware of the passage of time, its results, the transformation of our own desires into events. What differentiates the past from the present is precisely its out-of-reach objectivity; there is no more should-be; being is so consumed that it has ceased to exist. The details are already lost in the dust of time. Who was afraid of life, afraid of night, afraid of being taken, afraid of being kept?

The young woman's voice is the most militant:

> The dictatorship of the proletariat is a desperate struggle, bloody and bloodless, violent and peaceful, military and economic, educational and administrative, against the forces and traditions of the old world.

The title *On the Passage of a Few People Through a Rather Brief Unit of Time* is of interest because of Debord's identification of life with the "passage of time." The Institute of Contemporary Art borrowed this title for their Situationist exhibit cata-

Henri Bergson

logue and translated unité, not as "unit," but as "period," which mutes Debord's intended critique of what Henri Bergson (1859–1941) called scientific time, or *t*. Echoing Maine de Biran, Bergson argued that the primary inner experience was the "flow" of life, not the mechanistic motion of the hands of a clock. What Debord is saying here is that a *unit* of time (a year, hour, second, etc.) in no way corresponds to the way time acted on their lives in an irreversible way. Bergson called the experience of time as an active and ongoing process "real duration," and maintained that trying to represent it with spacial images (such as a clock) was an abstract illusion. Whereas Debord never cited Bergson and certainly opposed Bergsonism, he clearly echoes Bergson's insistence on the qualitative irreducibility of experienced time and Bergson's observation that people erroneously identify themselves with external images rather than with the experience of "real duration." Bergson's theories had been so widespread in France for so long that Debord wouldn't have had to read the Nobel Prize winner's books to be aware of them—Bergson's ideas were in the air. Of course for Debord, this apprehension of time was colored with the Hegelian preoccupation with the self-conscious creation of history with acts of negation, as well as the Marxist analysis of the spreading of commodity characteristics to all production, social relations and time. Nothing rings as hollow for Debord as the dictum: time is money. Money is the mechanism that enables humans to exchange their abstract units of work time (exchange value or monetary value is subsequently transformed into use value). By the time Debord wrote *Society of the Spectacle,* he was applying Marxist categories ("temporal surplus value") and rhetoric ("the violent expropriation of their time") to his analysis of time. But of all Debord's ruminations on, and attempts to represent this flow time, nowhere is he more insightful than when he speaks of the history of revolution, when years could be measured in decades or even centuries; and of the high evaluation he gave to the May '68 graffiti "Quick," which reflects the fact that what would normally take ages to change, changes overnight in a revolution.

One of the few still shots from the film *On the Passage...* pictured in Debord's *Complete Cinematic Works* is of the old Paris market, les Halles, where virtually all the agricultural produce entered the city, and where it was Debord's rite to watch the sun rise. Before it was turned into an ultra-modern shopping mall by Pompidou in the 1970s, les Halles was the heart of Paris. In *The Assassination of Paris,* Louis Chevalier reports that the decision to close the market was made in 1959 (but the government didn't plan to move the operation until 1966):

> Thus, les Halles, for a few more years, repelled all assaults, survived and even lived, as if the prospect of disappearing, more and more real after 1964, meant, at least for the young, a hatred of life. "Let's live while we may, it's not at Rungis [where the market would be moved] that we'll be able to laugh about things." Such was the caption for an elaborate cartoon by Moisan in Le Canard. Rungis! It is as if one had said the Big Bad Wolf. But soon, even at les Halles, there wasn't much laughing. From 1968, as far as young people were concerned, there was hardly any—certainly not in May 1968—except for some stragglers from the Latin Quarter preaching revolution to some poor prostitutes waiting to hook a client. "We will miss les Halles!" they said in my bistro in Moliere's old house. They already missed it, obliged to serve (and with some disdain), God knows what drinks made with mineral water, even whiskey, to the antique dealers who were now their clients. Here where only yesterday Silenus was pouring red wine for the young gods of Olympus.

Critique of Separation, another twenty minute, 35mm, black and white film was shot in September and October of 1960 and edited in January–February, 1961. Before the film actually begins, the voice of Caroline Rittener (who also played the young girl) cites a passage from Andre Martinet's *Elements of General Linguistics* ("When one dreams how natural and advantageous it is for man to identify his language with reality, one imagines the degree of sophistication he needed to disassociate language and reality, and make each an object of study") as posters announcing the film flash by on the screen: SOON, ON THIS SCREEN—ONE OF THE GREATEST ANTI-FILMS OF ALL TIME!—REAL CHARACTERS! AN AUTHENTIC STORY!—ON A THEME NEVER BEFORE CAPTURED ON FILM... Debord did the voiceover himself; the music was by Francois Couperin, Bodin and Boismortier. Many of the images were from comics, passport photos, press photos and other films, often "supercharged with subtitles, [that are] very difficult to follow at the same time as the commentary."

The opening sequence has Debord picking up a young girl at a cafe terrace, but the commentary implies that while this is pleasant, it's not enough: "What true project has been lost?" Next the narration turns against the "false, isolated coherence, dramatic or documentary, as a substitute for a communication and an activity that are absent" in cinema. Time rolls on, wasted. As spectators we remain children. The alternative is to "contest the totality," but even this adventure is tainted by the "whole range of legends transmitted by cinema or in other ways; part of the whole spectacular sham of history"—illustrated by knights in a Hollywood film. By following a poetic interpretation of dreams as they "illuminate moments previously lived in confusion and doubt" with a critique of the "sector of rulers" (Khruschev, de Gaulle, Eisenhower, Franco, the Pope) Debord draws a line between personal history and spectacular history that dissolves when he shifts to a riot in the Congo: "But it's always far away. [...] It makes us disappointed in ourselves. At what moment was choice postponed? [...] I let time slip away. I lost what I should've defended." In a particularly brilliant passage, Debord describes the way the boredom of daily life makes art alluring, adding: "This is a paradox to reverse, to put back on its feet."

The texts and technical descriptions of Debord's first three films were published as *Against Cinema* by Jorn's Institute of Comparative Vandalism in 1964. In his introduction "Guy Debord and the Problem of the Accursed," Jorn points to Godwin's inspiration of Shelly, Wordsworth, Blake and others, and notes that it's only by having solidarity with this "bad passion" that rules get broken. Over time the "accursed" was transformed into the romantic concept of misunderstood genius, but false explanations like this have nothing to do with Guy Debord.

According to Jorn the "most informed" critiques of the time recognized Debord as one of the biggest innovators in the history of cinema. Jorn mentions the influence of *Howlings in Favor of Sade* on Resnais' *Hiroshima mon amour,* but adds: "One ignores that his film activity is only a tease, a chance, a mediocre instrument to make a precise demonstration of his more general capacities." Debord inspired the silence

Guy Debord gets the girl in *Critique of Separation*

that John Cage introduced in music and the monochrome paintings of Yves Klein. The early Philippe Sollers novel *The Park* owes a debt to Debord, as does the "mania to communicate by comics detached from their original meaning, that is now the strike force of new American painting." Debord is the "the great exception" who transforms and corrects the rules of the "human game" to correspond to the new realties of his time. Jorn:

There are no "misunderstood geniuses," innovators poorly known naturally. There are only those who refuse to become known by being portrayed in striking discord with what they really are, those who don't want to let themselves be manipulated to appear in public in a misunderstood way, and by this alienated fact be reduced to the state of instruments hostile to their own cause [...] Guy Debord isn't badly known, he is known as being bad.

Chapter Nineteen

"I knew Gilles' taste for spending the night in a long march, where an open cafe becomes a precious port of call on the streets where the sleep-walker doesn't surrender." Of the many portraits in Michele Bernstein's novels that depict her life with Debord, one that stands out is of "Gilles" reading a novel by Kast and the journal *Socialisme ou Barbarie,* published by the group of the same name (1949–1965). Debord reportedly had a subscription to the journal, attended the meetings and might've been a member for a short time. The prime movers of the group were Cornelius Castoriadis and Claude Lefort. Castoriadis, a Greek, became a communist in his youth in the resistance, then broke with the Stalinists at the time of the Athens uprising in 1944 and joined the Trotskyist Fourth International. Writing under the pseudonyms Cardin, Chaulieu, Coudray and Delvaux, Castoriadis' voice dominated the forty issues of the journal. Lefort had been a student of Merleau-Ponty and joined the Trotskyist P.C.I. (International Communist Party). Socialism or Barbarism was highly critical of the rise of the bureaucratic class in both the East and the West, a point that the S.I. would continually echo. Armed with economic statistics, the S&B writers showed that managers in the East and corporate, union, and welfare bureaucrats in the West, comprised the bureaucratic class that completely encompassed the classical bourgeoise. The contraries were no longer found in proprietors and labor, but between order givers and order takers, managers and managed. These bureaucracies create alienation by their natural tendency to create cliques and competition for control among "specialists." Factories were no longer the place of socialization. To unify life and production, Socialism or Barbarism advocated the council communist organizational model, (based on the Russian soviets of 1905 and 1917, the council revolts in Germany and Italy after WWI, and Hungary in 1956) that would figure so large in Debord's *Society of the Spectacle* and elsewhere. It was Socialism or Barbarism that first trumpeted the "generalized self-management" platform that was on everyone's lips during May '68.

In the summer of 1960, Debord was looking for allies, and praised *Socialisme ou Barbarie* writer Pierre Canjeurs for underscoring the alienation of "the race to consume" in a society that thwarts creativity. Debord and Canjeurs soon co-authored

"Preliminaries Toward Defining a Unitary Revolutionary Program." Here, Debord clearly refutes the charge by critics that Situationists have no idea about Marxist concerns such as production and surplus-value. In regard to production, Debord and Canjeurs assert:

For the capitalist class, dominating production entails monopolizing the understanding of productive activity, of work. To achieve this, work is on the one hand more and more fragmented, i.e. rendered incomprehensible to those who do it; and on the other hand, it is reconstituted as a unity by specialized agencies.

The first sentence in the essay deals with surplus value in a way that makes it central to cultural revolution:

Culture can be defined as the ensemble of means through which a society thinks of itself and shows itself to itself, and thus decides on all aspects of the use of its available surplus-value; that is to say, it is the organization of everything over and beyond the immediate necessities of the society's reproduction.

According to the authors, work is absurd (and must be transformed by worker management of production); science obfuscates more than it clarifies; life is equated with useless consumption: "The world of consumption is in reality the world of mutual spectacularization of everyone, the world of everyone's separation, estrangement and nonparticipation." Everyone either relates to each other through the spectacle or through work in an inhuman science-fiction world that divides people into directors and executors, authors and spectators. Revolutionary art suffers from the same spectator-spectacle relation because the revolutionary expression is destroyed by "the reactionary element present in all spectacles." Revolutionary artists, according to the authors, must shatter the spectacle. The essay ends with sections on autonomous self-realization and "utopian practice":

Utopian practice makes sense, however, only if it is closely linked to the practice of revolutionary struggle. The latter, in its turn, cannot do without such utopianism without being condemned to sterility. The seekers of an experimental culture cannot hope to realize it without resuming the efforts of the cultural avant-garde toward the critique of everyday life and its free reconstruction.

Other *Socialisme ou Barbarie* writers wouldn't fare so well, particularly a certain Chatel in Debord's "For a Revolutionary Judgment of Art." Written in February 1961 while the lab work for *Critique of Separation* was underway, it's perhaps understandable that Debord finds Chatel's critique of Goddard insufficient. Chatel considered *Breathless* to be a "valuable example" of a film that relates to the revolutionary project. Naturally Debord disagrees on the grounds that only a film that questions film's "function as a spectacle" even begins to play the revolutionary game. Art criticism only rates as "a second-degree spectacle" and tries to elevate the role of the spectator of cinematic spectacles. "Revolution is not 'showing' life to people," Debord tells us, "but making them live."

Despite this short-lived attempt to ally with the post-Trotsky left, Debord continued to use "daily life," as formulated by Lefebvre, as the axis of Situationist analysis. In "Situationist Positions on Circulation," for example, Debord treats transport as a supplement to work that reduces free time—this is reminiscent of Lefebvre's "constrained time," which isn't work, but time spent on repeated formalities and obligations. For Debord, the automobile isn't transportation, but the "sovereign good of an alienated life." It exasperated Debord to see Paris architecture revised to accommodate cars (the mass destruction of housing), and he foresaw the day when cars would be forbidden in ancient cities. This prediction was only slightly less fanciful than his suggestion that by 1979 we would be flying around in personal helicopters. These ideas show us where Debord differed with the prevailing use of new technologies—he wanted the circulation of people and things to conform to the pleasures of his drifts. The urban games played by Situationists would dissolve separations such as work-leisure, and collective-private life, "paving the way with their experiments for a human journey through authentic life."

In an unsigned editorial note in *Situationist International* #4, Lefebvre's "theory of moments" (whereby the transformation of a moment is a defining aspect of a free act) is discussed in relation to the "construction of situations." The differences between moments and situations seem more apparent than real—the attempt to make the distinction is, however, revealing. A constructed situation, like a moment, is composed of ephemeral instants. But a situation is somewhere between an instant and a moment, and because of the way it favors chance, situations can't be repeated the way a moment could be because a situation is a perishable work of art. Whereas Lefebvre lists types of moments, situations combine and slip into new situations with such fluidity that every given situation escapes definition. The best "constructed moment" is therefore a series of irretrievable situations "attached to a theme" (a "situationist theme," we're told, is a "*realized* desire"). But this constructed moment is, unlike Lefebvre's natural moment as discussed in his *La Somme et le Reste,* irretrievable, which seems like an artificial distinction as soon as one recognizes the fundamental role of context—the S.I. editorial claims that the space-time aspect of situations distinguishes them from moments, which are predominantly defined by their temporal aspect. It's not possible to clarify this without speculating about both sides.

What's clear is that Debord was looking for ways to collaborate with Lefebvre without allowing the older professor to get the slightest upper hand.

In May 1961, Debord presented *Perspectives For Conscious Alterations in Everyday Life* to Lefebvre's Group for Research on Everyday Life as a tape recording "to break with the appearance of pseudocollaboration, of the artificial dialogue established between a lecturer 'in person' and his spectators." The speech is peppered with jokes about sociologists who disputed the existence of everyday life because for them, every aspect of life could be the object of some specialized research (Debord accepts Lefebvre's definition of everyday life as being, "what remains after one has eliminated all specialized activities.") Debord shows his scorn for these sociologists who haughtily think that workers must be infected with the "virus of everyday life" because they had no specialized activities. The reality of the situation is actually the reverse—everyday life infiltrates specialized activities to a greater extent than the sociologists are aware.

The class divisions in society impoverish everyday life by making people time-poor, and unable to make full use of the little free time that comes their way. Debord cites Lefebvre's application of Lenin's theory of unequal development to everyday life to make his own analogy—everyday life is more than merely a lagging sector, it's colonized, "a sort of reservation for the good natives" whose creative force makes the society, but who don't freely create the history they live. It's interesting to note that Debord's concept of the "colonization of daily life" is echoed without acknowledgement by the German philosopher Jurgen Habermas with his phrase the "colonization of the lifeworld." Instead of promoting life, communication, and self-realization, everyday life is the "realm of separation and spectacle." Debord is critical of the technologies that became part of everyday life in his time because they reduce independence and creativity. But it's precisely this poverty of daily life that exposes its possible richness, which could in turn lead to the reinvention of revolution.

Here Debord reverses the perspective of the sociologists and flatly states that everyday life has been disarmed, and needs to be rearmed by questioning everything that's external to it. Although Debord is critical of love and drugs here, it's only because they're now so trite. He wants new vices, passions, uses for life, and a new model for revolution that denounces everything that transcends everyday life. The only alternative to the revolutionary transformation of everyday life is the "reinforcement of modern slavery." Here, perhaps more so than anywhere else, we see Debord acknowledging the central place Lefebvre's everyday life had in revolutionary theory and practice. Raoul Vaneigem (a Belgian scholar of Roman philology who joined the S.I. in 1960, jokingly referred to as the "Vampire of Borinage" by Debord), would be widely identified with this concept in the English-speaking world by the translated title of his 1967 classic: *The Revolution of Everyday Life.*

Debord's break with Lefebvre would come in 1963, when the latter plagiarized (thesis by thesis, almost word for word) the legendary *Theses on the Paris Commune* by Debord, Vaneigem and Attila Kotanyi. The S.I. tract "To the Trash Can of History" was never refuted by Lefebvre:

> ... Henri Lefebvre was writing a book about the Commune and asked the Situationists for a few notes that would assist him. These notes were communicated at the beginning of April 1962. We thought it would be good to pass a few of these radical theses, on such a subject, into a book accessible to a wide public.

The S.I. thought that Lefebvre had left the group Arguments, which the S.I. was boycotting, and it was in part on these grounds that they assisted Lefebvre. Naturally, Debord was angry when he found out that Lefebvre had published the fourteen theses as if they were fourteen unnumbered paragraphs he had written as the conclusion to his book on the Commune in the last edition of *Arguments.* For Debord and the Situationists, *Arguments* might have done some good translations, but it was too full of the feeble thoughts of university professors and others who played the State's game. Lefebvre had been a rare exception to the rule of non-collaboration with university types. Debord shared Lefebvre's philosophy of history, but Debord especially liked the way Lefebvre identified with Marx's famous 11th Thesis on Feuerbach: "Philosophers have only *interpreted* the world in various ways; the point, however, is to *change* it." As Lefebvre put it, his friendship with Debord was "a love story that didn't end well."

Adolphe Thiers

Before delving into this important collaborative work by Debord, Vaneigem and Kotanyi (reportedly written in a few hours), I'll provide a thumbnail sketch of the Paris Commune. Students of history will recall that Napoleon III declared war on Bismark's Prussia on July 14, 1870; and then surrendered a few months later. The Empire fell and the IIIrd French Republic (1871–1873) was proclaimed while, simultaneously, the German Empire was proclaimed. The conservative Adolphe Thiers was the first president of the IIIrd Republic. Still hoping the National Guard could beat the Prussians who were preparing a siege of Paris, Thiers armed 384,000 working class men. Meanwhile, the leftist Faure lead an insurrectionary demonstration at Hotel de Ville that prompted Marx (in London) to warn Parisians not to overthrow the new Republic.

Even though the Prussian army had encircled Paris, the people of the city still paraded in honor of Liberty and staged more demonstrations at the Hotel de Ville. On October 27, Thiers agreed to Bismark's harsh peace terms and used the 200,000 French war prisoners then released for the "pacification" of Paris. Less than a week later, leftists and radical National Guard battalions marched on Hotel de Ville trying to establish a Commune of Paris reminiscent of the communes of the Middle Ages— free, self-determined cities. Government troops counter-attacked, arresting the leaders and dispersing the insurrectionary force.

On January 7, 1871, in defiance of the Government of National Defence, the Republican Central Committee of the Twenty Districts of Paris called for the establishment of a Commune of Paris to fight the Prussians. The German Empire was proclaimed in the Hall of Mirrors at Versailles as the siege of Paris continued to inflict hardships on the population of the city. At the end of January, insurrectionary demonstrations were mounted by National Guard battalions opposed to Thiers' surrender to the Germans. Severe repressions ensued. The armistice was signed. German troops occupied the Champs Elysees; and to prevent clashes, cannons were moved to Montmartre.

In February, nationwide elections created a heavily monarchist National Assembly. Thiers retained power as Head of the Executive Power. By the end of the month, civilians, National Guardsmen, women and children had moved more artillery from the center of the city to Montmartre and surrounding districts. Prussian troops briefly occupied Paris at the beginning of March, and when they left, a power vacuum developed. The National Assembly moved to Versailles and promulgated measures that provoked the working class of Paris; measures such as the discontinuance of the moratorium on rents and payment of commercial bills, and cancellation of daily pay for the National Guard. The military governor of Paris sentenced the revolutionaries Blanqui and Flourens to death in absentia.

The Federation of the National Guard that was formed in protest to the government surrender to the Germans organized a democratically elected Central Committee that endorsed the republican form of government. Thiers sent the army to confiscate the cannons in Montmartre, but the troops refused to fire on the women and children in the van who were winning the sympathy of the troops. The next day, March 19, the Central Committee of the National Guard called for elections for a Commune of Paris. Commues were proclaimed in Lyons, Marseilles and Toulouse, and attempted in Narbonne and Sainte-Etienne. On March 26, 1871, the Commune of Paris was proclaimed and communards moved into Hotel de Ville under a red flag. Socialists, neo-Jacobins, anarchists, pacifists, humanitarians, Marxists and a strong contingent of women shared power with the Central Committee of the National Guard.

Church and state were separated (indeed, the Archbishop of Paris would be executed). Government employee salaries were limited to the pay of a skilled worker. Despite the exaggerations of the destructive force of Communard kerosene bombs in the international press, Marx expressed his solidarity in his "Address to the People of Paris," which would later become his famous *Civil War in France.* Women's groups (The Union of Women, the Committee of Women, Association of Women for the Defense of Paris and Aid to the Wounded and the Woman's Vigilance Committee) acted heroically as the government in Versailles began to march on Paris. The Commune decreed that abandoned factories and workshops be transferred to worker-owned cooperatives and the occupation of vacant lodgings.

On May 1, power in the Commune was delegated to a Committee of Public Safety (an act that was opposed by a minority). Pro-Versaille newspapers were outlawed, national pawnshops were forced to return objects, neighborhood clubs were formed, and on May 16, the Vendome Column was toppled. A few days later, the Versailles armies (mostly provincials and former war prisoners) entered Paris. In a week of bloody fighting, the Communards burned memorials of the empire and executed hostages. The Versaillais shot tens of thousands of Communards—many more were jailed and hundreds were executed. The most vivid expressions of the legacy of the commune were by Lenin in 1917 on the eve of revolution, and by French women who evoked it during the resistance to Nazi occupation in 1944, and again by those "recommunizing" Chinese bureaucratic structures in Shanghai in 1976, and of course in the events of May 1968 in Paris.

In his essay "The Permanence of the Commune" Richard Greeman makes an excellent, point-by-point analysis of Debord and his fellow Situationist's *Theses on the Paris Commune* (the theses are in roman and Greeman's commentary is in italics):

▼▼▼ 1 ▼▼▼

The classical workers movement must be reexamined without illusions, particularly without illusions regarding its political and pseudo-theoretical heirs, for they possess only the heritage of its failures. The apparent successes of this movement are its fundamental failures (reformism or the setting up of a state bureaucracy) and its failures (the Commune or the Asturias revolt) have remained open successes, for us and for the future.

Here we have the theoretical basis for the rejection of the so-called "realists" of the Left, the official Socialists and Communists, by the revolutionary masses of 1968. The parties of the "Senile Left" were pushed aside in practice precisely because they insisted on limiting the movement to practical "successes" (e.g. the 10% wage-raises negotiated by Grenelle in order to end the general strike and twice rejected by the workers; the electoral circus

The Fall of the Vendome Column

imposed by the parties on the masses as a substitute for direct action). These "successes" were in fact defeats for the working class, while the actual process of the open and ongoing revolt was the first real success the European workers had seen since 1936. This lesson in practice has not been lost, for the process of rethinking working-class history has continued in France since 1968 from precisely the viewpoint suggested above, as witness the dozens of new books reviving the traditions of its apparent "failures:" the early Soviets, the Humanism of the young Marx, the Sparticists, the anarchists, etc.

▼▼▼ 2 ▼▼▼

The Commune was the greatest festival of the 19th century. On a fundamental level, the rebels seemed to feel they had become the masters of their own history, not so much on the level of "governmental" political decisions as on the level of daily life in that Spring of 1871 (note how everyone played with their weapons: they were in fact playing with power). This is also the sense in which we must understand Marx: "The greatest social measure of the Commune was its own existence in acts."

The Spring festival, the playing with power, the euphoric sense of release and self-mastery, the joy of at last feeling real, responsible, human, the pressing urge to transform daily life, the recognition of the seriousness of "play"—how better to express the essential spirit of the 1968 May Revolt?

▼▼▼ 3 ▼▼▼

Engels' phrase: "Look at the Paris Commune—that was the dictatorship of the proletariat" should be taken seriously as the basis for recognizing what is not the dictatorship of the proletariat (i.e. the various forms of dictatorship over the proletariat, in the name of the proletariat).

This fundamental criticism of all so-called "socialist" states, drawn from the example of the Commune, lays the basis for the rejection of bureaucratic Communism by the masses of 1968 and draws the dividing line between the "Old" and the genuinely "New" Left. The May–June Revolt broadcast this fundamental idea to the world with its popular slogan [a diversion of a phrase by Diderot]: "Humanity will at last be happy when the last capitalist has been hanged with the guts of the last Stalinist bureaucrat." It is also, as we have seen, the basis of the Chinese Ultra-Left's rejection of its regime.

▼▼▼ 4 ▼▼▼

Everyone has correctly criticized the disunity of the Commune, the obvious lack of a leadership apparatus. But since we today feel that the problem of political apparatus is much more complex than the self-proclaimed heirs of the Bolshevik-type apparatus will admit, it is time to consider the Commune not only as an example of revolutionary primitivism whose errors are to be transcended, but as a positive experience the whole truth of which has not yet been rediscovered or worked out.

To many observers, the May revolt owned its vigor, its expansiveness, its creativity and initiative to the very absence of a traditional revolutionary party-apparatus and to its rejection, partial or total, or the various self-proclaimed vanguards (Communists, Trotskyists, etc.). These apparatuses, with their passion for leading and their pre-formulated slogans and orders appeared positively divisive at times in their efforts to substitute themselves for the self-development of the mass movement. Subsequent to May–June 1968, many on the French Left have concluded, like the critics of the Commune earlier, that the ultimate downfall of the movement was due to the absence of a coherent, recognized leadership. Although many new groupings have been formed, ostensibly to fill that gap, it is significant that this question of the relationship between vanguard leadership and the spontaneous self-development of the masses is being reconsidered within these very groups.

▼▼▼ 5 ▼▼▼

The Commune had no leaders. And this at a time when the idea of the necessity of leaders was universally accepted in the workers' movement. The official guides of the Commune were incompetents (if compared with the level of a Marx, a Lenin, or even a Blanqui). On the other hand, the "irresponsible" acts of the time are precisely those which should be claimed as the heritage of the revolutionary movement of our time (even if circumstances limited most of them to the purely destructive level—the most famous example being the rebel who, when a suspect bourgeois insisted that he had never had anything to do with politics, replied, "That's precisely why I'm going to kill you."). [This parenthetical statement was omitted from Greeman's essay for some reason!]

The May–June Revolt, likewise, had no leaders, despite the efforts of the press and government to turn such popular figures as Danny-the-Red into super-stars. Moreover, in almost every case its most "irresponsible" (and destructive) acts marked positive turning-points in its development, e.g., the imprisonment of the manager of Sud-Aviation in his office by the workers, the attack on American Express, the student "scandals" of Nanterre, the occupation of public buildings (the Sorbonne, the Odeon), the throwing of paving-stone, etc. What "responsible" leader could possibly sanction such actions? Yet how would the movement have deepened without them?

▼▼▼ 8 ▼▼▼

The Paris Commune was vanquished less by the force of arms than by the force of habit. The most shocking practical example is the refusal to resort to arms to take over the Bank of France when money was needed so badly. Throughout the Commune's period in power, the Bank remained a Versaillese enclave in Paris, defended by a few rifles and the myths of property and theft. Other ideological reflex-habits were generally ruinous (the resurrection of Jacobinism, the defeatist strategy of barricades—a throwback to 1848, etc.).

The May–June 1968 Revolt, with all its audace, was marked by the same unconscious timidity and conservatism. Several months afterward, I interviewed participants who expressed outrage at the fact that the banks had been left untouched and that no one had even bothered to "liberate" paper, presses, and printing equipment during the period when the police were powerless to prevent it, and when the material means to continue revolutionary agitation were painfully lacking on the Left. Others felt the official radio-TV should have been seized and used, rather than merely boycotted. Similarly, the conservative weight of the trade unions and official "Left" parties, although ignored during the ascendent stages of the revolt, managed to reassert itself when the movement began to wane. This "dead hand of the past," which today includes not only Jacobinism but every form of reformism and Communism, still weighs heavy on the present, although the French events of 1968 and the rise of a world-wide New Left have done some to counter its effect. It is the counter-revolution within the revolution that is the hardest to combat.

▼▼▼ 11 ▼▼▼

Theoreticians who reconstitute the history of this movement from the omniscient viewpoint of God, which characterized the classic novelist, have easy work proving that the Commune was objectively doomed, that it had no possible transcendence. It should not be forgotten that for those who lived the event, the transcendence was there. *The same could be said for the "events" of May–June. In the Spring of 1968, the attitude of those who stood aloof from the rebellion (e.g., the Communists) was already that of omniscient hindsight: "no revolution is possible here." However, the feeling of the mass of actual participants was best expressed in the popular slogan, "Everything is possible." Like the Communards of old, the youth and workers of France experienced their revolt as actuality; as possibility, as a future that lay open before them; this in contrast to the Old Left dogmatists for whom history, and hence the future, is determined. These contrasting viewpoints reveal two totally opposed conceptions of revolutionary praxis.*

▼▼▼ 13 ▼▼▼

The social war, of which the Commune is one moment, still continues (although its surface conditions have changed a good deal). As for the task of "making conscious the unconscious tendencies of the Commune" (Engels), the last word has not been said.

This last thesis takes the Commune out of "history" and returns it to its place in revolutionary process. The Commune's meaning, therefore, is not just something to be worked out in theory, but also in practice. May–June 1968 certainly reaffirmed the Situationists' thesis that this struggle still continues (a thesis that was not so obvious in 1962), while its actuality added another "moment" to the revolutionary process, a "moment" whose unconscious tendencies, like those of the Commune itself, are to be elucidated, both theoretically and in the practice of the next stage of revolt. This revolutionary conception of history as process (uniting theory and practice) was clearly alive in the consciousness of the May–June rebels, who united present and future in their favorite slogan, "This is only a beginning; continue the struggle!" This slogan remained popular long after the last barricades had been swept away. The process of elucidating and digesting the meaning of 1968 continues to this day.

Greeman skipped over several theses. Thesis 6 deals with the positive aspects of arming of the population, and with the problems (seen again in the Spanish revolution) in coordinating grass roots military actions. Thesis 7 lauds the Commune's "revolutionary urbanism," its occupations and "understanding social space in political terms." Thesis 10 criticizes the timidity of the Communards who thwarted the burning of Notre Dame in "the name of eternal aesthetic values." Thesis 12 makes the point that the explosive power of the Commune was pitted against the interdependence of all conservative forces at that time: "In the same way, the interdependence of presently prevailing banalities (rightist or leftist) is a measure of the inventiveness we can expect of a comparable explosion today." Thesis 14 argues against interpreting the Commune simply as a nationalist, anti-German resistance—the Commune was instead the "inevitable battle" between the classes. Those who want to assess the legacy of the May 1968 revolution and the Situationist role in it, should consider this Situationist assessment of the Commune.

Chapter Twenty

With the *Theses on the Paris Commune* and the proceedings of the VIth S.I. conference in Anvers, both in 1962, the group had clearly entered a new, more radical phase. While the S.I. was simultaneously an artistic avant-garde and research organization on the liberation of everyday life, these activities now depended more directly on revolutionary theory and practice. The S.I. looked to the example of Dada, which could've been realized in the Spartakus revolt by coinciding with the revolutionary practice of the German proletariat. But the demise of Spartakus ensured the withering away of Dada. To their credit, the S.I. understood early on that the revolutionary intelligentsia could only "realize its project by suppressing itself; that the 'intellectual party' can really exist only as a party that supersedes itself, a party whose victory is at the same time its *own disappearance.*"

The S.I. decided at Anvers that working groups would be divided regionally into a sort of "anti-NATO" to fight against the "spectacle of possible war" as they put it in the editorial "The Geopolitics of Hibernation," published six months prior to the Cuban missile crisis in October 1962. Early that year, at a meeting of the Central Council in Paris, the German Situationists (primarily artists) associated with the journal *Spur* were excluded. In the Spring, Jorgen Nash (Jorn's brother) quit the S.I. to form another Bauhaus to make art objects for sale. Although he perpetrated the scandal of cutting the head off the Little Mermaid in Copenhagen, Nash's claim of creating a Second Situationist International was actually a short-lived bluff: "According to Scandinavian Situationist philosophy action is the result of emotion. Emotion is a primary non-reflective intelligence; passionate thought/thinking passion. We are not saying that the French method (action precedes emotion) cannot be used successfully. We merely say that our two outlooks are incompatible..." It was decided by the real S.I. as early as 1962, that groups who wanted to enter the S.I. should remain autonomous.

1963—the assassination of Kennedy, the big miners strike in France, clashes between Mods and Rockers in England, Soviet and Chinese crop failures: none of these events impressed Debord as much as the revolutionary students in Caracas who mounted an armed attack on an exhibition of French art, stealing five paintings as collateral for the release of political prisoners. "This is clearly an exemplary way to treat the art of the past, to bring it back into play in life and reestablish priorities." In *The Situationists and New Forms of Action in Politics and Art* Debord goes on to describe the way Bakunin wanted to use art on the barricades to inhibit the advancing troops during the Dresden insurrection. Debord is also delighted to report on the disclosure by the British "Spies for Peace" of the bomb shelter for the political class known as Regional Seat of Government #6. Following the disclosure, the secret military headquarters were invaded, officials were photographed against their will and security phones were blocked by "the continuous dialing of ultrasecret numbers that had been publicized." The S.I. subsequently staged the "Destruction of RSG 6" demonstration in Denmark, under the direction of J.V. Martin whose mock bomb shelter and thermonuclear maps of World War III served as props. Debord contributed five programmatic directives that were hung on the wall.

As mentioned above, Asger Jorn's Scandinavian Institute of Comparative Vandalism published the scripts of Debord's first three films as *Against Cinema* in 1964. This was also the year that he dropped the use of the hyphenated Guy-Ernest in favor of the simple Guy.

1964 was also the year of the Free Speech Movement in Berkeley that culminated with the occupation of Sproul Hall and the subsequent repression that sparked the anti-war movement. This "festival" qualified as a "scandal" (high praise) for the Situationists. Meanwhile in the Soviet Union, Brezhnev deposed Khrushchev in a coup d'etat. McLuhan and Marcuse published, respectively, their *Understanding Media* and *One-Dimensional Man,* but there is no reason to doubt Debord's word that he never borrowed anything from these people (no reference to Marcuse would appear in the S.I. journal until 1966, and complete translations of his work wouldn't appear until after the events of May '68; the "sage of Toronto," as Debord facetiously referred to McLuhan in 1988, was never mentioned in the journal). Jacques Ellul's *Propaganda* was, however, lauded for describing, "the unity of the various forms of conditioning, to have shown that this advertising-propaganda is not merely an unhealthy excrescence that could be prohibited, but is at the same time a remedy in a generally sick society, a remedy that makes the sickness tolerable while aggravating it."

In 1965 Jagger was singing "I Can't Get No Satisfaction" as miniskirts hit the streets of London. The Greatful Dead got together in San Francisco and Lefebvre began teaching sociology at Nanterre. This was also the year Malcolm X was murdered. The S.I. didn't publish its journal that year, rather several tracts, including "Address to Revolutionaries of Algeria and of all Countries:"

The disintegration of the revolutionary image presented by the international Communist movement is taking place forty years after the disintegration of the revolutionary movement itself. This time gained for the bureaucratic lie—that supplement to the permanent bourgeois lie—has been time lost for the revolution. The history of the modern world pursues its revolutionary course, but unconsciously or with false consciousness. Everywhere there are social confrontations, but nowhere is the old order liquidated, even within the very forces that contest it. Everywhere the ideologies of the old world are criticized and rejected, but nowhere is 'the real movement that suppresses existing conditions' liberated from one or another 'ideology' in Marx's sense: ideas that serve masters. Everywhere revolutionaries, but nowhere the revolution.

The cover of *Against Cinema*

The tract scrutinized Ben Bella's failed effort to create an authentic version of socialist self-management: he ruled the same way that he lost power—"by a palace revolution." It went on to denounce every false representation of proletarian revolution in the east and in the west. The authors (Debord's voice is prevalent) called for a total critique of spectacular consumption that would be "illuminated by the inverse project of a liberated creativity." The hubris of Situationist claims about modern society producing its own modernized negation continues to dazzle and amaze—at the time these claims surely inspired confidence. Clandestinely circulated in Algeria, this radical S.I. tract must've put the group on the line: "The option is now between the militarized bureaucratic dictatorship and the dictatorship of the 'self-managed sector' *extended to all production and all aspects of social life.*"

Just as Vaneigem had used his Situationist International essay "Basic Banalites"—

a very Kojevian master-slave interpretation of slavery, servitude and modern dispossession—as a dry run for his *Revolution of Everyday Life,* Debord's "The Decline and Fall of the Spectacle-Commodity Economy" was a prefiguration of *Society of the Spectacle.* In addition to being an incisive analysis of the Watts riots, the essay is also Debord's most sustained discussion of the spectacle up to that point.*

At the time, the tract was hastily translated in New York and distributed across the United States.

You'll recall that in August, 1965, 10,000 blacks were involved in a pitched battle with 15,000 police and National Guard—the wreckage and carnage would amount to forty million dollars and thirty-four killed (twenty-eight blacks).

Kids playing with stolen cash register

Somewhere between 3,000 and 4,000 people were arrested. It was only the previous January that President Johnson outlined his "Great Society" to eliminate poverty. According to Debord, the "flames of Watts *consummated* the system of consumption." By this he means that the blacks in Watts achieved the extreme consumption of the potlatch festival. They destroyed the exchange-value of commodities by stealing them, and thus destroyed their commodity status. The cop, Debord tells us, is the:

… active servant of the commodity, the man who completely submits to the commodity, whose job it is to ensure that a given product of human labor remains a commodity, with the magical property of having to be paid for, instead of becoming a mere refrigerator or rifle—a passive, inanimate object, subject to anyone who comes along to make use of it.

Debord is extremely critical of nonviolence as a strategy, and characterizes King's conduct at Selma as the cowardly spectacle of a potential confrontation. At the end of the essay he clearly champions armed resistance. Whereas the legality of the Civil Rights movement is irrational given the universal hierarchy imposed on people by the spectacle-commodity, "looting is a *natural* response to the unnatural and inhuman society of commodity abundance." In this light it's interesting to recall the

---

* The essay was originally signed by the S.I. in 1965 and again in *Situationist International* #10 in 1966. It was reissued by Belles Lettres in 1993 as a pamphlet with Debord claiming authorship.

"Legality and Illegality" chapter of Lukacs *History and Class Consciousness*. Revolutionary movements, according to Lukacs, rarely get beyond the legalistic-opportunistic phase despite being swept up in the romanticism of illegal activity. Illegal tactics are necessary for many reasons, but above all, for the "revolutionary self-education of the proletariat" if it is to liberate itself from capitalist life-forms and the bourgeois legal system. In his essay, Debord deplores American racism, but disagrees with black nationalists and calls on whites to rally to the black revolt against the commodity and the State. By insisting on accounting for the riot as the way worker-consumers instinctively challenge the logic of capitalism (even Martin Luther King admitted that Watts was a class riot, not a race riot) Debord hopes to incite class solidarity where racial solidarity would be absurd. Before discussing the blacks' *minority* spectacle, Debord makes the extravagant claim that, "The Los Angeles rebellion is the first in history to justify itself with the argument that there was no air conditioning during a heat wave."

> When California authorities declared a "state of insurrection," the insurance companies recalled that they do not cover risks at that level—they guarantee nothing beyond survival. The American blacks can rest assured that as long as they keep quiet they will in most cases be allowed to survive. Capitalism has become sufficiently concentrated and interlinked with the state to distribute "welfare" to the poorest. But by the very fact that they lag behind in the advance of socially organized survival, the blacks pose the problems of life; what they are really demanding is not to survive but to live. The blacks have nothing of their own to insure; their mission is to destroy all previous forms of private insurance and security. They appear as what they really are: the irreconcilable enemies, not of the great majority of Americans, but of the alienated way of life of the entire modern society. The most industrially advanced country only shows us the road that will be followed everywhere unless the system is overthrown.

Chapter Twenty-one

In 1966, Madam Mao entered political life at 52 as a cultural consultant to the Chinese Army—she was sympathetic to the insolent Red Guard youth and quickly paved the way for the proclamation of the Chinese Cultural Revolution (the widely-distributed 1967 S.I. tract "Explosion Point in China" denounced it as a bureaucratic power play that spread the Maoist ideology in the street). The Diggers organized to distribute food after the San Francisco ghetto riot of 1966 and attempted to construct a "free city." In Mississippi, Stokely Carmichael launched his Black Power platform. The Provo phenomenon erupted in Holland, soliciting disaffected youth into its ranks to transform Amsterdam through provocations such as the famous White Bicycle Plan (free communal transport in the form of white bikes).

In July 1966, the S.I. held its VIIth Conference in Paris. As Pascal Dumontier points out in his excellent work *Situationists and May '68: Theory and Practice of Revolution (1966–1972)*, the question of organization is one of the principle theoretical problems posed by revolutionaries. Debord and his wife Michele Bernstein were the only original members of the S.I. to have survived the purges, and he was certainly one of the primary protagonists; but according to Dumontier, "no source could pretend that Guy Debord was the uncontested master of the S.I." There were only four exclusions and two resignations between 1962 and 1966; relatively few compared to the ritual exclusions prior to the schism in 1962. The exclusions and resignations would pick up again in 1966 as the S.I. sought to further radicalize itself along the lines outlined in this key document drafted at the VIIth Conference (1966) and reprinted during the month of May, 1968.

MINIMUM DEFINITION OF REVOLUTIONARY ORGANIZATIONS

Since the only purpose of a revolutionary organization is the abolition of all existing classes in a way that does not bring about a new division of society, we consider any organization revolutionary which consistently and effectively works toward the international realization of the absolute power of workers councils, as prefigured in the experience of the proletarian revolutions of this century.

Such an organization makes a unitary critique of the world, or is nothing. By unitary critique we mean a comprehensive critique of all geographical areas where various forms of separate socioeconomic powers exist, as well as a comprehensive critique of all aspects of life.

Such an organization sees the beginning and end of its program in the complete decolonizaton of everyday life. It thus aims not at the masses' self-management of the existing world, but at its uninterrupted transformation. It embodies the radical critique of political economy, the supersession of the commodity and of wage labor.

Such an organization refuses to reproduce within itself any of the hierarchical conditions of the dominant world. The only limit to participating in its total democracy is that each member must have recognized and appropriated the coherence of its critique. This coherence must be both in the critical theory proper and in the relationship between this theory and practical activity. The organization radically criticizes every ideology as a separate power of ideas and as ideas of separate power. It is thus at the same time the negation of any remnants of religion, and of the prevailing social spectacle which, from news media to mass culture, monopolizes communication between people around their unilateral reception of images of their alienated activity. The organization dissolves any "revolutionary ideology,"

The S.I. in Paris

unmasking it as a sign of the failure of the revolutionary project, as the private property of new specialists of power, as one more fraudulent representation setting itself above real proletarianized life.

Since the ultimate criterion of the modern revolutionary organization is its totalness, such an organization is ultimately a critique of politics. It must explicitly aim to dissolve itself as a separate organization at its moment of victory.

Excerpts from "Report of Guy Debord to the VIIth Conference of the S.I. in Paris," which point to Debord's role as the bow of the ship cutting through the chaotic currents of the time, were printed the Debord-Sanguinetti collaboration *The Veritable Split in the International* (1972). In this 1966 "Report" Debord discusses what can be done with Situationist theory and how it can be communicated to revolutionaries around the world. Clearly, Debord has his eyes set on expanding the influence of the S.I. far beyond any "happening" or "teach-in" or other form of pseudo-revolt. Here he even rips into the notion of festivals that is dear to him:

I also reject the contentment or the menace of discontent with regard to the S.I. that would manifest themselves around the exigency according to which we should be, as it were, organizers of days of festival. We do not have to answer to such a demand for particular festivals. We must leave this dimension to individuals; that is to say not to obstruct anyone practicing an inevitably half-witted collectivism. [...] The search for a sort of "festival in the S.I." would lead to the trivial practice of entertainment in society, which is certainly not bad in itself, but would be bad for us because it would be coated with an ideology of play: that is, an attempt at collective play, but aggravated by a sort of doctrine of play. [...] In the alienation of everyday life, the possibilities of passions and of play are still very real, and it seems to me that the S.I. would perpetrate a grave misconception by letting it be understood that life is totally reified outside of situationist activity (which in concept implies a mystic rescue—see some persons who address themselves to us at present having this impression).

Debord was striving to make the S.I. the preeminent revolutionary organization in the world, and nothing up to that point in time served to communicate Situationist theory so much as the pamphlet "On the Poverty of Student Life: Considered in its Economic, Political, Psychological, Sexual and Especially Intellectual Aspects, with a Modest Proposal for its Remedy," and the scandal it provoked at the University of Strasbourg. As the story goes, extremists who ran on the platform of destroying the student union won control of it, and of the funds at its disposal. Friends of these extremists contacted the S.I., who suggested that the students write a critique of the student movement and society. It seems that the students agreed more with the S.I. than with each other, and Mustapha Khayati, a Paris-based Tunisian member of S.I. who had acted as liaison with the students, ended up writing the text (with only a few significant changes from "Paris," i.e. Debord). Khayati was certainly up to the task of popularizing the S.I. given his experience in writing a preface for a Situationist dictionary ("Words will not cease to work until people do") and translating Situatonist theory to third world revolutionaries ("The only people who are underdeveloped are those who see a positive value in the power of their masters").

The pamphlet *On the Poverty of Student Life* is remarkable for its total critique of student unions, the university, various forms of false opposition (the French left, the Provos, Zen, Ghandiism, Chinese Cultural Revolution, the American New Left, the black and anti-war movement), and cultural commodities such as Goddard, Robbe-Grillet, etc. No attempt was made to mask the Situationist influence, and the text is peppered with terms such as "desires," "spectacle" and "ideology." The pamphlet calls for students to become proletarians, and concludes:

Proletarian revolutions will be festivals or nothing, for festivity is the very keynote of the life they announce. Play is the ultimate principle of this festival, and the only rules it can recognize are to live without dead time and to enjoy without restraints.

Publication of *On the Poverty of Everyday Life* was preceded by a series of antics by the pro-situ students of Strasbourg. A professor who had tried to establish contact with the S.I., only to be rebuffed by Debord, was pummeled with tomatoes. Andre Bertrand's comic strip *The Return of the Durruti Column* (cowboys discussing reification in words plucked from Bernstein's novels and toothbrushes discussing the relative lack of merit of the entire spectrum of French political groups) began to appear around campus. The student union periodical published an article by Black Mask (a radical U.S. group: "Revolution burns inside us like the streets of Watts"), a critique of the Provos, Zengakuren (a Trotskyist Japanese group, with whom the union was in contact). Anticipating the publication of the pamphlet on November 22, the students scheduled a press conference for November 23.

All the big shots of Strasbourg came to the ceremonial opening of the university, hence they were the first to read the pamphlet. A rector was quoted as saying: "These students have insulted their professors. They should be dealt with by psychiatrists. I don't want to take any legal measures against them—they should be in a lunatic asylum... As for their incitement to illegal acts, the Minister of the Interior is looking into that." The uproar was augmented at the following day's press conference when it was announced by the students that they intended to dissolve the union. The scandal was reported across the country:

> Their doctrine, if this term can be used in describing their delirious lucubrations,... is a sort of radical revolutionarism with a nihilist basis... A monument of imbecilic fanaticism, written in a pretentious jargon, spiced with a barrage of gratuitous insults both of their professors and of their fellow students. It constantly refers to a mysterious Situationist International.

Khayati immediately had the students issue a communique stating that no member of the student union was a member of the S.I., and clarifying the fact that the S.I. was Marxist and not anarchist or post-Surrealist. While the union leaders were unable to bring the question of the union's dissolution to vote at a general assembly, they did get a good show of solidarity from many of the students in the region immediately following the publication of the pamphlet. The attempt to cancel the election results that had put the pro-situs in power failed. The elections were upheld and the pro-situs represented Strasbourg University at the national student union convention in Paris—they presented a motion to dissolve the union. The motion was rebuffed, but it did find sympathizers in students in Nantes who would provoke a scandal the following year that inspired the legendary Nanterre insurrection.

The pamphlet "On the Poverty of Student Life" was translated into numerous languages and reprinted numerous times in France. Cohn-Bendit, or Danny-the-Red, was spokesman for the students at Nanterre and thus no friend of the S.I. Nonetheless, he acknowledged that "the Strasbourg pamphlet acted as a kind of detonator... we did all we could to distribute the pamphlet" (other partisans of the Nanterre struggle such as Jean-Pierre Duteuil of the Liaison of Anarchist Students also acknowledged the influence of Situationist ideas). On the campus of Strasbourg itself, a war of words erupted between those student radicals in favor, and those now out of favor with the S.I.—a conflict that wouldn't die down until April 1967. The S.I. would continue to fan the flames on campuses across the country with its tract "The Misery of Sexology, The Sexology of Misery" that ridiculed the psychologists who commented on student sexuality a moment when birth control was, for the first time, legalized in France.

Chapter Twenty-two

In November 1967, the firm that had published Michele Bernstein's novels (Buchet-Chastel) published Debord's 221 theses as *Society of the Spectacle* despite concern that readers would buy the book under the mistaken impression that it dealt with celebrity lifestyles (in French "spectacle" means show or performance). And after years of delay, Vaneigem's *The Revolution of Everyday Life* was published by Gallimard in December, so it was natural for critics to review them together. *Le Monde*:

> It's the tune that makes the song: more cynical in Vaneigem and more icy in Debord. The negative and provocative violence of their phraseology leaves nothing standing among what previous ages have produced—except perhaps Sade, Lautreamont and Dada... A snarling, extravagant rhetoric that is always detached from the complexity of the facts upon which we reason not only makes the reading disagreeable, but also staggers thought.

By 1968 the tone had changed—*Le Nouvel Observateur* raved that Debord's book was "the *Capital* of the new generation."

Looking back on the initial publication of the book in his *Preface to the Fourth Italian Edition of Society of the Spectacle* (1979), Debord explained his intentions:

> In 1967, I wanted the Situationist International to have a book of theory. The S.I. was at this time the extremist group that had done the most to bring back revolutionary contestation to modern society; and it was easy to see that this group, having imposed its victory on the terrain of critical theory, and having skillfully followed it through on that of practical agitation, was then drawing near the culminating point of its historical action. So it was a question of such a book being present in the troubles that were soon to come, and which would subsequently carry the book to the vast subversive sequel that these troubles couldn't fail to open up.

By the time Debord wrote that preface, the book had already been reprinted dozens of times in as many years and translated into numerous languages. Aside from a few typos, Debord never changed a word and prided himself on having been proven correct by the events of history. When Debord looked back at this book in his *Comments on the Society of the Spectacle* in 1988, he stated that the essence of the spectacle was "the autocratic reign of the market economy having acceded to an irresponsible sovereignty, and the totality of new techniques of gov-

From the comic The Proletariat as Subject and Representation, to publize the first edition of *Society of the Spectacle*

erning that accompany its reign," adding, "When I began the critique of spectacular society, one certainly noticed—given the times—the revolutionary content that could be discovered in this critique, and it was naturally felt to be its most troublesome element." What then, is "the spectacle?"

As the title of the book indicates, the spectacle is the unifying principle of modern society—in other words, when Debord refers to "the spectacle" he's actually referring to the "society of the spectacle" as a whole. As was pointed out several times earlier in the book, Debord explicitly ties his concept of the spectacle to Marx's critique of the commodity. Recall, for example, the fact that the first sentence of the first thesis of *Society of the Spectacle* opens with a diversion of Marx's opening line from *Capital:* "All life in societies under the reign of modern conditions of production displays itself as an immense accumulation of *spectacles*." The hyphenated construct of the "spectacle-commodity" in Debord's essay on Watts requires us to bear in mind that every time Debord mentions "the spectacle," he is referring to the "spectacle-commodity." The spectacle is shorthand for the *society of the spectacle-commodity.*

With this in mind, it's not surprising that there is no singular definition of the spectacle. At different points in the book, the spectacle is variously referred to as the "concrete inversion of life" or "the sun that never sets on the empire of modern passivity" or "the bad dream of modern society in chains." The thirty-four theses in the first chapter, "The Perfection of Separation," were published by themselves in

Situationist International #11 (October, 1967), which tells us that Debord felt confident they were a good representation of the concept of the spectacle. While this fragment shouldn't be mistaken for the whole of the book, it underscores the central theme of separation. In his *Spirit of the Laws,* Montesquieu was the first to remark that tyranny depends on isolation of the tyrant from his subjects and isolation of subjects from one another. For Debord, the spectacle is the tyrant that thwarts the natural human situation of acting and speaking together; not merely using crude, time-tested means of orchestrating isolation such as mutual fear, but with the multifaceted methods of separation of the modern political economy that go to the heart of existential alienation.

Before scrutinizing the first chapter, let's look at the contents to get an overview of *Society of the Spectacle:*

I. Separation Perfected
II. The Commodity as Spectacle
III. Unity and Division within Appearance
IV. The Proletariat as Subject and as Representation
V. Time and History
VI. Spectacular Time
VII. The Organization of Territory
VIII. Negation and Consumption within Culture
IX. Ideology Materialized

I read *Society of the Spectacle* as follows:

A. Chapters I, II, III and VI focus on the concept of the spectacle and spectators.
B. Chapters VII and VIII relate to the theories and practice of unitary urbanism, and cultural subversion that Debord developed while in the L.I. and S.I.
C. Chapters IV, V and IX represent a wide-ranging revolutionary strategy of proletarian self-organization into workers' councils when the revolutionary moment arrives—the qualitative leap of revolutionary transformation of the totality in a moment of total history.

The first chapter is prefaced with a quote from Feuerbach's *The Essence of Christianity* that makes the point that it is always only illusions that are sacred, adding, "the highest degree of illusion becomes the highest degree of sacredness." The long history of denunciation of idolatry, and the theoretical "denigration of vision in twentieth-century French thought" described in Martin Jay's *Downcast Eyes* often leads people to narrowly identify Debord's concept of the spectacle with media images.

Debord very explicitly states that although the spectacle is "a pseudo-sacred entity," the "mass media" is only a "glaring superficial manifestation" of the spectacle. While the spectacle is "specifically the sector which concentrates all gazing and all consciousness" it is *not*, echoing Marx, "a collection of images, but a social relation among people mediated by images." The spectacle, Debord tells us in thesis 16, "is the true

reflection of the production of things, and the false objectification of the producers." In other words, Debord is making a Marxist critique of the economy that highlights the production of "image-objects" and the way this process subjugates workers. To paraphrase Debord, the spectacle isn't the world of vision, it is the vision of the world promoted by the powers of domination.

What, you ask again, *is* "the spectacle"?

Debord is often accused of being difficult to understand. At the risk of reducing his sophisticated analysis, I'll try to describe the spectacle to those readers who fail to understand the spectacle as Debord's update of Lukacs' interpretation of reification and fetishism in *History and Class Consciousness*. The easiest way is to equate the society of the spectacle-commodity with the entire economic ecology that none of us can escape: the spectacle as the economy and its self-representation. By economy here, I mean the economy understood in all its historical and political significance. Korsch, it might be remembered, highlighted the principle of historical specification whereby a theme such as fetishism, however general, always had an element of historic specificity that illuminated the specific character of modern bourgeois society. A specific theme can, in turn, be generalized and used to dissect bourgeois society, which was how Debord used "the spectacle." And because fetishism and the spectacle are historically specific, they can be changed, at least theoretically, by the historic intervention of people who act against these fetters to their freedom. This is much more difficult than it sounds because, as people consume the object-images that circulate in a society governed by this meaning-making machinery, they become part of the spectacle. Indeed, they become the spectacle.

If we read the first chapter backwards, we begin with thesis 34's assertion that the spectacle is the accumulation of capital to the absurd point where it becomes an image. While capital had attained the magical ability to reproduce itself long before 1967, Debord's claim still seemed excessive. But now, with financial capital accounting for more and more of the economy each quarter it makes perfect sense to rail against the spectacle of speculation and images of capital denoted by inflated, unfathomable numbers. Capital no longer requires a real capitalist, an entrepreneur who invests in the means of production. Instead, capital has become an absurd abstraction, like the zeros used to arrive at an unreal figure like 7,000,000,000,000. Even the people who daily deal with such figures have no idea what they represent.

Thesis 33 is a clear, if partial, expression of reification and what Debord means by the perfection of separation:

> Separated from his product, man himself produces all the details of his world with ever increasing power, and thus finds himself ever more separated from his world. The more his life is now his product, the more he is separated from his life.

Debord's formulations can read like Zen koans, but they're worth the trouble to decipher. Imagine a worker producing something with all the power of industrial techniques—his labor-power having been transformed into the commodity of wage labor that he sells on the open market to the proprietor of the means of production. The product he produces is distributed globally to consumers who have no consciousness of his hand in the production process. He is thus separated from this product that goes on to take its place in the world, and for this reason he is separated from his world. The more he works and identifies himself with his work and what he produces, the more he is separated from the unified life of a forgotten past; say, in the communal cities of the Middle Ages where the economy was regional and the unity of existence—however cruel—was tied to the land, the sun, the seasons and holidays. Rather than the laborer employing the means of production, the means of production employ the laborer in the society of the spectacle. As Marx pointed out in his discussions on the commodification of labor, labor is a unique commodity, the consumption of which leads to production of commodities *and* of surplus value. All the value-creating power of labor-power produces the profits that enable the capitalist to buy more people and means of production. As mentioned in earlier chapters, Debord didn't value work in the least, so it's understandable that he objected to human life being used as an object like any other commodity even more than Marx. Rather than finding the realization of humanity in work, Debord sees the realization of humanity in festivals and in revolution itself.

Thesis 32 states that the spectacle "corresponds to a concrete manufacture of alienation." For Marx, the key to alienation is the alienation of labor; he recognized it as the basis of all other forms of alienation (notably ideological alienation as false consciousness, which Debord takes up in Chapter IX). The theoretical foundation of alienation is objectification, or the passage of active human forces from a form of motion to the form of an object engaged in the process of a subject's activity. In his early works, Marx referred to the fact that humans remake and humanize the objective world, creating the world of culture. The way

...it demands more from men without quality.

humans utilize these products can result in "deobjectification," as humans connect with the object of their activity. In Debord's society of the spectacle, this connection is lost to alienation, separation and reification. The objects are subjects and vice versa as humans constantly serve the economy as producer-consumers of spectacle-commodities. The spectacle imposes this system of relations on us, and the only way to reconnect with the objects in this world is to steal them and use them for revolutionary ends (as Debord describes in Chapter VIII where he deals with "Negation and Consumption in Culture" and concepts such as *détournement*).

Thesis 31 is self-evident:

> The worker does not produce himself; he produces an independent power. The success of this production, its abundance, returns to the producer as an abundance of dispossession. All the time and space of his world becomes foreign to him with the accumulation of his alienated products. The spectacle is the map of this new world, a map which exactly covers its territory. The very powers which escaped us show themselves to us in all their force.

Debord's references to territory, explored in detail in Chapter VII, suggest that he is using the end of the first chapter as an outline for the book. Thesis 30 loosely corresponds to Chapter VI "Spectacular Time" where Debord deals with the condition of the spectator as a being who is of profit to the contemplated object: "the more he contemplates the less he lives; the more he accepts recognizing himself in the dominant images of need, the less he understands his own existence and his own desires." Recall here Debord's earlier works that equated life with time to understand why he despised the spectacle as the denial of life. The powers of spectacular domination dispossess humans of their time; Debord opposes the spectacle to life itself. This coincides with Debord's redefinition of the proletariat as those who have no power over their lives, and life is the force that has power to constitute itself as the subject that plays the game of history.

Thesis 29 is simultaneously very revealing and somewhat confusing. The spectacle originates in and expresses the massive loss of unity of the world in the alienating labor and production that Debord refers to here as "abstract," which allows him to make the claim that the spectacle's "*mode of being concrete* is precisely abstraction." He goes on to say that "one part of the world *represents itself* to the world and is superior to it." This "one part" is the part the spectacle chooses to show or display. We have to be careful not to confuse a single definition of the spectacle with the general concept, but here Debord argues by definition that, "The spectacle is nothing more than the common language of this separation" of fragments of the world. In a brilliant proposition Debord states that "The spectacle reunites the separate, but reunites it as separate," which is something I'm sure all of us have felt at one time or another. The spectacle is the illusion of unity in a fragmented world.

According to Debord the entire economic system is founded on the *circular production of isolation*—all the technological gadgets selected by spectacular domination "are also its weapons for the constant reinforcement of the conditions of isolation of 'lonely crowds'" (thesis 28). Taken in isolation, a phrase such as "the success of separate production as production of the separate" doesn't make much sense, but in the context of this discussion the meaning is readily apparent, and this formulation gives the language of theory a poetic ring. Debord consistently used what he called Marx's "insurrectional style, drawing the misery of philosophy out of the philosophy of misery": specifically the inversion of the genitive by replacing the subject with the predicate, and generally the inversion of the second of two parallel phrases called chiasmus.

Separation, isolation, alienation—these words are basically synonyms. Although Debord didn't bandy the word freedom around, freedom from separation, isolation and alienation was his ultimate goal. "There can be no freedom outside of activity," Debord states in thesis 27, "and in the context of the spectacle all activity is negated." At first, this sounds too totalizing, but again, try to think of an activity that doesn't somehow serve the economy, that isn't lost in labor proper or the labor of consumption (including the consumption of images)—not even books escape commodity status unless they're stolen or given away.

In thesis 26, "the progress of accumulation of separate products and the concentration of the productive process" assure that "unity and communication become the exclusive attribute of the system's management." This separation "is the *proletarianization* of the world." If we recall the classic conception of the proletariat as appendages of machines, as immiserated workers deprived of owning the means of production we see that Debord is redefining the proletariat in terms of its inability to communicate and unify in a world where spectacle-commodities talk to each other and unify the world: "every view of accomplished activity and all direct personal communication among producers is lost" due to the "incessant refinement of the division of labor into a parcelization of gestures which are then dominated by the independent movement of machines."

> Separation is the alpha and omega of the spectacle. The institutionalization of the social division of labor (the formation of classes), gave rise to a first sacred contemplation—the mythical order with which every power shrouds itself from the beginning. The sacred has justified the cosmic and ontological order which corresponded to the interests of the masters; it has explained and embellished that which society could not do. Thus all separate power has been spectacular, but the adherence of all to an immobile image only signified the common acceptance of an imaginary prolongation of the poverty of real social activity, still largely felt as a unitary condition. The modern spectacle, on the contrary, expresses what society can do, but in this expression the permitted is absolutely opposed to the possible... (excerpt from thesis 25)

In a formulation reminiscent of Gramsci's elaboration of the concept of hegemony (the way the ruling class sought to legitimize and totalize its domination), Debord defines the spectacle as "the existing order's uninterrupted discourse about itself, its laudatory monologue." The spectacle is "the self-portrait of power in the epoch of its totalitarian management of the conditions of existence," or again, "It is the diplomatic representation of hierarchic society to itself, where all other expression is banned." In thesis 6 Debord states that the spectacle is the permanent and "total justification of the existing system's conditions and goals." Debord wants to make it very clear when he states that the spectacle is "a social relation among people, mediated by images" that he is talking about the nature of relations between the classes. It should be added that the spectacle separates people within the same class; this intra-class divisiveness assures that everyone is alienated, separated and subjugated, not just workers. The techniques and technical apparatuses of the spectacle may change, but the form remains the same because the spectacle is "the product of the division of social labor and the organ of class domination."

Contrary to the goal of Marxism to "realize philosophy" the spectacle "philosophizes reality." As we saw above, in exactly the same way Debord was critical of art, Marx was critical of philosophy, which Debord called a "separate thought and the thought of separate power," comparable to religion. More than just being the representation of part of the world to the world, the spectacle is a world unto itself, a "fallacious paradise" like heaven that appears as though it exists here on earth: "The spectacle is the technical realization of the exile of human powers into a beyond; it is separation perfected within the interior of man." In short, even internal representation provides a platform for the spectacle to constitute itself.

The shift from an existence centered on *being* to a life based on *having* was a decisive shift in the consciousness of existence. Debord describes the way consciousness—in its spectacular phase—shifted the axis of existence from *having* to *appearing:* "The language of the spectacle consists of signs of the ruling production, which at the same time are the ultimate goals of this production." But things that appear in the spectacle don't really exist? It doesn't matter because the "means of the spectacle are simultaneously its ends"—it simply wants to develop itself by sucking everything into its orbit, thereby negating everything (even life itself) by reducing it to appearance. Debord's critique of the spectacle, "exposes it as the visible negation of life, as a *negation* of life which *has become visible*." As with Lukacs' concept of reification, the world is inverted, and what appears to be alive is really dead. How does this happen? The spectacle invades life, then "reality rises up within the spectacle, and the spectacle is real."

> The images that are detached from every aspect of life flow into a common stream where the unity of life can never be reestablished. Partially considered reality deploys itself in its own general unity as a pseudo-world apart, as an object of contemplation. The specialization of images of the world finds its attainment in the world of the autonomized image where the liar has lied to himself. The spectacle, in general and as the concrete inversion of life, is the autonomous movement of the non-living. (thesis 2)

In the second chapter "The Commodity as Spectacle," Debord defines the spectacle as a moment in the development of the world of the commodity, the moment predicted by Lukacs when the commodity becomes the "universal category of society as a whole." Debord gets no satisfaction from the cornucopia of industrially produced commodities; indeed, the system of commerce is the "perfected denial of man" because the political economy has come to dominate all spheres of life.

> The spectacle is a permanent opium war which aims to make people identify goods with commodities and satisfaction with a survival that increases according to its own laws. But if consumable survival is something which must always increase, this is because it continues to contain privation. If there is nothing beyond increasing survival, if there is no point where it might stop growing, this is not because it is beyond privation, but because it is enriched privation. (thesis 44)

Debord makes interesting use of the philosophical categories of quality and quantity by associating the spectacle with the same quantitative development as the commodity, which is self-evident given the superabundance of the spectacle. Although the spectacle excludes the qualitative, it is "subject to qualitative change," and by this he means change for the worse. While we are witnessing the emergence of the qualitative market (organic produce and the like), it is miniscule in comparison to the continuing, massive expansion of the cheap commodities and even cheaper images.

Debord goes on to apply value theory to the spectacle, revealing that use value has to be fabricated as a spectacular illusion to serve exchange value:

> The real consumer becomes a consumer of illusions. [...] The spectacle is not only the servant of pseudo-use, it is already in itself the pseudo-use of life. [...] At the moment of economic abundance, the concentrated result of social labor becomes visible and subjugates all reality to appearance, which is now its product. Capital is no longer the invisible center which directs the mode of production: its accumulation spreads it all the way to the periphery in the form of tangible objects. The entire expanse of society is its portrait.

The third chapter, "Unity and Division within Appearance," highlights the contradictions of a system of satisfaction that doesn't fully satisfy; how dissatisfaction is then sold as a commodity; and how the "eternal" constantly changes in the system of spectacular domination. He writes about the unity of misery in a world that divides spectacular tasks by positing the distinction between the concentrated spectacle and the diffuse spectacle.

The concentrated spectacle corresponds to fascism and the former Eastern bloc countries.

> The concentrated spectacle belongs essentially to bureaucratic capitalism, even though it may be imported as a technique of state power in less developed, mixed economies, or in advanced capitalism at certain moments of crisis. Bureaucratic property itself is, in effect, concentrated in such a way that the individual bureaucrat only relates to the ownership of the global economy through an intermediary, the bureaucratic community, and only as a member of this community. Moreover, the production of commodities (less developed in bureaucratic capitalism), takes on a concentrated form: the commodity held by the bureaucracy is the totality of social labor, and what it sells back to society is wholesale survival. The dictatorship of the bureaucratic economy cannot leave the exploited masses any significant margin of choice—the bureaucracy itself has to choose everything and any other external choice, whether it concerns food or music, is a choice to destroy the bureau-

cracy completely. The dictatorship must be accompanied by permanent violence. [...] Wherever the concentrated spectacle rules, so does the police. (thesis 64)

The diffuse spectacle corresponds to what is generally associated with the American-style commerce:

The diffuse spectacle accompanies the abundance of commodities, the undisturbed development of modern capitalism. Here each commodity is justified in the name of the grandeur of the production of the totality of objects—the spectacle is the apologetic catalogue of this totality. Irreconcilable claims crowd the stage of the unified spectacle of the abundant economy. Likewise, different commodity-celebrities simultaneously support their contradictory projects for the provisioning of society where the spectacle of automobiles requires a perfect circulation which destroys the ancient cities, and where the spectacle of the city itself needs museum districts. Thus satisfaction (already problematical), which is supposed to come from consuming the totality, is immediately falsified in that the consumer can only touch a succession of fragments of this commodity happiness, fragments in which the quality attributed to the whole is absent. (thesis 65)

By far the biggest and most important chapter of *Society of the Spectacle* is chapter IV, "The Proletariat as Subject and as Representation" (the chapter that the Italian section of the Situationist International printed in their journal). Debord begins by affirming the *subject* of history, the master of life who exists as "consciousness of his game" (thought of history coinciding with the "long revolutionary epoch inaugurated by the rise of the bourgeoisie"). Debord then turns to a critique of Hegel's interpretation of history that reconciled his thought with the bourgeois revolutions of the XVIIth and XVIIIth Centuries. Nonetheless, Debord is quick to point out that, "All the theoretical currents of the *revolutionary* workers' movement grew out of a critical confrontation with Hegelian thought—Stirner and Bakunin as well as Marx."

Naturally, Debord openly lauds the way Marx "ruined" Hegel's contemplative philosophy of history, but he is much more sly in the way he supports Marx's continued application of Hegelian dialectics. On the one hand, the "truth" of Marx's theory is inseparable from its use of Hegelian method. On the other hand, Debord quotes a long passage from Eduard Bernstein's (1850–1932) *Evolutionary Socialism: A Criticism and Affirmation* that is critical of Marx's Hegelian "historical self-deception" in predicting proletarian revolution in Germany in 1947. Without really saying so, Debord opposes Bernstein by embracing the connection in Marx "between the dialectical method and historical *partisanship*." That said, Debord rips into the scientific-deterministic elements in Marx's thought, characterizing them as "bour-geois" and "ideology."

The weakness of Marx's theory is naturally the weakness of the revolutionary strug-gle of the proletariat of his time. The working class did not set off the permanent revolution in Germany in 1948; the Commune was defeated in isolation. Revolutionary theory could not yet achieve its own total existence. The fact that Marx was reduced to defending and clarifying it with cloistered, scholarly work in the British Museum caused a loss in the theory itself. The scientific justifications Marx elaborated about the future development of the working class and the orga-nizational practice that went with them became obstacles to proletarian con-sciousness at a later stage. (thesis 85)

In other words, Debord supports the partisan forecast of revolution in the *Communist Manifesto,* but he is highly critical of Marx's "scientific" and "linear" pre-dictions that unified economic development, class struggle and revolutionary trans-formation.

... But in the observable reality of history, as Marx pointed out elsewhere, the "Asiatic mode of production" preserved its immobility in spite of all class con-frontations, just as the serf uprising never defeated the landlords, nor the slave revolts of Antiquity the free men. The linear schema loses sight of the fact that the *bourgeoisie is the only revolutionary class that ever won;* at the same time it is the only class for which the development of the economy was the cause and consequence of its taking hold of society. The same simplification led Marx to neglect the eco-nomic role of the State in the management of a class society. If the rising bour-geoisie seemed to liberate the economy from the State, this took place only to the extent that the former State was an instrument of class oppression in a *static econ-omy.* The bourgeoisie developed its autonomous economic power in the medieval period of the weakening of the State, at the moment of feudal fragmentation of balanced powers. But the modern State which, through Mercantilism, began to support the development bourgeoisie, and which finally became its State at the time of "laisser faire, laisser passer," was to reveal later that it was endowed with the central power of calculated management of the *economic process.* With the concept of Bonapartism, Marx was nevertheless able to describe the shape of the modern statist bureaucracy, the fusion of capital and State, the formation of a "national power of capital over labor, a public force organized for social enslavement," where the bourgeoisie renounces all historical life which is not reduced to the economic history of things and would like to "be condemned to the same political nothingness as other classes." Here the socio-political foundations of the modern spectacle are already established, negatively defining the proletariat as the *only pretender to historical life.* (thesis 87)

Throughout this chapter Debord restates the need for "unitary historical thought" so as to avoid the theoretical insufficiencies that engendered the specialists who ended up representing the proletariat. The subsequent chapter, "Time and History," is his take on world history, but in the present chapter he gives his assessment of the revolutionary workers' movement.

The International Workingmen's Association: As early as *The German Ideology* Marx explicitly stated that each new dominant class has to present its ideas as the only rational, universally valid one to carry out its aims. But elsewhere, such as in his polemic with Bakunin, Marx argued that workers would act democratically (in the broadest sense of the term—democracy in all social relations not merely in sphere of state politics), and that the dictatorship of the proletariat would constitute a brief phase. Bakunin voiced his doubts, which proved correct, in *Statism and Anarchy:*

Thus no matter from which side you look at the question, you will always arrive at the same, sad conclusion—the rule of the majority by a privileged minority.... However these representatives will be passionately convinced, as well as educated, socialists. The terms educated socialists and scientific socialism, which are encountered continuously in the writing of the Lasalleans and the Marxists, themselves demonstrate that the alleged popular state will be nothing more than the despotic rule of the popular masses by a new and numerically small aristocracy of real or imagined scholars. The people have not been educated and will, therefore, be freed entirely from the cares of government, and placed entirely into the governed herd. A fine liberation! The Marxists sense this contradiction and, recognizing that this scholarly government would be the most burdensome, offensive, and despicable in the world, that in spite of the democratic reforms it would be a real dictatorship, console us with the idea that this dictatorship will be temporary and short.

Debord characterizes Marx's criticisms of Bakunin in terms that might well be applied to Debord and his fellow Situationists, although Debord would obviously disagree:

[Marx] denounced Bakunin and his followers for the authoritarianism of a conspiratorial elite which deliberately placed itself above the International and formulated the extravagant design of imposing on society the irresponsible dictatorship of those who are most revolutionary, or those who would designate themselves to be such. Bakunin, in fact, recruited followers on the basis of such a perspective: "Invisible pilots in the center of the popular storm, we must direct it, not with a visible power, but with the collective dictatorship of all the allies. A dictatorship without badge, without title, without official right, yet all the more powerful because it will have none of the appearances of power." Thus two ideologies of the workers' revolution opposed each other, each containing a partially true critique, but losing the unity of the thought of history, and instituting themselves into ideological authorities. Powerful organizations, like German Social-Democracy and the Iberian Anarchist Federation faithfully served one or the other of these ideologies; and everywhere the result was very different from what had been desired.

Despite the fact that Debord is critical of anarchism—he calls individualist anarchism "laughable"—he acknowledged that anarchism led "the most advanced model of proletarian power of all time" in Spain in 1936. And despite the merit of anarchism's "rejection of existing conditions in favor of the whole of life," he would call anarchism the "ideology of pure liberty" for its attempt to realize an ideal. In the film version of *Society of the Spectacle* the camera switches back and forth between portraits of Marx and Bakunin with subtitles that cleary express Debord's preference for Marx.

The Second International: When Debord puts the word *professors* in italics and describes the way they were empowered by the social-democratic organization, we hear the scorn he has for these purveyors of the scientific ideology of "orthodox Marxism." When they educated the working class, they turned the workers into passive apprentices of socialist revolution and propagated the contemplative historical perspective. These were reformist, union bureaucrats who engaged in "legalistic agitation."

... The profound social upheaval which arose with the first world war, though fertile with the awakening of consciousness, twice demonstrated that the social-democratic hierarchy had not educated revolutionarily; and had in no way transformed the German workers into theoreticians: first when the vast majority of the party rallied to the imperialist war; next when, in defeat, it squashed the Spartakist revolutionaries. The ex-worker Ebert still believed in sin, since he admitted that he hated revolution "like sin." "The same leader showed himself a precursor of the socialist representation which soon after confronted the Russian proletariat as its absolute enemy; he even formulated exactly the same program for this new alienation: "Socialism means working a lot." (thesis 97)

Debord describes Lenin as "faithful Kautskyist," a reference to the leader and theoretician of the German Social-Democrats and the Second International. While Lenin was ready to acknowledge Kautsky's Marxist historical research, he certainly wasn't faithful when he wrote *The Proletarian Revolution and the Renegade Kautsky* (Kautsky was against the Russian Revolution). But what Debord is getting at is that Lenin managed the proletariat like the Kautskyists of the Second International, only with a peculiar Russian twist that enabled Lenin and his fellow "professional revolutionaries" to create the "profession of the absolute management of society." Readers interested in finding out more about the deficiencies of Kautsky's thought might want to read Karl Korsch's *Anti-Kautsky*. You would be hard-pressed to find anyone more implacably opposed to the Russian Revolution than Debord:

> The historical moment when Bolshevism triumphed *for itself* in Russia, and when social-democracy fought victoriously *for the old world,* marks the inauguration of the state of affairs which is at the heart of the domination of the modern specta-cle: the moment when the *representation of the working class* radically opposes itself to the working class. (thesis 100)

The Third International: Debord devotes numerous long theses to the development of the Bolshevik regime into bureaucratic rule and the institution of state capitalism. He is predictably contemptuous of the way the communist parties of the Third International were used by Moscow to support bourgeois governments abroad to garner support for Russian diplomatic initiatives, "sabotaging the entire revolutionary move-ment." The commodification of labor was fully disclosed by Stalin's industrialization, which was accompanied by "the reign of terror within the bureaucratic class itself." The control of historical knowledge in the Soviet Union, its falsification and abolition, cre-ated a "perpetual present" that he would later say characterized the "integrated" specta-cle that appeared in the West in the 1980s. "Between the two world wars," Debord writes in thesis 109, "the revolutionary workers' movement was annihilated by the joint action of Stalinist bureaucracy and of fascist totalitarianism which had borrowed its form of organization from the totalitarian party experimented with in Russia."

The Fourth International is not spared Debord's scorn:

> Here the identification of the proletarian project with a hierarchic organization of ide-ology stubbornly survives the experience of all its results. The distance which separates Trotskyism from a revolutionary critique of the present society allows Trotskyism to maintain a deferential attitude toward positions which were already false when they were used in a real combat. Trotsky remained basically in solidarity with the high bureaucracy until 1927, seeking to capture it so as to make it resume genuinely

Bolshevik action externally (it is known that in order to conceal Lenin's famous "testament" he went so far as to slanderously disavow his supporter Max Eastman, who made it public). Trotsky was condemned by his basic perspective, because as soon as the bureaucracy recognizes itself in its result as a counter-revolutionary class internally, it must also choose, in the name of revolution, to be effectively counter-revolutionary externally, *just as it is at home*. Trotsky's subsequent struggle for the Fourth International contains the same inconsistency. All his life he refused to recognize the bureaucracy as the power of a separate class, because during the second Russian revolution he became an unconditional supporter of the Bolshevik form of organization. (thesis 112)

Thus Debord was against the Trotskyists who applied their "neo-Leninist illusion" to underdeveloped countries to seize State power or implement a bureaucratic industrialization of the economy. As mentioned earlier, Lukacs' *History and Class Consciousness* was a huge influence on Debord, but Debord doesn't spare his poison pen when it comes to Lukacs' subsequent reversals and toeing of the party line. The council communism advocated by Anton Pannekoek is, for Debord, the answer to the central question of proletarian organization. Revolutionary organizations, such as the Situationist International, would dissolve when councils came to power: "At the revolutionary moment of dissolution of social separation, this organization must recognize its own dissolution as a separate organization" (the S.I. *would* dissolve prior to the "dissolution of social separation," but Debord clearly saw the writing on the wall and didn't want to see the S.I. deformed by the spectacle). As for the new proletariat, Debord had his finger on the pulse of his times:

The new signs of negation multiplying in the economically developed countries, signs which are misunderstood and falsified by spectacular arrangement, already enable us to draw the conclusion that a new epoch has begun: now, after the workers' first attempt at subversion, it is capitalist abundance which has failed. When anti-union struggles of Western workers are repressed first of all by unions, and when the first amorphous protests launched by rebellious currents of youth directly imply the rejection of the old specialized politics, or art and of daily life, we see two sides of a new spontaneous struggle which begins under a criminal guise. These are the portents of a second proletarian assault against class society. When the lost children of this still immobile army reappear on this battleground which was altered and yet remains the same, they follow a new "General Ludd"* who, this time, urges them to destroy the *machines of permitted consumption*. (thesis 115)

---

* General Ludd, leader of the British workers who rioted and destroyed textile machinery between 1811 and 1816 in the belief that it would diminish employment.

One of the often repeated criticisms of Debord and his fellow Situationists is the apparent contradiction between advocacy of workers' councils and the denunciation of work. For example, the British section of Solidarity in 1972: "The Situtationists... constantly talk of 'workers' (sic) councils... while demanding the abolition of work! Unfortunately they seem to confuse attacks on the work ethic and on alienated labor, both of which are justified and necessary, with attacks on work itself." As I understand them, the Situationists thought that the grubby work that really needed to be done would become so generalized in a revolutionary situation that each individual would have to do very little of it (and the less of it the better). Debord's graffiti NEVER WORK was made at a time when such inordinate amounts of time and energy went into production that work was not "necessary." Vaneigem's position was very clearly stated to be for the ten hour work week. Presumably, work in a post-revolutionary world would not be the alienated work that it is in the society of the spectacle. While the Situationists may have extoled the virtues of Huizinga's *homo ludens* (man the player), it's doubtful that they had any illusions about the extent to which *homo faber* (man the maker), would always be a part of the human being. Their scorn was generally reserved for the *homo economicus,* and those of the right and left who valued work for its role in the economy. Despite the reference to the anti-technological figure General Ludd, Debord doesn't seem to have a problem with machines taking over much of the heavy lifting of production to free humans from it—the "machines of permitted consumption" weren't power plants or even refrigerators, but automobiles and televisions.

The concept of "post-workerist" Marxism would be picked up by Toni Negri and others in the 1970s in Italy, and by the New York based *Zerowork* journal. To my mind, the zerowork goal has value for its utopian appeal; and as a former handy man in exchange for rent, I can say many apparently grubby jobs can actually become ludic chores.

Debord tells us in Chapter V, "Time and History," that humans are identical to time. But this time is experienced differently—a "static society organizes time in terms of its immediate experience of nature, on the model of *cyclical* time" and the dominant class "possesses for itself alone the irreversible time of the living." Cyclical time corresponds to nomads, and even more so to agrarian societies: "Eternity is internal to it; it is the return of the same here on earth. Myth is the unitary construction of the thought which guarantees the entire cosmic order surrounding the order which this society has in fact already realized within its frontiers." Debord characterizes these societies as "frozen" and as being characterized by "absolute conformism in existing social practices." Myths and chronicles give meaning to the cyclical time experienced by peasants, and provides the cover of illusion for the masters who have appropriated the time of others and thus acquired "temporal surplus value." These masters are free to wage wars of conquest and escape cyclical time by living the "event-oriented succession of powers." When Debord writes about "irreversible time" he's writing about the "event-oriented" history favored by most Marxists. Note, however, that the irreversible time of the historical event is transformed into a "general movement" of things (the production-consumption of commodities) by the bourgeoise—a sort of ersatz irreversible time.*

---

* It surprises me, considering Debord's use of this "irreversible time" construct, that Greil Marcus would attribute what he calls the "reversible connecting factor" to Debord in his *Lipstick Traces.* Marcus sets this concept up with two incredible quotes from Carl Jung about how "There is no lunacy people under the domination of an archetype will not fall prey to" opposite photos of Jewish corpses at Buchenwald in 1945. I say "incredible" because Carl Jung was the president of the International Society for Psychotherapy from 1933 to 1939 and presided over its Nazified German section and co-edited *Zentralblatt fur Psychotherapie* with Reichsmarshall Goring's cousin. Incidentally, there is no way that Jung wouldn't have been intimately aware of what his psychiatric brothers were up to—as Dr. Peter Breggin M.D. has clearly documented: "German psychiatry was responsible for developing the idea of mass sterilization and mass murder, and German psychiatry systematically murdered 100,000 or more patients as a prelude to Hitler's extermination program—everything from the first extermination centers to the gas chambers and crematoriums." In an wild leap, Marcus follows Jung's description of compulsiveness engendered by the activation of an archetype with the following passage:

> This was Jung's account of Nazism. In it was the power principle Debord would grasp: the reversible connecting factor, the idea that the empty repetitions of modern life, or work and spectacle, could be detourned into the creation of situations, into abstract forms that could be infused with unlimited content. But the situationist idea was at bottom a Dada idea, and Jung's account of Nazism needs only an excision of its specific examples to serve as an account of what the dadaists sought in the Cabaret Voltaire. Dada was a protest against its time; it was also the bird on the rhinoceros, peeping and chirping, but along for the ride. Dada was a prophecy, but it had no idea what it was prophesying, and its strength was that it didn't care.

My interpretation of this passage is that Marcus seems to transfer his attitudes onto Debord and Dada. The partisans of Dada may have acted blindly from moment to moment, but they were perfectly aware that they were annihilating bourgeois art and burning their boats behind themselves. As discussed in previous chapters, situations are irrepeatable; they exist in a unique time and space, and hence have nothing to do with "abstract forms"—specific examples simply can't be excised from their historical context

In his discussion of Greece, Debord flatly states, "Only those who don't work, live" because they are the only ones who have the power and temporal surplus to create and live their own history. His treatment of the age that gave birth to democracy and history is rather brief in *Society of the Spectacle,* using it merely to mark the dream of "universal" history (unifying the world known to the Greeks). Yet he frequently returns to the Greeks in his post-Situationist writings on democracy and strategy.

The fall of Rome witnessed the rise of what Debord calls semi-historical religions; the monotheistic religions "which grew out of Judaism are abstract universal acknowledgments of irreversible time that is democratized—opened to all—but in the realm of illusion." Born in profoundly historical struggles, these religions nonetheless distorted time into an eschatological orientation: "Eternity is the element which holds back the irreversibility of time, suppressing history within history itself by placing itself on the other side of irreversible time as a pure punctual element to which cyclical time returned and abolished itself."

Evoking Huizinga's *The Waning of the Middle Ages* in spirit if not in name, Debord writes of the "melancholy of the demise of a world" that was deeply felt by Debord himself—a character in Michele Bernstein's *La Nuit* remarked to Debord's character: "There's something mediaeval about you," as if he were one of the drunken poets living in the margins of the Latin Quarter in the XIIIth Century who composed the verses glorifying vice of the *Carmina Burana.* Debord's interpretation of the millenarian peasant revolts is informed by Mannehiem's chapter on "The Utopian Mentality" in *Ideology and Utopia,* and not by Norman Cohn *(The Pursuit of the Millenium),* whom Debord takes to task for identifying modern revolutionary expectations as continuations of the religious passion of millenarianism. Debord draws

---

as the author of *Lipstick Traces* wishes because each one of Marcus' oxymoronic archetypes of iconoclasm are creations of specific historical conditions. The experimental behavior advocated by the Situationists strove to be consciously and resolutely opposed to "the practical conditions of present oppression," and explicitly *not* some belated revival of Dada. To say that Debord found a "power principle" akin to one exploited by the Nazis is a smear, and nowhere does Debord use the phrase "reversible connecting factor" as Marcus claims. What emerges from the above passage by Marcus is that he misapplied an objectionable archetype category to connect Dada, Nazis and Debord. The "reversible connecting factor" is actually Marcus' sloppy brand of structuralism that he pegged on Debord's use of historical events such as the Albigensian Crusade and historical figures like Jack the Ripper. Debord was a particularly harsh critic of structuralism: "the *apology for the spectacle* institutes itself as the thought of non-thought, as the *official amnesia* of historical practice." No wonder, then, that Debord would mention Greil Marcus in the same breath as the *Times of London,* which "vomited" some baseless agent-baiting claims at Debord (in *"This bad reputation..."* 1993).

heavily on Mannehiem's interpretation of ideology in the last chapter of *Society of the Spectacle,* but it's well worth looking at Mannehiem's take on the orgiastic chiliasm (the doctrine that Christ will personally reign on earth during the millennium) of the anabaptists in *Ideology and Utopia:*

> The decisive turning-point in modern history was, from the point of view of our problem, the moment in which "Chiliasm" joined forces with the active demands of the oppressed strata of society. The very idea of the dawn of a millennial kingdom on earth always contained a revolutionizing tendency, and the church made every effort to paralyze this situationally transcendent idea with all the means at its command. [...] The "spiritualization of politics," which may be said to have begun at this turn in history, more or less affected all the currents of the time. [...] It is at this point that politics in the modern sense of the term begins, if we here understand by politics a more or less conscious participation of all strata of society in the achievement of some mundane purpose, as contrasted in the achievement of acceptance of events as they are, or as they are controlled from "above." [...] Even though this stage is, as already indicated, still very far removed from the stage of "proletarian self-consciousness," it is nevertheless the starting point of the process gradually leading to it. [...] The Chiliast expects a union with the immediate present. Hence he is not preoccupied in his daily life with optimistic hopes for the future or romantic reminiscences. His attitude is characterized by a tense expectation. He is always on his toes awaiting the propitious moment and thus there is no inner articulation of time for him. He is not actually concerned with the millennium that is to come: what is important for him is that it happens here and now, and that it arises from mundane existence, as a sudden swing over into another kind of existence. The promise of the future which is to come is not for him a reason for postponement, but merely a point of orientation, something external to the ordinary course of events from where he is on the lookout, ready to take the leap.

This fatal point of orientation, this waiting for a sign from God, was what defeated the millenarians. They didn't take conscious possession of their historical operation, and were thus doomed. The Renaissance, so dear to Debord that he would spend part of his years of exile in Florence, didn't suffer this illusion:

> The new possession of historical life, the Renaissance, which finds its past and its legitimacy in Antiquity, carries with it a joyous rupture with eternity. Its irreversible time is that of the infinite accumulation of knowledge, and the historical consciousness which grows out of the experience of democratic communities and of the forces which ruin them will take up, with Machiavelli, the analysis of

desanctified power, saying the unspeakable about the State. In the exuberant life of the Italian cities, in the art of the festival, life is experienced as enjoyment of the passage of time. But this enjoyment of passage is itself a passing enjoyment. The song of Lorenzo di Medici considered by Burckhardt to be the expression of "the very spirit of the Renaissance" is the eulogy which this fragile feast of history pronounces on itself: "How beautiful the spring of life—which vanishes so quickly." (thesis 139)

The bourgeoise, with the abhorrent values they placed on labor, succeeded in liberating labor time from cyclical time—so much productivity was released in labor (the production of commodities and the accumulation of capital) that historical conditions were transformed. With mass production, irreversible "profoundly historical" time was transformed into the "time of things"—humans began to consume history on a daily basis, "but only in the form of the history of the abstract movement of things which dominates all qualitative use of life." This is what is meant by the slogan "Historical consciousness is consciousness of daily life" voiced by the Italian section of the Situationist International in their journal.

> ... The ruling class, made up of *specialists in the possession of things* who are themselves therefore a possession of things, must link its fate with the preservation of this reified history, with the permanence of a new immobility *within* history. For the first time the worker, at the base of society, is not materially a *stranger to history* because it is now the base that irreversibly moves society. In the demand to live *the* historical time which it makes, the proletariat finds the simple unforgettable center of its revolutionary project; and every attempt (thwarted until now) to realize this project marks a point of possible departure for new historical life. (thesis 143)

Until this demand of the proletariat to live historical time is met, what Debord calls "unified irreversible time" or the movement of universal history will continue to be the abstract, fragmented units of production-consumption time. I've added the hyphen and "consumption" where Debord only identifies production because many workers produce very little and their service to the economy and their experience of bourgeois time has as much to do with consumption as production. In other words, the masses are now needed more as consumers than producers. The conclusion to Debord's analysis of "Time and History" is summed up in the following sentence: "With the development of capitalism, irreversible time is *unified on a world scale.*"

Perhaps the most concrete indictment of the spectacle is in the next chapter, "Spectacular Time," but this severe attack is muted for listeners who haven't been paying close attention. Perhaps part of the reason Debord is said to be so difficult to

read is that people attempt to read a thesis in the middle of the book without having comprehended the development of thought up to that point. If you don't understand what Debord means by cyclical time, for example, pseudo-cyclical time is
meaningless. You will recall that cyclical time was time rooted in the seasons,
months, weeks, days, and the alternations of real labor that was the true source of
wealth of ancient societies. While the ancient myths fostered illusions of eternity,
people really lived in cyclical time.

> Pseudo-cyclical time is the time of consumption of modern economic survival, of
> increased survival. Here daily life continues to be deprived of decision and remains
> bound, no longer to the natural order, but to the pseudo-nature developed in
> alienated labor; and thus this time naturally reestablishes the ancient cyclical
> rhythm which regulated the survival of pre-industrial societies. Pseudo-cyclical
> time leans on the natural remains of cyclical time and also uses it to compose new
> homologous combinations: day and night, work and weekly rest, the recurrence of
> vacations. (thesis 150)

Time becomes a commodity and losses all qualitative dimensions, a fact which
makes the expression "quality time" (as in "I *spent* quality time with the kids") laughable: "But being the by-product of this time which aims to retard concrete daily life
and to keep it retarded, it must be charged with pseudo-valuations and appear in a
sequence of falsely individualized moments." People don't use their free time to consume commodities, commodities consume their free time. From tourist vacations to
daily image-consumption, time is appropriated in an unnatural way for the sake of
the production.

> Here this commodity is explicitly presented as the moment of real life, and the
> point is to wait for its cyclical return. But even in those very moments reserved for
> living, it is still the spectacle that is seen, reproduced and becoming more intense.
> What was represented as genuine life reveals itself simply as more genuinely spec-
> tacular life. (thesis 153)

Debord rails against "vulgarized pseudo-festivals, parodies of dialogue and the
gift" as he advances the thesis that reality is changing, but people experience this
change as a mere illusion. This is the inverse of cyclical time where change is lived in
the face of the illusion of eternity. The illusion of pseudo-cyclical time is the "*advertisement* of time" and the never-ending expansion of homogenous consumption—
the real changes are in the processes of production. Consumers have the illusion of
change as fashions come and go on a pseudo-cyclical basis, but nothing really

changes other than fact that domination continues to create more effective ways to exploit labor and accumulate capital.

Personal history is as illusive as world history for spectators because they can't possibly be conscious of "time really lived" in opposition to the pseudo-cyclical time of economic quarters and planned vacations:

> This individual experience of separate daily life remains without language, without concept, without critical access to its own past which has been recorded nowhere. It is not communicated. It is not understood and is forgotten to the profit of the false spectacular memory of the unmemorable.

At the beginning of a supposedly informed discussion on Debord in *Telos* (#86 Winter 1990 pp 81–102) that is full distortions and obvious gaps of historical knowledge, Russell Berman states that "the spectacle thesis occluded the concreteness of lived experience." This is far from the case—Berman conveniently omits the radical aspect of Debord's critique of the spectacle: "the obvious and secret necessity for revolution." And if we look at Debord's more autobiographical works, such as the collage *Memoires,* his *Panegyric* and his film *In Girum...* we see Debord's refusal to forget and his development of a seductive language of daily life to communicate what he really lived.

> The natural basis of time, the actual experience of the flow of time, becomes human and social by existing for man. The restricted condition of human practice, labor at various stages, is what has humanized and also dehumanized time (as cyclical time and as separate irreversible time of economic production). The revolutionary project of realizing a classless society, a generalized historical life, is the project of a withering away of the social measure of time, to the benefit of a playful model of irreversible time of individuals and groups—a model in which independent federated times are simultaneously present. It is the program of a total realization (in the context of time), of a communism which suppresses "all that exists independently of individuals." (thesis 163)

Berman also makes the even more laughable claim that "domestic intelligence services have been gradually dismantled since Watergate" in the U.S., when in fact, "domestic defense" budgets have ballooned and are considered to be the new boom industry by the military-industrial-entertainment-complex. The other participants in the *Telos* discussion muster equally weak arguments. Paul Piccone calls Debord "Adorno gone mad," and he discusses terrorism in Western Europe in the 1970's as if he is completely unaware of the well-documented cases against the "black orchestra," or neo-Nazi involvement in the infiltration of left-wing groups, arrest of the leaders so that infiltrators could take over and subsequent perpetration of terrorist acts. The Italian government has gone so far as to concede its involvement in many of these incidents, but Piccone still hangs on to the idea that terrorism was the "last gasp" of 1968ers (the Situationists, as is well known, were anti-militant and anti-terrorist). David Pan, for his part, states: "Clearly out of gas by thesis #220, he abruptly closed *Society of the Spectacle* with a sudden appeal to the workers' councils as the agency of redemption—an appeal totally unwarranted by the earlier presentation." It would seem that Pan neglected to read the references to workers' councils in chapter IV, and he is either confused or disingenuous if he thinks that Debord would grant domain of universal history to intellectuals, or anyone else other than the proletariat. Debord claimed with pride that the best readers of *Society of the Spectacle* were in the factories of Italy where, in the autumn of 1969, the council movement was such a threat that right-wing forces associated with military intelligence, the P2 Masonic lodge and the police put their campaign of false terror into high gear:

> The workers of Italy can be held up as an example to their comrades in all countries for their absenteeism, their wildcat strikes (which no particular concession can manage to appease), their lucid refusal of work and their contempt for the law and all Statist parties—they know the subject well enough by practice to have been able to benefit from the theses of *Society of the Spectacle,* even when they read nothing but mediocre translations of it.

Society of the Spectacle's Chapter VII, "The Organization of Territory," was the only chapter reprinted by the short-lived American section of the S.I., highlighting the relevance of his theses related to architecture "aimed at the poor" for North America. Debord brings all the knowledge acquired in the L.I. and S.I. experiments in unitary urbanism to bear on the problem, and concludes that "Proletarian revolution is the critique of human geography through which individuals and communities have to create places and events suitable for the appropriation, no longer just of their labor, but of their total history." It almost goes without saying that Debord was a thoroughly urban creature who envisioned revolutions occurring exclusively in cities. It could be argued that revolutions sometimes migrate from city to country and back again, but Debord does make a good case about the way the landscape is now designed to manufacture apathy in accordance with the laws of spectacular separation. And to refute David Pan again, I quote thesis 179:

> The greatest revolutionary idea concerning urbanism is not itself urbanistic, technological or esthetic. It is the decision to reconstruct the entire environment in

accordance with the needs of the power of Workers' Councils, of the *anti-statist dictatorship* of the proletariat, of enforceable dialogue. And the power of the Councils, which can be effective only if it transforms existing conditions in their entirety, cannot assign itself a smaller task if it wants to be recognized and to recognize itself in its world.

The first *Telos* commentator, Russell Berman, makes the inane claim that contrary to his beloved Adorno no "genuine art or genuine popular, perhaps populist culture" appears in Debord. Where was Berman when Debord describes, at length (theses 205–209), the insurrectional style of diverting pre-existing cultural products for revolutionary ends? This practice has turned thousands, perhaps millions, into anti-artists with relatively little effort. This is the communist anti-art that Debord practiced in his journals, tapes, books and films—a critical practice that he unified with social practice and hoped would be superseded along with all culture in the creation of total history with proletarians world-wide. Cultural activity, albeit its negation, doesn't get more populist than that. Incidentally, Debord's books continue to be widely read by his intended audience, i.e., those contesting the established order; and his films had an even wider audience when they were shown. An entire generation of Europeans experienced a Situationist education. Adorno, meanwhile, wrote in an impenetrable academic style suited exclusively for academics, and his atonal musical compositions were anything but populist. What Russell meant to say about Adorno (the author of an indefensibly bogus critique of jazz), was that no "genuine popular, perhaps populist culture" appears in Adorno's life.

Aside from his attacks on cultural history's "preservation as a dead object in spectacular contemplation," the reformism of sociology, the anti-historicism of structuralism, and the above-mentioned discussion of the "insurrectional style," Debord also makes an interesting thesis on the baroque in the penultimate chapter: "Baroque is the art of a world which has lost its center. The last mythical order in the cosmos and in terrestrial government that was accepted by the Middle Ages, has fallen." Debord sees the theatrical festivals of baroque art as being a positive choice of life over eternity, "where every specific artistic expression becomes meaningful only with reference to the setting of a constructed place, a construction which is its own center of unification; this center is the *passage* that is inscribed as a threatened equilibrium in the dynamic disorder of everything." Subsequent art movements were increasingly fragmented, and when combined with the advent of museums for the souvenirs of art, this ultimately led to the "complete negation of the artistic sphere."

On the face of it, the last chapter, "Ideology Materialized," is by far the weakest chapter. Only by recognizing the expressly partisan essence of the book can we begin to come to grips with Debord's one-sided use of ideology and false consciousness.

Ideology is a pejorative term in most Western Marxist lexicons—Russian Marxism-Leninism claimed, with pride, to be a truly scientific ideology, but by the Fifties in the West, ideology was just a bad word that denoted a reactionary class-bound perspective. While the ideological distortion of facts is what commits the reactionaries to act as they do, those who level the charge of ideology with even more commitment than the reactionaries are somehow above the charge. Debord naturally makes polemical use of the term, and considers his views to be vastly superior to anyone beholden to an ideology. The apparent weakness in Debord's reduction of the complexities of reality into two Manichaean blocks of truth and falsehood, life and the spectacle could be interpreted as a strength because it puts everything in strategic terms. For Debord, to live was, to paraphrase Shakespeare, to stomp the heads of kings. In his monograph on Debord, Anselm Jappe makes the point that for Debord there almost a Platonic conception of authentic reality and truth in opposition to falsified models of the world, to which Debord might respond, the role of revolutionaries, at least since 1789, has been to bring their subjective truth to the world. My personal interpretation of ideology relies on Volosinov's equation of ideology with individual words as outlined in the first chapter of his *Marxism and the Philosophy of Language*—most theoretical words are not ideologically neutral but value-laden (with values drawn from ideologies as Vygotsky makes clear in his *Thought and Language*).

Debord begins the last chapter with the statement that "Ideology is the basis of the thought of a class society in the conflict-laden course of history," which stresses the point that while his opponent's consciousness might be socially determined, Debord's is somehow free from a similar social determination. By refusing the needs and desires of that cause reification, Debord implies that reifications and ideological thoughts can be broken, here and now. This wasn't without precedent—in a letter to Franz Mehring, Marx wrote: "Ideology is a process accomplished by the so-called thinker—consciously, it's true—but with a false consciousness. The real motive forces impelling him remain unknown to him [...] he imagines false or apparent motive forces." Readers struggling to come to grips with the phrase "false consciousness" can consider it to be roughly synonymous with "ideology"—the former being slightly more diffuse than a concretized manifestation of the latter. According to Mannehiem, whom Debord draws on in this chapter, consciousness is false "if it is oriented with reference to norms, with which action in a given historical setting, even with the best of intentions, cannot comply," or in theory when "in a given practical situation it uses concepts and categories which, if taken seriously, would prevent man from adjusting himself at that historical stage." Law is perhaps the best example of this because it attempts to deny the historical fact that everything is wound up in the historical process of conflicts and struggles. As Jospeh

Gabel, the French interpreter of Mannehiem, points out "These views are highly akin to those of young Marx."

Gabel, whom Debord quotes from *False Consciousness,* makes the point that the French translation of Manneheim's 1929 *Ideology and Utopia* in 1956 was made from a very poor English translation. The translators' modifications reduced the book in order to simplify it, and added numerous remarks to the body of the work, such as an erroneous definition of false consciousness. Gabel also asserts that "The absence of a veritable definition of the Marxist notion of 'consciousness,' which is often used in practice as synonymous with 'knowledge' or even 'thought' paved the way for a theoretical interpretation that, when arrived at its logical conclusion, threatens to reduce to a banality all the theory of false consciousness."

The only legitimate use, according to Gabel, of "ideology" and "false consciousness" corresponds to Manneheim's original historicist and dialectical use of the terms—not the polemical use of the terms. The "total" conception of ideology is said to have democratic, pluralist viewpoints as its natural corollary. Debord's citation of "total ideology" that he quickly defines as "the despotism of the fragment which imposes itself as pseudo-knowledge of a frozen *totality, the totalitarian vision*" is derived from Manneheim's distinctions between "total," "general" and "non-evaluative" ideologies. But these distinctions tend in practice to be blurred beyond recognition. The positing of a total ideology, such as the spectacle, could logically only be opposed by the plurality of viewpoints found in total democracy.

In the context of this discussion of Mannheim we should quickly examine the often repeated phrase "totality" (as in "contest the totality" with total revolution) often used by Situationists. Mannheim's use of this term is sometimes translated as a "global historical schema" to be applied to the profundities of historical becoming—past and present. So when Vaneigem says "Think globally, act locally," his imperative is to transcend all provincial, socially-conditioned perspectives of the world and its history. With a dialectical conception of history, a person can move easily in and out of various historical epochs and thereby recognize the need for social change at a given moment. This global understanding enables a person to resist the temptation to take up with causes that issue from flawed forms of historical consciousness—an example of this would be Michel Foucault's support for the Iranian revolution simply because Khommeni was anti-American. A totalizing or dialectical perspective wouldn't fall into this trap.

In *Marxism and Totality,* Martin Jay traces the concept of totality from the ideal of "Hellenic unity" to its variations in contemporary Western Marxism. This highly informative account suffers from the contemplative perspective of an academic, which leads the author to denigrate concepts such as Karl Korsch's assertion that theory must follow practice (we have seen, on the contrary, how the S.I.'s theory of drifts and diversion did indeed follow their practice). What Jay shows us, as he demonstrates the operation of totality in the thought of Vico, Rousseau, Kant, Schiller, Hegel, is just how flexible this concept can be. The holistic view of history developed by Hegel in *Phenomonology of the Mind* would loom large in young Marx and the anti-scientific, historicist Marxists of Central Europe (Lukacs and Korsch). The Surrealists were reportedly the first in France to deploy the concept in its Hegelian-Marxist usage, and as was mentioned above, Lefebvre discovered Hegel via Breton. Of particular relevance to Debord is how Lefebvre theorized "open" and "closed" totalities and chastised Lukacs for not foreseeing the eventuality of a closed totalitarian totality created by Stalin. The totality Lefebvre sought was open-ended and dynamic—Debord was a partisan of this open-ended conception of the totality of history, even in his somewhat more pessimistic (he would say realistic) later works.

As I will demonstrate in the next chapter, Debord was an effective advocate of total democracy in the May '68 revolution and practiced what he preached. So, while Debord would use the polemical aspect of "ideology" to denounce opponents (a Manniechian conception of good and evil), we should bear in mind the positive aspect of the negative concept of spectacular totality. This implies support for total democracy—support Debord would express in deeds. But to turn back to the critique of the spectacle, for Debord, "the spectacle is ideology par excellence"

> ... because it exposes and manifests in its fullness the essence of all ideological systems: the impoverishment, servitude and negation of real life. The spectacle is materially "the expression of the separation and estrangement between man and man." Through the "new power of fraud," concentrated at the base of the spectacle in this production, "the new domain of alien beings to whom man is subservient... grows coextensively with the mass of objects." It is the highest stage of an expansion which has turned need against life. "The need for money is thus the real need produced by political economy, and the only need it produces" (*Economic and Philosophical Manuscripts*). The spectacle extends to all social life the principle which Hegel (in the *Realphilosophie of Jena*) conceives as the principle of money: it is "the life of what is dead, moving within itself." (thesis 215)

Debord then draws on Gabel's use of psychiatric categories such as schizophrenia in the latter's *False Consciousness,* which is much too medi-cynically clinical for my taste. But it highlights the importance of historical understanding—the mentally ill often have little recollection of their own personal histories much less of world history. People no longer have encounters, but the "illusion of encounters," and because people aren't recognized by others, "every individual becomes unable to recognize his own reality;" all that people recognize is the mirror-image of the spectacle, and they imitate it via exchanges with the spectacle-commodity economy. This almost implies that people are sick because they don't have recognitions of world history. The use of "ideology" to denounce rivals and opponents cast all debate in terms of a polemic. This was a way to sharpen one's wits and continually restate the debate in the terms of class war. Class consciousness was the arm that Debord used against the false consciousness of his enemies who conspired for the spectacle. When the revolutionary moment came, Debord was in a position to express his views on direct democracy very effectively and easily—out of one side of his mouth he defended the democratic process in the General Assembly of the Sorbonne and out of the other he denounced all views that were insufficiently radical.

The last thesis of the book is more prescriptive than the above critiques, and warrants being read and reread:

> Emancipation from the material bases of inverted truth—this is what the self-emancipation of our epoch consists of. This "historical mission of installing truth in the world" cannot be accomplished either by the isolated individual, or by the atomized crowd subjected to manipulation. But now, as ever, truth can be installed by the class which is able to effect the dissolution of all classes by bringing all power into the dealienating form of realized democracy, the Council, in which practical theory controls itself and sees its own action. This is possible only where individuals are "directly linked to universal history," where dialogue arms itself to make its own conditions victorious. (thesis 221)

This wide-ranging book served as Debord's playbook in the power struggles in the Sorbonne in May '68. His calls to radicalize the striking workers in France and his denunciations of capitalism and so-called "socialism" in Russia and China, in concert with his revolutionary comrades, wouldn't have been possible without the lessons Debord learned to be able to write *Society of the Spectacle*—lessons that enabled him to instantly assess the situation and generate demands. Vaneigem's *Revolution of Daily Life* may have been more inspirational to the graffiti writers in the days of May '68, but as we will see, Debord had a much more direct role in the events (Vaneigem arrived in Paris late and went on an infamous "vacation")—Debord and his cohorts set up shop in the Jules Bonnot room of the Sorbonne (renamed after the notorious anarchist bank robber) openly expressing support for Makhno (the notorious anarchist general) over Lenin and Trotsky to let people know where they stood. Without a very generous, democratic conception of the proletariat such as Debord's chapter IV in the context of a view of history such as in chapter V, Debord wouldn't have had the foundation for the total opposition to the totality of the spectacle. In order for the proletariat to be the subject of the history it lived, it had to have a total "thought of

Raoul Vaneigem and J.V. Martin

history" that engenders modes of thought and action that reject bourgeois legality and capitalist life-forms. The amazing way Debord put his demoniacally poetic spin on Hegel and Marx (and their descendents) and the incredibly fortuitous way he was able to embody—however briefly—the revolutionary story told in *Society of the Spectacle* is what makes Debord's story so inspiring.

Chapter Twenty-three

It was in December, 1967 that Vaneigem's *The Revolution of Everyday Life* was published by Gallimard. This *Treatise on How to Live,* as a literal translation of the French title reads, has done as much to spread sabotage and subversion as any book I know. With his own references to writing the book at cafes and the legend about his dismissal from his high school teaching post for preaching free love, we can almost catch a fleeting image of a free-wheeling young Raoul drifting through the streets of Paris and Brussels. He sneers back at those who would make him feel like an object, all the while feeling the humiliation worthy of a Rousseau. Violently atheist, inspiring in his denunciation of the "disgrace of work" and the "dictatorship of consumption," Vaneigem is widely read, albeit in flawed translations—many, if not most of the people who have become interested in the S.I. came to it via *The Revolution of Everyday Life.*

For that reason, and because this is a book on Debord, I'll forego a detailed exposition of this influential tome and encourage readers to check it out for themselves.
Rather than a series of concise, numbered theses as with Debord, Vaneigem divides
his book in half and fills the expansive pages with literary references and cynical sim-
iles such as "like arsenic in jelly." The first part is his lyrical critique of "The
Perspective of Power," informed by his study of Roman philology, Hegel and Marx.
As with his "Basic Banalities," this is a very Kojèveian reading of Hegel and Marx,
that brings the master-slave dichotomy to the modern world. In fact, the chapter on
"Exchange and Gift," with its references to potlatch and sacrifice is more reminiscent
of that dissident student of Kojève, Georges Bataille, than any other S.I. text.
Vaneigem's profound critique of roles, the repetition of stereotypes or any other spectacular category provides still more evidence that Marcus' equation of the S.I. project with Jung's activation of archetypes is erroneous (cf. note pp. 145–146). Part of
Vaneigem's appeal is that he addresses the idea of freedom and sovereignty from an
individual perspective rooted in everyday life in his "Reversal of Perspective."

Those who speak of revolution and class struggle with explicit references to everyday life, without understanding the subversiveness of love and what's positive in
the refusal of constraints, they have a cadaver in their mouths.

These lines and many others from R.E.L. (as Vaneigem's book is referred to in
England) would find their way onto the walls of the Latin Quarter during the hot
days of May '68, even if Vaneigem wasn't there—actually he was there, but he went
on "vacation" for a week at the height of the events, which resulted in some acrimo-
ny between him and other members of the S.I. Looking back on the May Revolution,
Andre Stephane went so far as to say that "Vaneigem's very style is that of the slogans
of May. He seems, moreover, to have been at the origin of many of the most successful and poetic phrases.... The author of the *Treatise on Living* gives us a key for understanding the role and place of the *paranoiac mechanisms of our civilization.*"
  Aside from the release of Debord and Vaneigem's books, 1967 was a year of pre-
monition—Soviet dissidents protested in Moscow, anti-military German students
protested across the republic, riots in Berlin, Tunis.... "Burn this town down" was
shouted at the radical riots that rocked Newark, Detroit, Minneapolis, New York,
Washington, DC and many other cities in the summer of 1967. The C.I.A. set up
the illegal Operation Chaos to look into war protesters as Mao's efforts to bring
Chinese peasants into the Cultural Revolution created a virtual civil war. In the Fall,
agitation erupted at the University of Algeria and a deadly riot occurred in Tokyo.
French workers at Saint-Azire, the largest shipyard of the country, went on strike.
Che Guevara was killed in Bolivia in October and a week of mourning was held in

his honor in Paris in December. As we will see in greater detail below, the agitation and strikes at Nanterre in March and November (respectively) were premonitions of what would come the following year.

During the months of November and December 1967, Debord and Vaneigem were picked up by the cops and hauled in for questioning several times. The charge? Debord was the editor who published (in S.I.#11) Vaneigem's stolen comic strip images adorned with revolutionary phrases; the stolen strip was reproduced in Spain, Denmark and Holland. It's not clear why they were let go, but these sorts of comics would reappear in the Nanterre insurrection and, with a workers' council slant, in the revolution of May '68.

To digress for a moment, according to Douglas Pourch's *The French Secret Services,* the Interior Ministry under de Gaulle and Pompidou wasn't spying too closely on the extreme left—there was no information on Cohn-Bendit, for example, when the events erupted in 1968. Given his years of radical activity, Debord certainly had a file at the Renseignements Generaux de la Prefecture de Paris. According to the head of the French equivalent of the FBI, the DST (Direction de la Surveillance du Territoire), the Renseignements Generaux tried to blame May '68 on the C.I.A. and Mossad in order to get increased funds for counterintelligence. This claim was easily disproved, and Raymond Marcellin, the Interior Minister at the time, would later (*La Geurre politique,* 1985) blame May '68 on Maoists, other revolutionary groups and "Jews and Germans." After May '68, the Renseignements Generaux created a special "central operational brigade" to destroy left-wing groups through tested methods—burglary, agent provocateurs, phone taps, mail searches, etc. In *"This bad reputation..."* Debord asserts that "even in the pure S.I. of 1967 there were two provocateurs-infiltrators, perhaps three." It's impossible to say if this increased surveillance played a part in the dissolution of the S.I. a few years after May '68, but this pressure certainly didn't encourage a group that specialized in subversive scandals and knew it needed to democratize if it were to continue to exist in a viable way.

The protests and riots that had spanned the globe in 1967 continued in 1968: student protests against the docking of the U.S. aircraft carrier Enterprise at European ports; student agitation in Warsaw, Algiers, Berlin; riots in Rio de Janiero; the attempt on German radical Rudi Dutschke's life created solidarity marches in Paris, Rome, Vienna and London. But the activity that interests us here begins on January 8 with the famous incident between Cohn-Bendit and Minister Missoffe, in which the minister was publicly criticized by the German student at the inauguration of a swimming pool at Nanterre (a dismal suburb of Paris): "Your *White Book on Young People* doesn't say a word about the problem of sex!" It should be noted that the Enragés (sympathizers with, and future allies of, the Situationists) had prepared the student body for the event by telling everyone that the pool would become an excellent place for orgies. These Enragés of Nanterre, named after proto-anarchists in the French Revolution, were as fond of scandal as the Situationists, and following the swimming pool incident, more and more students began to imitate their radical tactics. Plainclothes cops were photographed by students on campus, and the pictures were posted. When the cops were sent in, they were thus easily recognized and chased away by anarchists and Enragés. In February, the Enragés circulated the lyrics to songs insulting the university administration and numerous professors. On March 22, the Enragés and other students occupied a campus administration building, giving birth to the March 22nd Movement, which, after many minor scandals in April,

The Enragés at Nanterre University

resulted in the closure of the university for two days on May 2. This was the act that spread the agitation to the Latin Quarter of Paris. Although the Enragés left the occupation early because of the presence of certain objectionable radicals (leaving their mark on the walls with slogans such as "Never Work" and "Take your desires for reality"), and discontinued their activity on campus, they were treated harshly by the authorities—Patrick Cheval was expelled from the university and Gerard Bigorgne was banned from all establishments of higher learning in France. Rene Riesel and Cohn-Bendit were scheduled to appear before a university commission on May 6.

Before going into the events of May, note that the best eyewitness account is Situationist René Viénet's *Enragés and Situationists in the Occupation Movement, France, May '68*. My account draws on this report, as well as the assessments made by Pascal Dumontier in *The Situationists and May 68* and Jean-Francois Martos' *History of the Situationist International*. Numerous other books deal with the subject, but none offer the same focus on the Situationist role. It should also be said at the outset that none of the Situationists, perhaps Debord least of all, sought to gain personal glory in a spectacular way. When the actions of the Situationists are described, we should bear in mind that Debord, Khayati, Viénet and later Vaneigem were the only Situationists in Paris at the time. In other words, Debord certainly had a hand in all Situationist activity during the occupation movement. It should also be noted that the first press run of *Society of the Spectacle* was sold out by May.

The first May Day parade in fifteen years took place in Paris on May 1, 1968. Scuffles errupted between the security detail of the major union federation, the C.G.T., and revolutionary students. As mentioned above, the Nanterre campus was

Rene Riesel and Daniel Cohn-Bendit

closed indefinitely on May 2. Meanwhile, students in Berkeley rebelled against the Vietnam war and copies of Che Guevara's memoir were burned by cops in Barcelona. The March 22nd Movement and the student union called for a meeting in the courtyard of the Sorbonne on Friday, May 3. Viénet was there:

> In itself, the meeting of May 3rd was banal: as usual three or four hundred hangers-on responded to the call. The few dozen fascists of the "Occident" group counter-demonstrated at the beginning of the afternoon on the Boulevard Saint-Michel. Several Enragés at the Sorbonne called for the organization of self-defense. Furniture had to be broken up as there were no clubs. Rector Roche and his policemen thought this would be sufficient pretext for an attack. The police and the gendarmerie mobile invaded the courtyard of the Sorbonne without meeting resistance. The students were encircled. The police then offered them free passage out

of the courtyard. The students accepted and the first to leave were in fact allowed to pass. The operation took time and other students began to gather outside in the quarter. The remaining two hundred demonstrators inside the Sorbonne, including all the organizers, were arrested. As the police vans carried them away, the Latin Quarter erupted. One of the two vans never reached its destination. Only three policemen guarded the second van. They were beaten up, and several dozen demonstrators escaped.

A week of street fighting ensued—students were arrested and sentenced to hard time. Police occupied the Latin Quarter. On May 6, the Enragé René Riesel and other students were to appear before a disciplinary commission at the Sorbonne. Demonstrations and riots erupted around the Latin Quarter. Barricades went up and were defended against the police. Suburban hoods (blousons noirs) had come to the center of the city to fight side-by-side with the students. Cars were burned; stores looted. Slogans were sprayed on the walls. The unions, including the student union,

were against the actions of the most revolutionary students and would alternate in their support—for and against (mostly against)—the demonstrations and occupations. According to Viénet, the Situationists were active in creating the barricades and defending them along with young and old workers, students and hoods on rue Gay-Lussac the night of May 10. As the post festum photos show, this had been a real combat zone where revolutionaries responded to the chloride gas grenades and bullets of the police with Molotov cocktails and paving stones.

On May 11, the unions called for a strike on May 13—much to the dismay of

Rue Gay-Lusac, May 11

Prime Minister Pompidou who had just returned from Afghanistan. He quickly agreed to release imprisoned students and allowed university buildings to be used to discuss education reform. Pompidou's biggest mistake was to promise to withdraw all police from the Latin Quarter. On Monday May 13, the police withdrew as one million protesters marched through the streets of Paris during the general strike. The students, meeting in the Champ de Mars, decided to occupy the Sorbonne; and at 9:30 p.m., it was declared an "Autonomous Popular University, open in permanence, night and day, to all workers."

Lyrical slogans and diverted publicity posters began to appear in the Sorbonne. Viénet reports that although the Enragé René Riesel's remarks about solidarity with looters and demands for absolute power to Workers' Councils weren't applauded as much as those speakers at the Grand Amphitheater of the Sorbonne who simply wanted university reform, Riesel did get elected by the General Assembly to the Occupation Committee—the institution of executive power in the occupied Sorbonne. Riesel would call for and defend "direct democracy at the Sorbonne" in the face of all the problems the Occupation Committee had in asserting its authority. The Occupation Committee was composed of fifteen members, "elected and revokable anytime by the general assembly." This was on May 14, the day when the Enragés and S.I. formed a joint committee and took up stakes in the "Jules Bonnot" room. By all accounts, Debord was very calm, even tranquil, during the occupation. Late in the day, workers at Sud-Aviation factory in Nantes occupied the plant and barricaded themselves in the company president's office. The only thing the Occupation Committee did on May 15, was send a telegram of support to the workers at the Sud-Aviation factory in Nantes. The S.I. reportedly participated in the debates before the General Assembly. According to Debord, only once in his life did he sign a prescriptive tract describing what needed to be done—this was signed on May 14 and distributed the next day.

FROM THE S.I. TO COMRADES WHO HAVE DECLARED THEMSELVES IN AGREEMENT WITH OUR THESES.

Comrades,

The student "revolt" of Paris began with a small group of "Enragés" of Nanterre over the last few months; René Riesel; Gerard Bigorne (expelled in April from all French universities for five years), etc. The group took pro-S.I. positions. The rest of the Movement of March 22nd" (more moderate and confused) found its leader in Danny Cohn-Bendit (anarchist from the group Black and Red) who accepted the role of spectacle celebrity mixed with a certain honest radicalism.

The appearance of these two comrades as well as five other leaders before the University Council unleashed the trouble of May 3. The street movement of May 6 (10 to 15,000 youth) began to be recuperated by the tardy support of the bureaucrats of the U.N.E.F., P.C. etc.

Everything bounced back superbly the night of May 10–11. A section of the 5th district was entirely closed by barricades and was in the hands of a little insurrection for close to eight hours. The forces of order that surrounded it used the last four hours to reduce it. We were 3 to 4,000 rioters strong (about half students, many high schoolers or bloussons noirs, a few hundred young and old workers).

Violent repression, as we expected. Faced with the loud protest of the entire bureaucratic left and the emotion in working class districts, the government pulled back. Almost all the Paris faculties were occupied and turned into clubs. What dominated was actually direct democracy with a base that wanted to put society in question, that wanted unification with workers, and which resolutely condemned Stalinist bureaucracy. Three positions appeared in the free general assembly of the occupation of the Sorbonne on May 14, 1968.

1. The first (between a third to half, but who say little) simply want university reform and are at risk of following the recuperation led by the professors on the left.

2. The second—of better stock—wants to pursue the struggle up to the destruction of the Gaullist regime or even of capitalism (all of the nuances of known leftists). Among them, the Federation of Revolutionary Students (Trotskyist Lambertist) which is badly discredited by condemning the barricades.

3. A third position (of a highly vocal minority) expressed by a declaration of Riesel (which will be communicated to you as soon as possible) wants the abolition of classes, of work, of the spectacle and of survival, and demands the absolute power of Workers' Councils.

The possible developments (in a declining order of probability) are as follows: a) exhaustion of the movement (at least to the degree that it remains with the students before the anti-bureaucratic agitation can win over more workers) b) repression (anticipating the arrest of a large number of rioters) if the movement radicalizes or is maintained for a long time without rocking the working class and dissolving the bureaucracies that control it c) social revolution.

Yesterday we constituted the Committee Enragé-S.I. that began posting the Sorbonne with radical, extremely coherent proclamations. We will continue. Riesel is a member of the first Committee of the Occupation of the Sorbonne (revocable every day by the base).

Do the maximum to make the agitation known, maintained and understood. The principal themes, in the immediate moment in France seem to us to be:

▼ Occupation of factories
▼ Constitution of Workers' Councils
▼ Definitive closure of the university
▼ A complete critique of all alienations; affirmation of the principal Situationist theses (in particular the diffusion of the S.I.'s "Minimum Definition of Revolutionary Organizations").

Paris, May 15, 1968
Guy-Mustapha-Raoul-René

Vaneigem arrived, only to leave for a week's vacation—The "Communique of the S.I. Concerning Vaneigem," written after his resignation described the situation:

> The first factory had been occupied the day before, and at this date the most imbecilic member of the most retarded group could not doubt that a very grave social crisis had begun. Nevertheless Vaneigem, much better informed, as soon as he had appended his signature to our circular, left the same afternoon to take his train to rejoin his holiday location on the Mediterranean, booked a long time ago. Several days later, learning abroad, through the mass media, what was proceeding in France (as predicted), he naturally set about returning, crossing with great difficulty the strike-bound country, and rejoining us one week after his ridiculous faux-pas. By then the decisive days, when we were able to do the most for the movement, had passed. Now we're well aware that Vaneigem truly likes revolution and that he in no way lacks courage. Thus one can only understand this as a borderline case of the separation between the rigorous routine of an unshakably orderly daily life and the passion, real but heavily disarmed, for revolution. (reprinted in *The Veritable Split in the International*)

The Enragé-S.I. Committee republished their "Minimum Definition of Revolutionary Organizations" on May 15th as the Occupation Committee found itself in a crisis. Thirteen of the fifteen members deserted the Occupation Committee for other committees, and the General Assembly confirmed eight members of a self-appointed Coordination Committee as an auxiliary to the Occupation Committee. A power struggle between the two committees ensued. In the courtyard of the Sorbonne, Riesel denounced the manipulations of the bureaucrats of the Coordination Committee and told them to face the General Assembly. When the members of the Coordination Committee explained their maneuvers publicly, they were forced by the General Assembly to slink away in shame.

On May 16, the Occupation Committee was reduced to Riesel and one other person. They were bivouacked in the Jules Bonnot room with the S.I., the Enragés and fifteen others. They established a security detail to get the means to disseminate the Occupation Committee's call for the "immediate occupation of all factories in France and the formation of Workers' Councils." Viénet, once again, gives us the eyewitness account:

> As has been shown above, the occupation committee had been stripped of all means at its disposal for the execution of the slightest activity. To distribute its appeal, it set out to reappropriate those means. It could count on the support of the Enragés, the Situationists and a dozen other revolutionaries. Using a mega-

Courtyard of the Sorbonne

phone from the windows of the Jules Bonnot Room they asked for, and received, numerous volunteers from the courtyard. The text was recopied and read in all the other amphitheaters and faculties. Since the printing had been purposely slowed down by the Inter-Faculty Liaison Committee, the Occupation Committee had to requisition machines and organize its own distribution service. Because the sound crew refused to read the text at regular intervals, the Occupation Committee had their equipment seized. Out of spite the specialists sabotaged their equipment as they were leaving, and partisans of the committee had to repair it. Telephones were taken over to relay the statement to press agencies, the provinces, and abroad. By 3:30 p.m. it was beginning to be distributed effectively.

One can only begin to imagine what it was like to be standing in the courtyard of the occupied Sorbonne as the entire country began to shut down. These exhilarating events terrified those people strongly opposed to fanning the flames of discontent. The saboteurs were being sabotaged by reformers who were afraid of the nation-wide wildcat. As factories around the country were occupied, the Occupation announced the occupations over the Sorbonne P.A. system. At 4:30 p.m., the Occupation Committee issued the tract "Vigilance!"

Comrades,

The supremacy of the revolutionary assembly can only mean something if it exercises its power.

For the last 48 hours even the capacity of the general assembly to make decisions has been challenged by a systematic obstruction of all proposals for action.

Up until now no motion could be voted on or even discussed, and bodies elected by the general assembly (Occupation Committee and Coordinating Committee) see their work sabotaged by pseudo-spontaneous groups.

All the debates on organization, which people wanted to argue about before any action, are pointless if we do nothing.

AT THIS RATE, THE MOVEMENT WILL BE BURIED IN THE SORBONNE!

The prerequisite of direct democracy is the minimum support that revolutionary students can give to revolutionary workers who are occupying their factories.

It is inexcusable that yesterday evening's incidents in the GA should pass without retaliation.

The priests are holding us back when anti-clerical posters are torn up.

The bureaucrats are holding us back when, without even giving their names, they paralyze the revolutionary awareness that can take the movement forward from the barricades.

Once again, it's the future that's being sacrificed in the re-establishment of the old unionism.

Parliamentary cretinism wants to take over the rostrum as it tries to put the old, patched-up system back on its feet again.

Comrades,

The reform of the university alone is insignificant, when the whole of the old world should be destroyed.

The movement is nothing if it is not revolutionary.

The best picture we have of Debord and his comrades at this point comes from these tracts, which were being issued one after the other. At 5:00 p.m. the Occupation Committee issued the tract "Watch Out!"

The Press Committee situation on the second floor, stair C, in the Gaston Azard library, represents only itself. It happens to be a case of a dozen or so student journalists anxious to prove themselves straight away to their future employers and future censors.

The Committee, which is trying to monopolize all contact with the Press, refuses to transmit the communiques of the regularly elected bodies of the general assembly.

Debord at the Sorbonne

The Press Committee is a Censorship Committee: don't have anything more to do with it.

The various committees, commissions, working parties can approach the Agence France Presse directly on 508, 45, 40 or the various newspapers:

Le Monde: 770 91 29

France-Soir: 508 28 00

Combat: leave a message with Robert Toubon, CEN 81 11.

The various working parties can, while waiting for this evening's general assembly where new decisions will be taken, address themselves to the occupation committee and the coordinating committee elected by the GA yesterday evening.

EVERYBODY COME TO THE GENERAL ASSEMBLY THIS EVENING IN ORDER TO THROW OUT THE BUREAUCRATS

At 6:30 p.m. on May 16, the Occupation Committee issued yet another tract "Watch Out for Manipulators! Watch Out for Bureaucrats!" that underscored the importance of the General Assembly that evening. The central issue for the Occupation Committee was to have the General Assembly vote on the Occupation Committee's appeal for the occupation of all factories. At 7 p.m., the Occupation Committee issued nine slogans ("Abolish Class Society," "Death to the Cops," etc.)

to be spread by all means possible. Despite the Occupation Committee's desire to press its case before the General Assembly, it decided to delay the meeting due to the call by leftist groups to march on the Renault factory at Billancourt. In a statement issued just before 8 p.m., the Occupation Committee postponed the General Assembly meeting to 2 p.m., on May 17.

The unions and government warned the students against the march on Billancourt, but the students made the trek under red and black flags anyway. The C.G.T. (the union federation) effectively prevented almost all contact between workers and students. The plan on the part of the student union and other groups was to carry out the Enragé-Situationist plan to march on the government-owned radio and TV station, following the example of Hungary, 1956. But on the night of May 16, "manipulators" managed to muck everything up. When most of the students were marching on Billancourt, the manipulators at the Sorbonne tried to call a general assembly. Delegates of the Occupation Committee denounced the meeting and the assembly disbanded.

The next day, May 17, the Occupation Committee sent volunteers to support Metro strikers and printed a tract by young Renault workers who supported the strike (against the union). The Occupation Committee also sent numerous poignant and humorous telegrams around the world that, while being pro-councilist, were also pro-anarchist. Many striking workers had come to the Sorbonne—the General Assembly of 2 p.m. was crowded and chaotic. The only issue discussed was another march on Billancourt. The General Assembly of 8 p.m. was controlled by people who prevented the Occupation Committee from discussing its activities, for which it was still seeking a mandate. Viénet states that the Occupation Committee didn't want to get more involved in the power struggles and compromises; and "announced that it was leaving the Sorbonne, where direct democracy was being strangled by the bureaucrats." The Situationists realized that they were blocked by the students and militants who only wanted a reform of the university.

The Enragés, Situationists and forty others formed the C.M.D.O. (Council for Maintaining the Occupations), a "councilist" organization rather than a "council" proper. The goal wasn't a Situationist power grab, but the promotion of autonomous organizations. The C.M.D.O., initially taking residence in the National Pedagogic Institute on the rue d'Ulm, was an uninterrupted general assembly that guaranteed egalitarian participation in debates. Three commissions were organized—the Printing Commission (publication and printing of C.M.D.O. publications), the Liaison Commission (ten cars and drivers to maintain contacts with occupied factories), the Requisitions Commission (to get supplies). On May 19, the C.M.D.O. published its "Report on the Occupation of the Sorbonne" and on May 22, "For the Power of Workers' Councils." All of the C.M.D.O. publications are reproduced in

Viénet's book. The major tracts, which would certainly include the "Address to All Workers" (May 30), had print runs of 150,000 to 200,000— impossible without the help of workers from occupied print shops. The Situationists took great pride in the fact that nothing in these tracts glorified, or even mentioned the Situationist International—above all these tracts called for worker autonomy. At the end of May, the C.M.D.O. moved to the basement of the School of Decorative Arts where it designed six striking posters composed of white letters on a black background. But none of these exemplary works (translated and published simultaneously in Italy, Japan, Denmark, Sweden, Portugal and Czechoslovakia when the Russian troops reestablished order after the Prague Spring) capture the spirit of the activity of the C.M.D.O. as one of the songs they composed:

THE COMMUNE'S NOT DEAD
At the barricades of Gay-Lussac,
The Enragés at our head,
We unleased the attack:
Oh bloody hell, what a party!
We were in ecstasy amongst the cobblestones
Seeing the old world go up in flames.

CHORUS: All that has shown, Carmela,
That the Commune's not dead (repeat)

To brighten things up, the combatants,
Fucking set fire to cars:
One match and, Forward!
Poetry written in petrol.
And you should have seen the C.R.S.
Really get their asses burnt!

(chorus)

Politicized, the blousons noirs,
Seized the Sorbonne,
To help them fight and destroy,
They put no faith in anybody.
Theory was realized,
The shops were looted

(chorus)

What you produce belongs to you,
It's the bosses who are the thieves.
They are taking the piss out of you,
When they make you pay in the shops.
While waiting for self-management,
We'll apply the critique of the brick.

(chorus)

All the parties, the unions,
And their bureaucrats,
Oppress the proletariat,
As much as the bourgeoisie
Against the state and its allies,
Let's form workers' councils.

(chorus)

The Occupation Committee,
Spits on Trotskyists,
Maoists and other prats,
Who exploit the strikers.
Next time there'll be blood spilt,
By the enemies of freedom.

(chorus)

Now that the insurgents
Have gone back to survival.
Boredom, forced labor,
And ideologies,
We'll take pleasure in sowing
Other May flowers to be picked one day.

FINAL CHORUS: All that has shown, Carmela,
That the Commune's not dead (repeat)

Grenelle Negotiations

Aside from the reports of the C.M.D.O.'s relations with other councilist organizations that come down to us from Viénet and the unattributed essay "The Beginning of an Era" in *Situationist International* #12 (the authorship of all the anonymous articles in #10, 11 and 12 was later claimed by Debord) not much else is known about the activity of the C.M.D.O. Certainly, a great deal of energy went into trying to establish links with other councilist organizations: "And the strikers' participation in the links established by the C.M.D.O. in and outside Paris never contradicted their presence at their own work places (nor, to be sure, in the streets)." It's easy to imagine the C.M.D.O. sitting around drinking wine and singing their songs, but the

record shows that they were quite busy communicating with revolutionary groups inside and outside of France. Yet not even Viénet's eyewitness account paints a vivid picture of the C.M.D.O. camped out in the basement of the School of Decorative Arts or distributing their tracts and posters around Paris.

Back to the big picture: Georges Seguy (on behalf of the workers) and Prime Minister Georges Pompidou negotiated the Grenelle Accords (named after the Parisian street) at the end of May. This agreement was rejected by the base of workers and no-one went back to work. The communists and union federations picked

de Gaulle with his helicopter

up on this and tried to get behind a "popular government." De Gaulle responded by saying that he would maintain power by all means, including civil war. The army was deployed around Paris and the bourgeoise marched in support of the government. At this point, the communist party was behind the strike movement and reportedly wanted to bring down the Gaullist regime, but they were actually just as much appeasers as the unions. The last C.M.D.O. tract "It's Not Over!" was issued on June 8, 1968—it attacked the unions, the communists and democratic socialists for trying to position themselves to win the next electoral campaign after the strike. The tract ends with emblematic slogans such as: "The emancipation of workers will be the creation of workers themselves or it will not happen." Repression, effected by the military in the streets of Paris, became increasingly severe; and by the second week of June people began to go back to work. The Odeon and Sorbonne were evacuated by the police on June 14 and 16.

The C.M.D.O. dissolved on June 15, and the most compromised Situationists went into exile in Brussels. This retreat was a source of pride for the Situationists. Given the fact that many of the C.M.D.O. had been arrested during the course of the revolution, it is fairly amazing that the Situationists escaped the dragnet. The official Situationist interpretation of the revolution is expressed in Debord's "The Beginning of an Era" (*Situationist International* #12):

> Since the defeat of the occupations movement, both those who participated in it and those who had to endure it have often asked the question: 'Was it a revolution?' The general use in the press and in daily conversation of the cowardly neutral phrase, 'the events,' is nothing but a way of evading answering or even formulating this question. Such a question must be placed in its true historical light. In this context the journalists' and governments' superficial references to the 'success' or 'failure' of a revolution mean nothing for the simple reason that since the bourgeois revolutions *no revolution has yet succeeded:* not one has abolished classes.

In this light, the S.I. did submit its own activity to a self-critique, but these shortcomings were negligible.

The main points that the Situationists stressed were:

1. May '68 was the first wildcat general strike in history.
2. May '68 was the largest strike to attack an advanced industrial country.
3. The revolutionary goals were more radical, modern and explicitly expressed than any previous revolutionary movement.
4. May '68 was NOT a student protest, but a proletarian revolution.
5. This proletariat was enlarged to include white-collar workers, delinquents, unemployed, high school kids and young hoods.
6. May '68 was a revolutionary festival that contained within it, a generalized critique of all alienations.

One truly amazing aspect of May '68 was the way the protest encircled the globe: Saturday May 11, 50,000 students and workers marched on Bonn, and 3,000 protesters in Rome; on May 14, students occupied the University of Milan; a sit-in at the University of Miami on May 15; scuffles at a college in Florence on May 16; a red flag flew for three hours at the University of Madrid on the 17th; and the same day, 200 black students occupied the administration buildings of Dower University; on May 18 protests flared up in Rome, and more in Madrid where barricades and clashes with the police occurred; on May 19, students in Berkeley were arrested; a student protest in New York; an attack on an ROTC center in Baltimore—the old world seemed to be on the ropes. On May 20, Brooklyn University was occupied by blacks, and occupations took place the next day at the University of West Berlin. On May 22, police broke through barricades at Columbia University. The University of Frankfurt and the University of Santiago were occupied on May 24.

Protests in Vancouver and London in front of the French Embassy on May 25. On Monday May 27, university and high school students went on strike in Dakar. Protests by peasants in Belgium on May 28. On May 30, students in Munich protested, as did students in Vienna the next day. On June 1, protests spread to Denmark and Buenos Aires. The next day the Yugoslav insurrection began. In Brasil, 16,000 students went on strike on June 6, followed by a large protest march in Geneva for democratization of the university. Even in Turkey, 20,000 students occupied the universities in Ankara and other cities. The chronology just keeps going as occupations, protests, scandals and barricades continued throughout the summer in Tokyo, Osaka, Zurich, Rio, Rome, Montevideo, Bangkok, Dusseldorf, Mexico City, Saigon, Cochabamba, La Paz, South Africa, Indonesia, Chicago, Venice, Montreal, Auckland. "What," people seemed to be asking, "if the entire world were transformed into a Latin Quarter?"

Chapter Twenty-four

The activity of Debord and the S.I. subsequent to May '68 began with the minor scandal of Riesel and Viénet intervening at the apartment of Jean Maitron, who had falsified Situationist positions in his publications. In another instance, the replacement of a statue of Charles Fourier on his pedestal at Place Clichy (empty since the Nazis removed the first statue) in March 1969 was reported in a very brief article in the mammoth final issue of *Situationist International*. We can only suspect that Debord and other Situationists were some of the "barricaders of rue Gay-Lussac" who placed the statue there. We do know that when the jury of the Sainte-Beuve Prize signaled that it intended to give the award to Debord for *Society of the Spectacle* (then a bestseller), he wrote his publisher that he was against all literary prizes and warned that "young Situationists" would be hostile to such a move.

The biggest concerns of the time were to set the record straight regarding Situationist activity during May '68 and to cut ties with "pro-situ" groups who either imitated the S.I., vulgarized it, or merely admired it. The distortions of the historical record have been discussed by others, and pro-situ groups are now legion. To illustrate what the S.I. was up against, consider the case of the pro-situ kid from the Strasbourg scandal who spread the rumor that Cohn-Bendit was telling people that he had slapped Debord at the Sorbonne. The kid later admitted that Cohn-Bendit had never told him such a tale. This story recalls the invitation to Debord's funeral that was circulated in January 1967 by people associated with one-time Situationist Jean Garnault, which, it should be noted, Debord took in good humor. It should also be noted that while the Situationists denounced the "Leninists" on the left (i.e. the majority of the left), the Situationists also denounced the repression against these same Leninists. This repression continued until amnesty was declared the summer of 1969, and was certainly a factor in the dissolution of the S.I. For all the bemoaning the "childish disorder" (yet another parody of Lenin) of pro-situs, Debord seems to have tolerated certain ones, if only momentarily. It's doubtful, for example, that Jean-Pierre Voyer (now on the extreme right) and Jean-Jacques Raspaud would've been able to publish their *Situationist International: protagonists/chronology/bibliography (with an index of insulted people)* with Editions Champ Libre (where Debord held considerable sway) without Debord's support. The real problem was the increasing manifestation of pro-situs within the S.I.

The VIIIth Conference of the S.I. took place in Venice in September 1969. Given their own premonitions and what we now know about the strategy of tension in Italy at the time, it was very bold for the S.I. to be stepping up its activity there—the same month the final issue of *Situationist International* was published. On July 28, 1969, Debord had "announced, by letter addressed to all the sections of the S.I., that after this issue he would cease 'to assume the responsibility, as much legal as editorial,' for the management of this review." He cited the need to rotate and share tasks, but he was trying to highlight the inactivity of the expanding French section.

The Conference of Venice constituted a second symptom, more manifest and of more weight. The VIII Conference of the S.I. was held in Venice from the September 25 to October 1, 1969, in a very well chosen building in the popular quarter of la Giudecca. It was constantly surrounded and watched over by a great number of informers, Italian or delegated by other police. One part of this Conference knew how to formulate good analyses on revolutionary politics in Europe and America; and notably to foresee the development of the Italian social crisis in the coming months, as well as the interventions which we would have to make in it. This debate certainly showed the most extremist, and the best informed, political grouping then existing in the world at work. But the best aspects of what the S.I. also signified (fundamental theory, critique and creation in the whole of life, or simply the capacity for real dialogue between autonomous individuals—"association in which the free development of each is the condition for the free development of all") proved to be completely absent. The "pro-situ" mind manifested itself in Venice in a grandiose manner. While some comrades systematically imitated the prudent silence of Vaneigem, half of the participants wasted three quarters of the time in repeating with great firmness the same vague generalities which each preceding orator had just affirmed; and all this was translated step by step into English, German, Italian and French. Each of these eloquent comrades evidently only aimed to underline that he was just as Situationist as the next, in such a way to justify his presence at this Conference (as if he could have found himself there by chance), but also as if an ulterior, more historical justification had not been abandoned in the sole pursuit of this formal recognition which should have been considered to be already assured. In short, the Situationists there numbered eighteen, they had the spirit of four. ("Notes to serve towards the history of the S.I. from 1969 to 1971" an appendix in *The Veritable Split in the International,* Guy Debord and Gianfranco Sanguinetti)

A few noteworthy events took place at the conference. One of the key Situationists, Mustapha Khayati, the author of the *Poverty of Student Life,* submitted his resignation. The S.I. didn't allow its members to simultaneously join other organizations, and Khayati wanted to look for proletarian elements in the Democratic Popular Front for Palestinian Liberation—he didn't find his fellow proletarians in Jordan, but when he returned to Europe, he was not allowed to rejoin the S.I.

Pascal Dumontier reports on the provisional statutes adopted at the conference:

The S.I. defined itself as "an international association of individuals, equal in all the aspects of its democratic management." It thus reaffirmed its conception of unitary organization that rejects the adhesion of already formed groups. Each member is recognized as being "responsible before the ensemble of the S.I." and "the general assembly of all the members of the S.I. has the only power to decide on the ensemble of theoretical and practical choices." If the unitary conception of the organization again highlighted the desire for coherent practice, the S.I. tried to develop its own democracy. The autonomy of national sections appears as the resolution reviving the organization that formerly constituted "one unique, united center." Each thus decides its activities, its publications, its contacts, its breaks, its unions, its exclusions, its financial management. The "democratization" of the S.I. drove it to acknowledge the right to openly constitute a tendency, and the need for a minority to split if it is in opposition on a fundamental question on the bases of agreement. The care over democratic practice conjugated itself with an effort at coherence between the autonomous sections. Thus, to coordinate the activities of Situationists, the S.I. suppressed the Central Council to adopt the principle of reunion of delegates of sections, elected on a precise mandate, that should hold between each Conference. This, in 1969, the S.I. shows its will to renew itself with new people and revised statutes. Taking their organizational practice during the events of May 1968 as a model, the S.I. seems to thus surpass the question of organization prior to 1968. (*The Situationists and May '68*)

Following the VIIIth conference, numerous people were excluded: Chevalier, Chasse, Elwell. Others would resign in short order: Beaulieu and Cheval. There were language problems that hindered the correspondence between sections; and the French section, for its part, instituted policies to promote internal discipline—each meeting was to be considered a "Conference" of the section "working quickly and well." These meetings were to begin in the morning, break, and begin again in the afternoon. If a problem couldn't be resolved in one day, it should automatically be brought up the next day. Members of the French section were required to be in Paris "almost in permanence" to follow up on the activity decided upon at the meetings. No outside obligation could justify missing a meeting—two unexcused absences were grounds for exclusion.

As the S.I. went into an organizational crisis, the Italian secret services planted and exploded bombs in Milan and Rome on December 12. The Italian section responded with the tract "Is the Reichstag Burning?" that denounced the provocation—it was posted on December 19, "during the hardest days of repression," at the Piazza Fontana and in front of the biggest factories in Milan. The tract also denounced the "errors of the old anarchists," and called the bombings the bourgeoise's "first act of civil war against the proletariat." The bombings justified the existence of the state to protect people of the right against false "anarchist peril." This was the state's response to the economic bust following the post-war boom. The unions had achieved some unity (between communists and non-communists) and used strikes to win major pay raises even as a slide toward bankruptcy began. The Italian Situationists were seen posting this tract and forced to flee. Despite the efforts of the Italian Anarchist Federation and the Interior Ministers of Italy and France to pin terrorist activity on the Situationists, the Situationists were unequivocal in their denunciation of terrorism, as in the article "On Repression" in *Situationist International* #12:

> To examine things from the point of view of the strategy of social struggles, one must, first of all, say that one should never play with terrorism. Moreover, even serious terrorism never had any historical efficacy where all other forms of revolutionary activity was rendered impossible by complete repression, and thus where a notable fraction of the population was brought around to the side of the terrorists.

Strange days had arrived. Armstrong and Aldrin were walking on the moon as a Japanese lathe operator threw herself off a speeding train after discovering that she had been poisoned by inhaling cadmium fumes while working for the Toho Zinc Co. It was discovered that the milk in American mothers' breasts had four times the amount of DDT permitted in cows' milk. A massive fish kill (millions of fish) in Europe's Rhine River was caused by leaking containers of insecticide that fell off a barge. In what must've been a disappointing moment for Debord, the marketplace Les Halles, "the belly of France," as Emile Zola called it, was finally moved to Rungis, near Orly Airport in 1969.

Alice Becker-Ho

Debord married his second wife, Alice Becker-Ho, in 1970. Press accounts, reprinted by Debord in *Considerations on the Assassination of Gerard Lebovici,* state that her mother was the owner of a restaurant where PRC journalists met, always under the surveillance of the D.S.T., or French equivalent of the American F.B.I. Debord, it should be noted, scoffed at these comments that tried to evoke "the daughter of Fu Manchu, the secret societies of Ancient China, the agents of bureaucratic China."

1970 was also the year of what would be called *The Debate of Orientation of the ex-Situationist International.* This internal documentation is more relevant than much of the Situationist correspondence collected at the International Institute of Social History in Amsterdam—as you might imagine by now, some of these letters deal with petty squabbles. Debord's letters are a notable exception, which is somewhat surprising given the petulant tone of his letters to people whose attempts to contact the S.I. he didn't welcome. To his Situationist comrades, even those with whom he had profound disagreements, Debord's letters are quite sincere and even (at times) kind. In Debord's first contribution to the "Orientation Debate"* (his notes written for a meeting of French and Italian sections), he called for increased intensity in the development of theory and practice so as to "stun the world." His thirst for scandal hadn't been quenched by May '68; he was growing impatient with the pretensions of his comrades, and was already calling into question the "justification" for the S.I.'s existence. He once again called for exclusions, beyond the merely "defensive" use of exclusions, so that each Situationist would be "admirable" for the others, as he ironically put it. The lack of other strong revolutionary groups in France and the "terrorist" provocation by the Italian state were, according to Debord, the issues to be discussed. He added:

> Despite their very great historical and programmatic interest, Workers' Councils of the past are evidently insufficient experiences, and real councilist organizations to come are still far from existing. A vague councilist style is developing, even among Christians. We don't have any way to arrange this, but to disarrange this, for the present. In the sense of the *total content* that Councils must attain, in the meaning of what the S.I. can and must do so that this power exists *in reality,* I reduce my thesis to a sentence: it's not so much Situationists who are councilists, *it's Councils who will have to be Situationists.*

Debord weighed in again in late March**, agreeing with others who would refuse all interest in readers of Situationist books and contacts with the "intellectual milieu." If autonomous groups formed, the S.I. must "strongly diminish contacts with them" and "give them as little chance as possible to bore us." Tony Verlaan's remark that members of the S.I. were "déclassés who want to abolish classes" while members of the "social base" were "pseudo-déclassés who dream of becoming a class" received Debord's agreement. This line of thought was never developed despite the clear implication that the two groups could conceivably unite as a sub-proletarian

---

* Document 4, written prior to March 17, 1970.

** Document 12.

class. In choosing how to meet the working class, Debord reminded the others that workers should come to the S.I., and not vice versa—workers were to remain completely autonomous of the S.I. He offered two suggestions for theoretical work: 1) Create a brochure or small book that would be the "inverse of the *[Communist] Manifesto*" called *Problems of the Classless Society* that "demonstrates all the possible and desirable characteristics of the next revolution, analyzing all *the difficulties,* the serious uncertainties and the truly obscure points that it will have to overcome;" 2) A book that establishes all the erroneous and correct interpretations of Marx as revealed in the last 125 years in the history of capitalism. He also proposed a collection of chronologically grouped quotations, and a *History of the S.I.* In this document, he first expressed his desire to bring *Society of the Spectacle* to the silver screen, and promised to train other Situationists in the medium.

In early July, Debord wrote a quick note to the others concerning what he described as imprudent phone calls to publishers, most likely concerning *Society of the Spectacle.* It's hard to say exactly what went on here, but Debord chastised the unnamed comrade(s) for their lack of discretion, and promised never to "communicate to members of the S.I. certain facts that *only concern me,* the negligent divulging of which might eventually be harmful." A few weeks later, he wrote sixteen theses under the title "Remarks on the S.I. Today," that go over all the minutiae of the organization's malaise. In discussing, somewhat cynically, the problems that the new editors were having in editing *Situationist International* #13, Debord mentions that he almost single-handedly edited #10, 11 and 12. These were by far the biggest issues, and in Debord's humble opinion, "the best in the series." According to Debord, Khayati wrote the essay on the Prague Spring, "Reform and Counter-Reform in Bureaucratic Power," but aside from a little help from Khayati in #10 and #11, Debord wrote *all* the anonymous articles. Debord was obviously becoming increasingly impatient with the "vague discontent" that he encountered with his comrades. Perhaps this malaise was caused by the exclusions, but it is evident that the solution Debord foresaw would come to pass. The small groupings of comrades (those with clear affinities or experiential ties) that Debord proposed was almost certain to break up the group. After all, here was the critic who defined separation as the "alpha and omega of the spectacle" proposing separate groupings.

Debord, Riesel and Viénet—members of the French section who had been at the barricades together in May '68—constituted a tendency on November 11 with a "Declaration."

> The crisis that has continually deepened in the S.I. in the course of the last year, and whose roots go back much further, has ended up revealing all its aspects; and has led to a more and more glaring increase in theoretical and practical inactivity. [...]

Considering that the S.I. has carried out an action that has been at least substantially correct and that has had a great importance for the revolutionary movement of the period ending in 1968 (though with an element of failure that we must account for); and that it can continue to make a significant contribution by lucidly comprehending the conditions of the new period, including its own conditions of existence; and that the deplorable position in which the S.I. has found itself for so many months must not be allowed to continue—we have constituted a tendency.

Our tendency aims to break completely with the ideology of the S.I. and with its corollary: the miserable vainglory that conceals and maintains inactivity and inability. We want an exact definition of the S.I. organization's collective activity and of the democracy that is actually possible in it. We want the actual application of this democracy.

[...] We want a radical critique—a critique *ad hominem.*
Without prejudging any later, more considered and serious responses they may make, we declare our disagreement with the American comrades, who have constituted a tendency on completely futile bases. [...] Other comrades have for months never undertaken to respond in any manner whatsoever to the mass of clearly burning questions pointed to by facts themselves and by the first, and increasingly specific, written critiques that we have been formulating for months. [...] We are quite aware that some of you have not wanted to respond.

[...] Considering that the crisis has attained a level of extreme gravity, we henceforth reserve the right—in accordance with Article 8 of the statutes voted at Venice—to make our positions known outside the S.I.

This "Declaration" had the desired effect. Vaneigem resigned on November 14, immediately after receiving the document. His short letter of resignation is a mixture of denial, blame, delusions of grandeur and pomposity. The "Communiqué of the S.I. Concerning Vaneigem" rips into him, picking his resignation letter apart point-by-point. For example, Vaneigem accused the signatories of the "Declaration" of "scheming tactics," but he never responded to the challenge to identify those tactics. And in his letter, Vaneigem went so far as to write, "It would be disarming naiveté itself to still want to save a group so as to save myself when I did not know how to make of it anything of what I really wanted it to be." There was no way Debord could allow that one to pass:

[He] forgets to pose for himself this cruel question: what did he ever, himself, try to say, to do, by arguing or by serving as an example, so that the S.I. could become even better, or closer to his proclaimed best personal tastes? Vaneigem did nothing towards such goals; though meanwhile the S.I. did not really remain as a consequence nothing! [...] Vaneigem has occupied an important and unforgettable place in the history of the S.I. [...] He had a lot of intelligence and culture, great daring in ideas, and all this was dominated by the truest anger against existing conditions. Vaneigem at that time had genius, because he knew perfectly how to go to the extreme in everything that he knew how to do. [...] The S.I. of the years 1961–1964—an important period for the S.I. as for the ideas of modern revolution—was heavily marked by Vaneigem, perhaps more so than by any other. It was in this period that he not only wrote the *Revolution of Everyday Life* and other texts which he signed in the review of the S.I. ("Basic Banalities", etc.), but also greatly contributed to the anonymous collective texts of numbers 6 to 9 of this review, and very creatively in all the discussions of this epoch. If he forgets it now, we don't. [...] The Situationists entered, with their epoch, into these more concrete struggles which deepened until 1968, and even more since. Vaneigem was already no longer there. [...] In the years 1965–1970, the fading of Vaneigem manifested itself quantitatively (he hardly participated in our publications any more except for three little articles which he signed in the last three numbers of S.I., and he was very often absent from meetings and when he attended, he generally kept silent) and above all qualitatively. His very rare interventions in our debates were struck with the sign of the greatest incapacity to envisage concrete historical struggles; they were marked by the feeblest escapes with regard to the maintaining of any relation between what one says and what one does, and even by the smiling forgetfulness of dialectical thought.

This "Communiqué" goes on and on in ways that tell us how much Vaneigem meant to Debord, and that Debord felt Vaneigem let him and the other members of the S.I. down.

Although the American section—reduced to Verlaan and Horelick—didn't want a split, the others felt that "their participation in our activities had been all the time too minimal for us to be able to continue to consider ourselves as co-responsible for what they would do." This is understandable when one reads the shrill correspondence between Verlaan and those Americans who were genuinely interested in Situationist theory—it doesn't seem that the S.I. was well-represented in the United States by these guys. Debord had no patience for their contradictory responses (without being acknowledged as such) to his letters.

The resignation of Christian Sebastiani, the "poet of the walls" of '68, was altogether different. His auto-critiques, the only Situationist prose we have of his, are crisply written, insightful and moving to read. Debord writes that there was much to like about Sebastiani, but:

What we reproach him with, and which had unfortunately to bring about the end of our collaboration, is that he did not really employ himself, as he should have, with managing the S.I.; and that even at the end of this crisis, he did not seem to recognize in theoretical terms all its depth.

The Orientation Debate was over—Debord had the last word: "In casting back into their nothingness the contemplatives and incompetents who counted on a perpetual membership in the S.I., we have taken a great step forward." A great step forward on a sinking ship.

▼ ▼ ▼

Before going on to describe the final dissolution of the S.I., Debord's publishing coups should be noted. In 1970, the Dutch publisher Van Gennep published all twelve issues of the journal *Situationist International* (1958–1969) in facsimile with a metallic silver cover. During the summer of 1971, Debord established both friendly and commercial relations with Gérard Lebovici, the proprietor of the publishing house Champ Libre. Financing his subversive books with the profits from the production of films starring Belmondo and Deneuve, Lebovici, or *le roi Lebo* as he was affectionately called, straddled two worlds—the spectacular world of his cinema production company and the anti-spectacular world of Situationist subversion. The initial encounter is described by Debord in response to the memoir of Gérard Guegan, then an editor at Champ Libre, who erroneously described the first meeting between himself, Debord and Lebovici.

Guegan always arranges things according to very instructive intentions, and hides the essential of what is. The publisher Buchet, his head spinning from the success of *Spectacle,* thought he had a chance to get more income by adding, unknown to me, a false sub-title to the third and fourth press run, stating that the book was quite simply about "Situationist theory." As soon as a copy Masperized this way appeared before my eyes, I wrote to Buchet (a little menacingly I acknowledge) a simple letter advising him that he was no longer my publisher. Lebovici learned of this and proposed to republish my book. I didn't ask anything of him that day; even as my reasons for acting were quite serious. I didn't forget that the only weakness of my position was this troublesome detail—I aspired to manifestly create justice for myself, despite my repugnance to bring to the terrain of vulgar judicial chicanery, a conflict of principle that was so evidently superior to it. [...] On that day Gerard Lebovici started down the path of crime that has since taken him so much further, seduced as he was in the first instance by the hooligan style, and without wanting to consider anything else. (*"This bad reputation..."*)

Debord was attracted to the aura of subversion that surrounded Champ Libre, and with false modesty, Debord would later write to a comrade that he didn't think that Champ Libre's pirate edition of *Society of the Spectacle* "lowered the subversive value" of the publishing house.

▼ ▼ ▼

To turn back to the dissolution of the S.I., we should take a glimpse at the Italian section, which came into being in January 1969 and was dissolved in September 1970. Paven (a member of the Italian section) resigned in February 1970, but this resignation was refused and transformed into an exclusion. In April, the Venezuelan member of the Italian section, Eduardo Rothe, was excluded; and in August the entire S.I. demanded the exclusion of Salvadori, who had tried to exclude Sanguinetti. In September 1970, Debord proposed to Sanguinetti that he dissolve the phantom Italian section and continue its activity in Amsterdam, New York or Paris—Sanguinetti chose the latter and joined Debord's tendency on December 8, agreeing with the criticisms leveled against Vaneigem. So when Viénet resigned (February 1971) for "personal convenience," and Riesel was excluded (September 1971) for "unscrupulous ambition," "lying wretchedly," and for being a "mediocre crook" (theft of S.I. funds), only Debord and Sanguinetti were left. It's true that J.V. Martin hadn't resigned, nor was he excluded. But Martin was apparently out of the loop, struggling with the Scandinavian section, of which, he was the only member.

Sanguinetti, a young but highly cultivated communist, was deported from France on July 21, 1971 by the Interior Minister and would remain under surveillance in Italy. He and Debord would sign the *Theses on the S.I. and its Time,* presumably in Italy. The *Theses* were published with several documents appended to it by Champ Libre in April, 1972 as *The Veritable Split in the International: Public Circular of the Situationist International,* a title that diverts that of the internal circular distributed by Marx and Engles on the *Supposed Splits in the International* (I.W.A.). These sixty-one theses, described by the Library of Congress as "incomprehensible to anyone who is not an International Situationist," are actually perfectly comprehensible to anyone who knows the history of the S.I. and the act of auto-dissolution by the S.I. The quote by Hegel that prefaces the book explains the rationale for the split:

One party proves itself to be victorious by breaking up into two parties; for in so doing, it shows that it contains within itself the principle it is attacking, and thus has rid itself of the one-sidedness in which it previously appeared. The interest which was divided between itself and the other party now falls entirely within itself, and the other party is forgotten, because that interest finds within itself the antithesis which occupies its attention. At the same time, however, it has been raised into the higher victorious element in which it exhibits itself in a clarified form. So that the schism that arises in one of the parties and seems to be a misfortune, demonstrates rather that party's good fortune. (*Phenomenology of Spirit*)

The theses trace the failures and successes of the S.I., adding a few new wrinkles to the Situationist perspective, such as a critique of pollution and an assessment of the global political economy and signs of proletarian consciousness. A great deal of the book is aimed at pro-situs:

He must postulate that his conduct is essentially good, because it is "radical," ontologically revolutionary. [...] He ignores dialectics because, refusing to see his own life, he refuses to understand time. Time frightens him because it is made of qualitative jumps, of irreversible choices, of occasions which will never return. The pro-situ disguises time to himself as a simple uniform space that he'll traverse, from error to error and from insufficiency to insufficiency, while enriching himself constantly. [...] And presently, although they all have something fundamentally Vaneigemist about them, all the pro-situs boldly give Vaneigem a donkey kick as he lies on the ground, while forgetting that they have never given proof of one-hundredth of his former talent; and they still salivate before the might of it, which they do not understand.

Perhaps the most interesting pro-situ critique is the class analysis of them in thesis 34 that equates pro-situs with "executives" or "managers" (cadres in French). Certain commentators, even those favored by the Situationists themselves such as Richard Gombin, state that the Situationists "are not Marxists," but they are clearly in that tradition, speaking in terms of class analysis of society and of the proletariat. After a long discussion of modern revolutionary history in thesis 35, for example, Debord and Sanguinetti state that, "The proletariat can only be defined historically, by what it can do and by what it can and must want."

In later theses, the authors flatly admit that many of the post-'68 purges were aimed at weakening the S.I., and this was one of the S.I.'s most important contributions to the revolutionary movement:

Never have we been mixed up with the business, the rivalries and the frequentations of the most leftist politicians or the most advanced intelligentsia. And now that we can flatter ourselves with having acquired among this rabble the most revolting celebrity, we will become even more inaccessible, even more clandestine. The more our theses become famous, the more we will ourselves be obscure. (excerpt from thesis 57)

Part III

**The
Clandestine
Years
1973–1994**

Celeste with Alice Becker-Ho

Chapter Twenty-five

At this point in his life Debord began to cover his tracks. Despite his Lettrist protestations against leaving "traces," the *Potlatch* and *Situationist International* journals left clear trails of his activities and public life. The fact that the internal S.I. correspondence and other archival projects were given to the International Institute of Social History in Amsterdam demonstrates Debord's desire to leave guideposts for posterity. But when he embarked on his solo career as a "retired" revolutionary, he chose to keep his cards much closer to his chest.

Why? Perhaps it was the desire to combat his fame, although this stand against celebrity-commodity status might have been calculated to engender still more fame. I wouldn't underestimate a very realistic sense of prudence on Debord's part. The authorities were turning a much more watchful eye on subversives like Debord; and as mentioned above, his cohort Sanguinetti had been denied entry into France by the Interior Minister. But this privacy might also be explained, in part, by his post-Situationist perspective that entailed a great deal of looking back at his personal history. Debord sensed that his greatest days of glory where behind him, and if he were to do justice to those cherished days of revolution, he would have to maintain an aura of dignity around his persona. To digress for a moment, it's clear that Debord generally aspired to act with honor. Given the dismay he elicited with his exclusions and harsh judgments, it's worth remembering that his high standards of conduct were the basis for his reproaches of others, even if those reproaches strike the bourgeois observer as being less than honorable. In order to avoid false charges of hypocrisy or being caught in a compromising situation by the spectacle that he genuinely detested, Debord chose to remain out of sight. From this position, well aware that his personal history was on-going, Debord was able to effectively rectify the predictable false reporting about himself and his works—often doing so with depreciative humor. As long as he was alive, he would try to have the last word on his persona and creations, usually judging his critics more severely than they judged him.

Skipping ahead, it seems that he wanted to have a posthumous last word on his persona in a way that highlights a few of the paradoxes of his character. The publication of his film contracts in February 1995, two months after his death, served to remind everyone of the malicious aspect of his persona. (I mention his *Contracts* here because it deals with his film contracts from 1973 on.) In letters to friends and in person, Debord could be sincerely humane. But the severity of his public judgments in *Potlatch* and *Situationist International* were not momentary aberrations of his character. These judgments would become more haughty, almost aristocratic, in his latter works—as if his ego knew no bounds. In his "Vindications" that served as a preface for *Contracts,* Debord claimed that "Nothing is equal in such contracts; and it's precisely this special form that makes them so honorable [...] They were all made to *inspire confidence in only one side:* that of the one who merited admiration." Although Debord made a quick reference to the "glory" his producer, Lebovici, brought to his profession by backing a subversive such as himself, Debord's letter to the publisher of the *Contracts* regarding the cover design begs a few questions. Debord suggested that the bateleur (juggler, buffoon, mountebank) plate from the Marsaille tarot deck be used on the cover because it implies "something that one could see as a certain mastery of manipulation." The classic interpretation given to the bateleur is that he is capable of mastering any new situation, and Debord certainly wanted to give the impression that he had mastered death. A strong Epicurean current ran through him; seen not only in his "Let us eat and drink for tomorrow we die" approach to life, but also in the peace of mind he gives voice to in his latter works, a serenity that only comes to those who have no fear of death. But what honor is there in manipulation? And did this include the manipulation of Lebovici, reportedly his friend and bene-factor, not simply a "producer" with whom he had contractual relations. Were these contracts published along with such repugnantly egotistical remarks to once again combat his fame? In any case, by this last act Debord effectively communicated that his desire to maintain his dignity didn't mean that he was above wallowing in the mud of manipulation and recriminations—and, as we will see, wallowing in the mud of the spectacle when he collaborated with French television.

In addition to learning he was well paid, *Contracts* informs us that Debord was liv-ing at 180 rue Saint-Martin (not far from where the Pompidou Center is now locat-ed) when he signed on with Lebovici's Simar Films to translate *Society of the Spectacle* into film on January 8, 1973. The building at this address has the aspect of a former flop house. In a letter from Lebovici, written a week after the signing of the contract, Debord and his wife had already changed addresses, moving up the street to a regal old building at 239 rue Saint-Martin. Although I personally think this is an erroneous line of inquiry (as I've made clear above), the same students of Debord who relish the use of an occult symbol from the tarot on the cover of *Contracts* will be delighted to learn that Debord's new address was only a few doors away from Paris' large Rosicrusian center. If Debord hadn't been such a hard-drinking communist, we might be able to imagine him taking a yoga class or reading Rosicrusian publications such as *The Mastery of Life.* Lest there still be any doubt, consider the cynical diversion of an infamous critique of Schiller's *Die Rauber* that Debord used as preview of the film *Society of the Spectacle*—scrolled white letters on a black background:

> When the idea occurred to me to create the world, I foresaw that there, one day, someone would make a film as revolting as *Society of the Spectacle.* Therefore, I thought it better not to create the world (signed): God

After having been well compensated and guaranteed complete artistic freedom by Lebovici's Simar Films, Debord created a veritable masterpiece in less than a year. And he did it the easy way—by using pre-existing footage: *Battleship Potemkin, October, New Babylon, Shanghai Gesture, For Whom the Bell Tolls, Rio Grande, The Charge of the Light Brigade, Johnny Guitar, Confidential Report,* advertisements, Soviet and Polish films, industrial films, American Westerns, news footage, the Sorbonne General Assembly in May '68, the murder of Oswald, political speeches and sorties over Vietnam... These filmed photographs accounted for the ninety minutes of images in Debord's first feature-length film.

In his essay "Dismantling the Spectacle: The Cinema of Guy Debord" (the major essay in the *On the Passage of a Few People Through a Rather Brief Moment in Time* catalogue published in conjunction with the Boston and London Institute of Contemporary Arts Situationist exhibits), Thomas Y. Levin lists the theses from the book *Society of the Spectacle* that were used in the film—Debord reportedly told Levin that he considered these hundred-odd theses to be the best ones. Citations not in the original book are also inserted into the film; texts by Clausewitz, the Committee of Occupation of the Sorbonne, Debord himself, Machiavelli, Marx, Tocqueville, Emile Pouget and Soloviev. Perhaps the most striking aspect of the film is the way Debord turns the cinema against itself, such as in the still shot of cinema spectators watching the silver screen through 3-D glasses (the now ubiquitous J.R. Eyerman photo on the cover of the Black & Red edition of the book), or the use of stills taken from films in a way that displays their sockets. Levin gives us the perspective of a Yale academic on this practice:

> Like the book *Society of the Spectacle,* Debord remarks that "its current cinematographic adaptation also does not offer a few partial political critiques but purposes instead a holistic critique of the extant world, which is to say, of all aspects of modern capitalism and its general system of illusions." As the cinema is one of the tools of this "system of illusion," its language must be revolutionized for it to serve other ends. The coherence of the text-image relations is thus neither one of illustration nor of demonstration but rather of détournement—"the fluid language of anti-ideology"—here defined as a mode of communication that contains its own critique. Employing a strategy reminiscent of Benjamin's *Passagenwerk* (Arcades Project) in its practice of citation without quotation marks, Debord insolently throws back at spectacular society the images with which it depicts itself. Indeed, one could say that Debord's critique consists in an *incriminating, analytical quotation of the spectacle.* This marks a turning point in the history of cinema that, according to Debord's Hegelian logic, is nothing less than the Aufhebung (sublation [i.e. obliteration]) of the medium: "In a way, in this film, the cinema, at the end of its pseudo-autonomous history, gathers up its memories." Debord's film is simultaneously a historical film, a Western, a love story, a war film—and none of

the above; it is a "critique without concessions," a spectacle that as such, like the double negative, reverses the (Hegemonic) ideological marking of the medium.

Yes, the film is all that, but it is also a very moving work of poetry. And I think that as VHS copies of the film circulate underground and an English version comes out, it will be increasingly recognized for its very poetic conception of revolution. The most moving aspect of the film is the way Debord brings together all these disparate images of the people with whom he shared the world. Debord wants to make it clear that this is really a film about contemporary society, especially when he begins with an astronaut space walking and the murder of Oswald. But this global view is, early on, given a heavy French accent—the use of Paris subway surveillance cameras and the incredible sequence of the CGT bureaucrat Seguy speaking to Renault workers about the Grenelle accords at the end of the May '68 events: "At the end of these discussions we accepted what was positive, and made it clear that there was still a lot left to be done." Nixon, Mao, Mitterand, etc. all make appearances, but the dominant images are of scantily clad women and military scenes.

My interpretation of the many bikini-clad women and the more pornographic images of women in the film is that Debord both enjoyed and opposed these objectifying images—they operate both as a lure of beauty and to incite revulsion (the exaggeratedly revolting striptease at the beginning, for example, can't be read any other way). The dialectical use of martial footage has a similar function—the charge of the Light Brigade in the Crimean War operating as a metaphor for the "lost troop" of the avant-garde; the footage of Eisenhower and U.S. aircraft carriers represents the more objectionable side of the war machine (certain underground publications have quite correctly, in my opinion, equated the society of the spectacle with the "military-industrial-entertainment complex").

For me, the following is the singularly most moving sequence in the film *Society of the Spectacle*:

"What the spectacle offers as eternal is based on change, and must change
In Budapest insurrectionary workers demolish a giant statue of Stalin: only with its base. The spectacle is absolutely dogmatic and
his boots are left.
at the same time cannot really arrive at any solid dogma. Nothing stops for it; this condition is natural to it yet most contrary
The camera pans across a woman up to her smiling face.
to its inclination.
The unreal unity proclaimed by the spectacle masks the class division on
Sequence on the activity in a cardboard packaging factory

which the real unity of the capitalist mode of production rests. What obliges the producers to participate in the construction of the world is also what separates them from it. What brings together men liberated from their local and national boundaries is also what pulls them apart. What requires a more profound rationality is also what nourishes the irrationality of hierarchical exploitation and repression. What creates the abstract power of society creates its concrete UNFREEDOM.

[Michel Corrette: Sonata in D Major, for cello and harpsichord.]

Close up of Durruti, the Spanish Anarchist leader.

Board: "Are we really living proletarians, are we really living? This age that we count on, and where everything we count on is no longer ours, can it be called a life? And can't we recognize how much we keep losing as the years pass by?"

Close up of a revolutionary sailor from Eisenstein's October—he shakes his head negatively. Durruti looks at him. The sailor repeats his negative gesture.

Board: "Rest and food, aren't they feeble remedies for the continual illness that belabors us? And this other thing that we call and is well known as the final illness, what more is it than a sudden attack of the last of the evil that we bring with us into the world at birth?"

The Petrograd sailor agrees. *The music fades away.*

While I'm no film critic, I've never encountered a montage as sophisticated as this with similar revolutionary content. The music is what really makes the last sequence work—the notes are incredibly stirring when accompanied by the text of Durruti asking proletarians if they're really living. The expressive face of the sailor shaking his head matches the resolve of the music perfectly.

At the end of the film, the music by Corrette is taken up again with footage from May '68, often as filmed photographs. The music continues over boards quoting Machiavelli and Tocqueville. Subsequently, there's another sequence from *October* showing Russian workers carrying away packets of leaflets as they come off the press, followed by a shot of the "Down With The Spectacular-Commodity Society" poster created by the C.M.D.O. in May '68. As the music continues over a shot of a burning barricade at night, Debord puts a little of his poetry into a caption:

But neither the wood nor the fire find any peace, satisfaction or ease in any warmth, great or small, or in any kinship, until the moment when the fire becomes one with the wood and they impart to each other their real nature...

This poetic sequence is followed by a board from Pouget's *Sabotage* about the necessity that impels workers to destroy their machines. The last strains of music

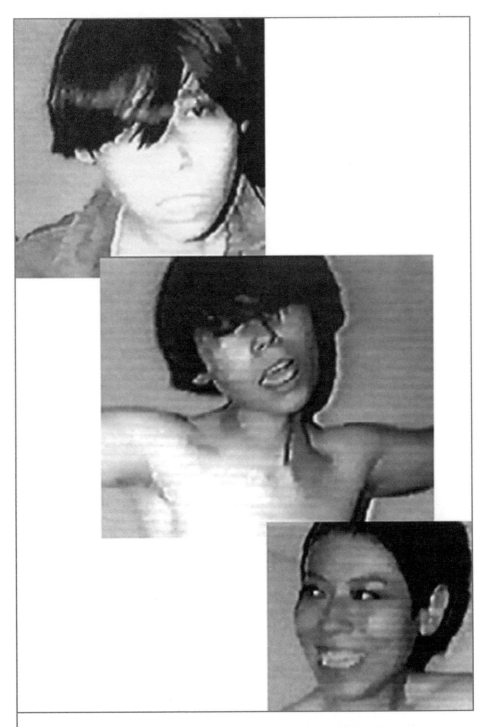

Stills of Alice Becker-Ho from the film *Society of the Spectacle*

end, but the imagery continues to follow the path of insurrection in France, Italy, Poland, Germany, the United States.

The poetry comes through nowhere in the film so much as in the dedication to his wife, Alice Becker-Ho at the beginning of the film:

> Since a particular feeling is only part of life, and not life in its entirety, life longs to range across the diversity of feeling. Thus life rediscovers itself in the sum of this diversity... In love, the separate still exists, but not longer as separate: as unified, and the living encounters the living.

The still photographs of his wife in this dedication display a childlike exuberance and playfulness. Alice prances around the bedroom in the nude, posing and smiling for her Guy. Debord would later remark that a critic was totally erroneous in his critique of the film except in his observation that Alice was "ravishing." One of the last sequences in the film is of Orson Welles as Arkadian at a masked ball in his Spanish castle—his toast to friendship is followed by photos of Chtcheglov and Jorn. One might think Debord was downright sentimental given this dedication to love and ode to friendship, if the latter wasn't followed by still more desperate military charges. The film concludes with Clausewitz' remarks on the use of strategic theory, which leads one to the conclusion that no matter how genuine and beautifully expressed his more sentimental feelings, the people that mattered to Debord were all ultimately *enfants perdus,* those lost to revolution.

In 1975, Debord released a short but highly characteristic film entitled *Refutation of all judgments whether for or against, which have been brought to date on the film Society of the Spectacle.* Needless to say, reviews of *Society of the Spectacle* were mixed, with support coming from unsuspecting corners such as conservative newspapers. According to Levin, *Refutation* is "A landmark in the history of cinema," because it's the first film that focuses on the reception of a prior film:

> Through an examination of the few real arguments to be found in eight representative reviews of his most recent film, Debord is able to establish a catalogue of the blind spots in their rhetorical strategies and to demonstrate their integral function in the economy of the spectacle. If the focus here seems to have shifted from the analysis of spectacle proper to an investigation of the economy of its reception—that is, film criticism or, more generally, art criticism—this is only because the two are, as Debord demonstrates, effectively synonymous.

The arguments against the film *Society of the Spectacle* are sometimes hilarious, but always specious—Debord handles them with great style and dismissive wit.

Another equally modestly gifted Jesuit pretends, on the contrary, to wonder, if to denounce the spectacle would not itself be to enter into the spectacle? One may easily see what such an extraordinary purism would like to obtain: that no one should ever appear in the spectacle as an enemy.

And again, at the end:

The specialists of the cinema said that its revolutionary politics were bad; the politicians among all the left-wing illusionists said that it was bad cinema. But when one is at once a revolutionary and a film-maker, one may easily demonstrate that their general bitterness derives from the obvious fact that the film in question is the exact critique of the society which they do not know how to combat; and a first example of the cinema which they do not know how to make.

In *Refutation,* Debord once again took his shots at the society of the spectacle—at the pollution that issues from the processes of production, the commodities and modes of distribution. Debord also takes jabs at the theorists Lyotard and Castoriadis, but the major subtext of the film is the Portuguese revolution of 1974-75. The revolution coincided with a coup by a leftist military junta headed by General Antonio Sebastiao Reveiro de Spinola. He took power from Marcelo Caetano, who had been dictator since Prime Minister Salazar's heart attack in 1968. The new regime resumed diplomatic relations with Moscow, raising fears in NATO that communists in the new Lisbon government would leak secrets. Debord illustrates his film with the Stalinists and socialists who denounced the revolution in its first few days, portraits of the provisional governments and footage of workers demonstrating in Lisbon.*

Debord was quite clear about the significance of the Portuguese revolution—it wasn't the strike wave, or the barricades to stop right-wing counter-demonstrations; nor was it the occupation of factories and houses, the open-air markets selling looted goods, the push for workers' councils, communal work arrangements, the popular assemblies, the creation of parks and social centers. The generalization of the concept of non-party politics was significant, but it wasn't the most significant factor

---

* The best account of these "two freest years in Portuguese history" is Phil Mailer's *Portugal: the impossible revolution?,* although one of Debord's comrades did write a short work entitled *La guerre sociale au Portugal* which Debord recommended to Lebovici for publication by Champ Libre. In a letter to Jaime Semprun, author of this book on Portugal, Debord mentions a letter "to the Portuguese" that I haven't been able to obtain.

either. It wasn't even the massive drunkenness—reportedly as many as five liters of wine were consumed per day by revolutionary workers, so a limit was set at four: Debord no doubt approved of the establishment of bars in factories! The real significance of the Portuguese revolution was the reason for its defeat—the reliance of revolutionaries on the military, which led to the commando raids and seizure of state power by "The Nine" who made the outrageous claim that they were the revolutionaries and that everyone else was counter-revolutionary. Many authentically revolutionary soldiers felt they had been betrayed, but the crisis was so confusing that they were helpless to stop the rapid reinstitution of state control.

CHAPTER TWENTY-SIX

In a long letter to Jamie Semprun (December 26, 1976), Debord responds to Semprun's request for support for a manuscript on revolutionary struggles in Spain that Semprun had sent to Champ Libre. The letter is illustrative both of Debord's limited role at the publishing house and his personal relations. Debord insists that he was never an associate or an employee of Champ Libre, that he had no responsibilities or rights in regard to it. He goes on to state that he always insisted on total rights and responsibilities in any activity that he engaged in, and he "never" used a pseudonym. According to the letter, he had no desire to be an editor, agent, director, etc. He was simply a writer who was published by Champ Libre. Skipping down Debord does concede that he did recommend two titles written by his contemporaries—Semprun's book on Portugal and Sanguinetti's brilliant fake known as *Censor,* which Debord slyly agrees was written in a "Debordist" style. Interestingly, Debord concedes that he gave Lebovici "a number of elements of response" to use in his replies to Vaneigemists, but denies having written letters signed by Lebovici. Debord implies that he recommended that classics such as Clausewitz and Gracian be republished by Champ Libre. But he insists that Lebovici is to "blame" for the *General Essay on Strategy* by Jean-Paul Charnay and has the "merit" of publishing Cieszkowski and Anacharsis Cloots. Debord also noted that the political books published by Champ Libre (Bakunin, Korsch, himself) don't reflect a unified worldview, and he agrees that this is the correct policy for a publishing house.

Debord then turns to his personal relations with Semprun, reminding his comrade that everyone has a "Stirnerian" (after the Young Hegelian exponent of egoism Max Stirner) right to use one's time and choose one's affinities as one pleases. Debord had a penchant for sometimes dining with a group of young unemployed workers, and when he took Semprun there one night, Semprun judged them harshly because they weren't talking revolution. Debord was more indulgent and simply wanted to be with them—following Semprun's harsh criticism of the young workers, his relationship with Debord was never the same. Debord:

> I'm glad you remember that, during the few months that we met fairly frequently, I treated you in a friendly way. It was sincere, and you surely merited it by your book on Portugal, so brilliantly written in overwhelming conditions of urgency, by the strength of all your positions, by the pleasure of your conversation, etc. After a while, and quite suddenly, a certain boredom seemed to constantly dominate the better part of each of our dialogues. I'm sure you had the same impression, because these things engender themselves dialectically more quickly than others. Understand for certain that I don't think that you're a boring person (you would be well founded to make the same reproach of me by extrapolating the same experience). [...] I'm much less inclined to try to elucidate or transform the atmosphere of certain relations because, on the one hand I still too frequently have the obligation to meet a number of people and because, on the other hand, I find pleasure in relative solitude.

As proof of his lack of involvement in Semprun's manuscript, Debord mentions that he was "absent from Paris for a very long time." We know from *Panegyric* that Debord spent some time in exile in Italy and Spain, and it could well be that he was in Italy in 1975 when Sanguinetti self-published his Censor "fake" (it was thought to have been written by some young polytech grad working at the Ministry of Economics or an elder authentic conservative). Sanguinetti's *The Real Report on the Last Chance to Save Capitalism in Italy* was translated by Debord and published by Champ Libre in 1976. While one can certainly hear Sanguinetti's accent in this, his first book, the work is almost too rich to believe that it was written when the author was still in his twenties without some assistance from Debord, then in his forties. In his letter to Semprun, Debord denies having written under other names, adding, "These sorts of noises were made around the *Real Report,* which is less extraordinary: one always suspects translators, and as we know Censor doesn't exist..." A very ambiguous denial, in my opinion. Sanguinetti would later write Debord asking for him to come back to Italy to assist Sanguinetti in another writing project (using the lure of one hundred liters of wine!). While it would be completely erroneous to misattribute Sanguinetti's book to Debord, I have one more reason for suspecting Debord had a hand in it. In this sublime post-Situationist work, Sanguinetti enumerates five aspects of political economy:

1. Progress of political lies.
2. Grandiose reinforcement of state power.
3. Isolation, or the perfection of the separation of people.

4. Unprecedented growth in the power of the economy and industry.

5. The existing hierarchy's development of secrecy and control in everything.

Debord would later enumerate precisely five aspects of the "integrated" spectacle in Italy and France (distinct from the concentrated and diffuse forms of the spectacle described above), in his *Comments on the Society of the Spectacle:*

1. Incessant technological renewal.
2. Integration of state and economy.
3. Generalized secrecy.
4. Unanswerable lies.
5. An eternal present.

Obviously there isn't a one-to-one correlation between these points, but I suspect that Debord was developing and reformulating points that he and Sanguinetti worked on together in the Censor book. As we will see below, Sanguinetti might've taken Debord's generous help a little too far in his next book—stating one position, having it rectified by Debord and then calling it his own. *The Real Report* is a "fake" inspired by the anonymous pamphlet by Marx and Bauer, *The Trumpet of the Last Judgment Against Hegel, Atheist and Antichrist?* that took a swipe at the Hegelian right from the right. Sanguinetti adopted the tone of a European conservative, an "authentic" conservative from another era who knew himself, his time and his enemies all too well. This is the opening line from the Preface:

> The author of this Report is afflicted with a great disadvantage: nothing, or almost nothing, seems to him as if it should be treated with a soft tone. The XXth Century thinks otherwise, and it has its reasons for this. Our democracy, craving the expression of personal opinions of an infinite number of brave people who don't have the time to form one, constrains everyone to speak about everything with a softness that we are, in our turn, obligated to excuse considering the necessities of time.

Sanguinetti sustains this trenchant tone throughout the book to show his fellow countrymen that they don't know how to write, and when they fail to recognize his diverted phrases, that they don't know how to read. The letter attributed to Louis XVIII was a famous fake by Paul-Louis Courier, and another letter attributed to a Russian diplomat was from a well-known passage by Nietzsche. There are long diversions of Shakespeare, Tocqueville and an entire page from *The Real Split in the International.* The rhetorical use of the word "necessary" and the method of looking at the consequences of an incident (such as the "historic compromise" between the

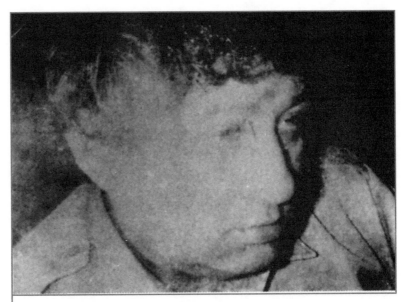

Debord at forty-five from *In girum...*

Christian Democrats and the Italian Communist Party) were deployed to suggest the arrival of a new Machiavelli.

The Italian press of the time thought that the author might be a young ministry official due to his extensive knowledge of economics:

> A few copies of this cynical and refined Report appeared in August, eliciting a whirlwind of interpretations... Is it a man from the right or left? What does he really want?... If someone consciously sought to create a success like this, and if he was an upstart, he would be a genius. Epocha (11-15-75)

What they had was a descedant of Machiavelli, or even a descendant of Dante, on their hands. Like Dante, Sanguinetti named names and compared capitalism with a sick man; and like Dante, who wrote for emperors, princes and cardinals, Sanguinetti sent the 520 copies of his book to the economic elite—industrialists, ministers and the most respected journalists. It's interesting to recall that according to Burckhardt, Dante was one of the earliest publicists to address pamphlets and political tracts to "the Great ones of the Earth." By quoting Dante at length, Sanguinetti invites this comparison with the great poet.

> *He replied: "The conscience that is dark with shame*
> *for its own deeds or for another's*

may indeed feel harshness in your words;
nevertheless, do not resort to lies,
let what you write reveal all you have seen
and let those men who itch, scratch where it hurts

Your cry of words will be like the wind
striking hardest at the highest peaks,
and this is greatly honorable

Dante, Paradise, Canto XVII

Reportedly, it was right after Sanguinetti got out of prison for a false arms possession charge that he gave the manuscript of the Report to the printer. Of his stay in Italy, reportedly in a XIVth Century house in Florence, Debord would later remark in his *Panegyric:*

In Italy I was certainly not well thought of by everyone, but I had the good fortune to meet the '*sfacciate donne fiorentine*' when I lived in Florence, in the Oltrarno district. There was that little Florentine who was so graceful. In the evenings she would cross the river to come to San Frediano. I fell in love very unexpectedly, perhaps because of her beautiful, bitter smile. I told her, in brief: "Don't stay silent, for I come before you as a stranger and a traveller. Grant me some refreshment before I go away and am here no more." At that time Italy was once again losing its way: it was necessary to regain sufficient distance from its prisons, where those who stayed too long at the revels of Florence ended up.

In 1977, Debord signed on with Simar Films, then managed by Lebovici's wife Floriana, to create his "sixth film"—the exact title of the film was left to Debord's discretion. The title would be a palindrome, a phrase that reads the same backwards and forwards: *In Girum Imus Nocte et Consumimur Igni* (we go around in circles in the night and are consumed by fire). Although the film was completed in 1978, it wouldn't be shown for another three years because no cinema would show it. But it was known in book form to readers of Debord's *Complete Cinematic Works,* which was published in 1978—another "critical" version of *In Girum...* was published in 1990 by Éditions Gérard Lebovici (formerly Champ Libre) with footnotes on quotes and new commentaries. The superb English translation by Lucy Forsyth, published by Pelagian Press, incorporates the stills from the first version and the notes from the latter. The critical version (with footnotes) opens thus:

I will make no concession to the public in this film.* Several
The actual audience of a cinema, staring fixedly in a perfect
excellent reasons justify such conduct to my mind and I shall give
reverse angle shot, faces the spectators, who therefore merely see them.
themselves on this screen.

Debord goes on and on, heaping scorn on spectacles, spectators and the society of the spectacle, illustrated by its neo-houses, neo-food and cars. The tone here is perhaps the most poetically trenchant of all of Debord's works. Consider a few of Debord's "Swifty's" such as "pseudo-criticism," "mystified ignoramuses," "spectacular superstitions," "mental degeneration," "the gibberish of dozens of paternalist professionalisms," "the conspicuous consumption of nothingness," "dismal junk," "overburdened servants of the void," "childish respect for images," "intellectual domesticity," "ridiculous dogmas," etc. Debord's contempt for images is summed up in the following axiom: "The existing images only serve the existing lies."

Naturally, Debord makes use of the existing images from films that he admired, such as Marcel Carné's *The Children of Paradise,* and others, such as *Zorro,* which were of no significance to him. The few images that he filmed himself were of such high quality that critics still qualify him as a great cinematographer. The poets and writers whose work he exploits—Homer, Sun Tze, Gracian, Omar Khayyam, Villiers de l'Isle-Adam, Alcuin, Stevenson, Pascal, Heraclitus, Hugo, Hegel, Percy Shelley, Villon, Musset, Bossuet, Shakespeare, Li Po, Ariosto, Dante, Machiavelli—are always writers he respects. Indeed, after the implacable judgments of the society of the spectacle, the film becomes the *Homage to the Things We Loved* that Debord had planned to film in the Sixties. These "things" encompassed not only his literary tastes, but also his beloved Paris, Florence, the houses he lived in, his obsession with war and historical engagement, his lovers, the friends who were by definition his equals—and above all—himself.

A significant portion of the film is concerned with Paris, which "no longer exists"—a place that was "so beautiful that many people preferred to be poor there, rather than rich somewhere else." By tracing the streets listed by Debord in *Panegyric*

---

* [Debord's note] "In 1978, this discourse was actually illustrated by a film. Such a genre of film never really had any place in 'the cinema,' just as it can now be seen that the cinema itself no longer has any place in society. The mere words, provided they are accompanied by some notes to aid comprehension, should be nevertheless instructive. Our time will have left few writings which consider quite bluntly the massive transformations which have effected it. What could those who have shared some of its combined illusions and ambitions say about it which would be true?"

to illustrate where he lived most of his life, we find a triangle that spans sections of the third, fourth, fifth and seventh districts of Paris. Art Blakey's "Whisper Not" is the tune that takes the viewer on a cinematic drift through these city streets. The poetry that Debord uses to describe this Paris evokes the burning of time in these sacred spaces with the scoundrels of his youth.

At a certain point, this vivid narrative on the labyrinth of Paris stops and Debord quotes his first film *Howls in Favor of Sade* using the black and white sequences. There are numerous references to Ivan Chtcheglov, and to other Situationists for whom "Nothing is true, everything is permitted," as the notorious Assassins liked to say. The still of Alice and Celeste illustrates the fact that Debord and Alice sometimes enjoyed the company of other women—lest there be any doubt, the subsequent nude of Celeste coincide with the voice over: "... and the people, and the use we made of time, all this constituted an *ensemble* very much like the happiest disorders of my youth." There are photos of Debord at various stages in his life, and the requisite cavalry charges by the Light Brigade as it rushes into the "Valley of Death" at Balaklava: "As these last reflections on violence still show, for me there will be no going back and no reconciliation. There will be no good conduct."

Rather than using the standard *"le fin"* to end his film, Debord used the subtitle: "To be begun again from the beginning." The note on this states that the film is worth being seen again to "achieve more fully its despairing effect." This ending also demonstrates the cycle suggested by the title—the actions of the L.I. and S.I. must be taken up again and again. The film was finally shown at Cinema Quintette-Pathe and in a pirate television screening at 4 a.m. on June 3, 1981—it would later enjoy a long run at the Studio Cujas, a famous Latin Quarter theater which Lebovici bought in order to show this and all of Debord's other films. The critical reception of the film (mixed) was published by Champ Libre (without any commentary) in a small booklet called *Refuse and Rubble Unpacked Upon the Release of In Girum Imus Nocte et Consumimur Igni.*

A more reliable assessment of Debord's cinematic work comes from Debord himself:

> It seems to me that my work [in the cinema], very succinct but extended over a period of twenty-six years, did indeed correspond to the principal criteria of modern art: (1) a very marked originality from the start and the firm decision never to do "the same thing" two times in a row, while still maintaining a personal style and a set of thematic concerns that are always easily recognizable; (2) an understanding of contemporary society, *id est* explaining it by criticizing it, since ours is a time which is distinctly lacking less in apologetics than in criticism; (3) finally, to have been revolutionary in form as well as in content, something which always struck

Baader and Meinhof

me as following the direction of all the "unitary" aspirations of modern art, toward the point where that art attempted to go beyond art.*

This attempt to "go beyond art" had an element of subversion and sabotage about it—as Sanguinetti would write, sabotage should be considered as one of the fine arts. Before examining the correspondence between Debord and Sanguinetti that precipitated Debord's 1979 *Preface to the Fourth Italian Edition of Society of the Spectacle* (henceforth *Preface*), it should be recalled that Europe had experienced the exploits of urban guerrillas since the late Sixties. The most notorious of these "terrorists" were the German Red Army Faction, two of whom—Andreas Baader and Gudrun Enslin—Debord pictured in *In Girum...* with the commentary taken from a Milanese riff-raff song "... the best of youth dies in prison."

The events immediately preceding these deaths in 1977 evoke the atmosphere in Europe at the time. On April 7, the German attorney general in charge of the Baader-Meinhof gang case and his driver were assassinated by sympathizers. Baader and two others were convicted and sentenced to life in prison for murder and other criminal activity—their political motives were discounted. On July 30, the head of the Dresdner Bank, Jurgen Ponto, was murdered by his granddaughter who was a Red Army Faction member. On September 5, five R.A.F. members kidnapped Hanns Schleyer, head of the German Industries Federation. They killed his entourage, then demanded a ransom and the release of Baader and ten other R.A.F. members. On

---

* From a letter to Levin, author of the essay "Dismantling the Cinema" cited above.

October 18, Baader was found shot dead in his cell in Stuttgart's Stammheim Prison. His partner, Gudrun Ensslin hung herself in her cell the same day—Schleyer was executed and West Germany turned into a virtual police state.

In Italy, terrorist activity would reach incredible levels—1,926 attacks in 1977 and 2,379 in 1978. On March 15, 1978, the Italian Red Brigade did the unthinkable and kidnapped the Christian Democrat politician and former Premier, Aldo Moro (architect of the "historic compromise" between the Christian Democrats and the Italian Communist Party). Five bodyguards were killed in the abduction. When the government rejected the Red Brigade demands to release their imprisoned comrades, the group held a people's trial and found Moro guilty. His body was found in a parked car in Rome on May 9, 1978. Before discussing Sanguinetti and Debord's reaction to these events, it should be noted that books such as Philip Willan's *Puppetmasters: The Political Use of Terrorism in Italy* and Stuart Christie's *Stefano Delle Chiaie: Portrait of a Black Terrorist* demonstrate very conclusively that the United States C.I.A. and local secret services had developed a "strategy of tension" that relied on agent provocateurs, infiltration and other means to impute blame for the worst terrorist acts on the left.

The chronology mentioned above is important for understanding the exchange between Debord (writing as "Cavalcanti," as in Guido Cavalcanti, the aristocratic poet who was a strong personal influence on Dante's early poetic endeavors) and Sanguinetti (writing as "Niccolo" Machiavelli). In his letter of April 21, 1978, Debord stated that the left couldn't have kidnapped Moro, but the enemies of the historic compromise could have done it. The "Stalinists" representing the organized left, were obliged to maintain their silence, therefore, according to Debord, the duty fell on Sanguinetti to expose this secret of official involvement in the abduction of Moro. Debord ended his letter by encouraging his friend:

> I knew a man who used to spend his time amongst the "*sfacciate donne fiorentine*," and who loved to carouse with the low company of all the drunkards of the bad quarters. He understood all that went on. He showed it once. One knows that he can still do it. He is therefore considered by some as the most dangerous man in Italy.

Sanguinetti let the opportunity to expose the truth slip away. In his reply to Debord, dated June 1, 1978, Sanguinetti wrote about where he was when he heard that Moro was kidnapped and how he was glad to run into an old acquaintance in order to have an alibi. Sanguinetti decided to go out to his country house in order to be seen by the townspeople—clearly he was wary of being falsely accused, and with good reason: at one point while the affair was going on, eighteen armed soldiers searched his house, and rumors spread in the locality that he was somehow involved. Terrorism was so widespread that an unseemly pro-situ group perpetrated a few attacks, including one against the dreaded "Stalinists." This troubled Sanguinetti as much as the misapplication of Situationist theory upset him because he lived in a district governed by the Italian Communist Party.

Sanguinetti admired Debord's interpretation of the Moro affair, almost agreeing with Debord on the grounds that the state was certainly lying as it usually did. But then Sanguinetti changed his mind for these reasons:

Aldo Moro

1. The sheer amount of terrorist acts and known groups led him to conclude that the Moro affair could have been proletarian terror responding to State terror—there were six acts of terror per day during 1977.
2. The secret services were "non-existent."
3. No false perpetrators were captured and claimed by the State.
4. Italy was in a fragile state and these terrorists wanted to exploit this fragility.
5. Terror did account for some tactical successes, despite its strategic flaws.
6. There was really no other field of action in Italy at that time due to its historical circumstances.
7. Terrorists were afflicted with the need to see themselves on television, like voyeurs.

This interpretation, while being very insightful, was not the one that Sanguinetti would use in his book *On Terrorism and the State*—he would revert back to Debord's interpretation. Sanguinetti's long letter offers a few surprising perspectives regarding Debord. It seems that pirate editions of *Society of the Spectacle* were circulating far and wide: even major bourgeois papers like *Corriere della Serra* and *L'Espresso* spoke of the spectacle and "the society of the spectacle" in regard to the Moro affair. Sanguinetti suggested that Debord write a preface for a real first Italian edition, a suggestion that Debord would take. Perhaps the following passage from the letter, reflects Sanguinetti's alleged sexism (he was reportedly militantly anti-feminist), and also the wild Seventies that were very much part of Debord's life:

> Perhaps you remember a whore from Naples or Rome who came to Caldaie one day, and who displayed so much pleasure when you caressed her pussy, with four hands. You remember perhaps that she had a brother who wasn't to be valued on a moral plane any more that her because they were both equally incestuous and didn't hide it. Well, it turns out that this brother met a well known terrorist—he didn't want to tell me the name, and I don't even remember his name or that of his whore of a sister. He told me, the brother, that despite his doubtful morality, he was astonished by the crazy offhandedness that reigned in this milieu that was ready for everything, and capable of many things (useless for our ends and too spectacular), as if he were back in the time of Nechaev and Dostoyevsky. Therefore, it's better for those of us who still believe in certain principles not to get mixed up with whores, incest and terrorists!

Sanguinetti closed his letter with the admission that he needed Debord's help and encouragement to write his planned "Remedy for Everything," adding that he had over one hundred liters of wine with which to welcome Debord should he be able to make the trip. Breaking the cadence of their letter exchange, Sanguinetti wrote Debord again on August 15. He proposed a "fake" similar to the Censor project called "Technical Solution to the Political and Social Question," only with more official-looking references, typesetting and printing. Then, Sanguinetti announced that his "Remedy for Everything" was already written, although he may well have been exaggerating—*On Terrorism and the State* was to have been the tenth chapter, but it was probably all he had written of the book other than the extravagant table of contents and "dedication to the bad workers of Italy and of all countries."

In this letter, Sanguinetti also communicated the astonishing activity of some factory worker friends of his who put *Society of the Spectacle* into play in their cake factory with wildcat strikes and by publicizing the fact that they had been required to put some sort of poison into the food—a few hadn't worked for years (while they were "on the job") and after the strike several were eventually paid indemnities! But Debord wasn't interested in all this. While he was quick to encourage Sanguinetti's "fake" and "Remedy for Everything" in his reply, Debord really wanted to know who had gotten to Sanguinetti to cause him to take up the analysis outlined in the seven points above (from the June 1 letter). Debord went so far as to ask Sanguinetti if he had been pressured by the authorities.

I don't have access to the correspondence that follows, so I can't share the amazement Debord certainly felt when he found out that Sanguinetti published his *On Terrorism and the State* (confirming Debord's analysis of the situation) with the subtitle "The Theory and Practice of Terrorism Divulged for the First Time." Both *On Terrorism* and Debord's *Preface* were published in April 1979 (although the Italian version of Debord's work didn't come out until May). According to Lebovici, the *Preface* was communicated to Sanguinetti in February, but Sanguinetti retained his objectionable subtitle. Naturally, comparisons were made between the two works, and it was even suggested by one of Debord's Dutch translators, Jaap Kloosterman, that they be published together. Debord replied in early 1981, that his friendship and collaboration with Sanguinetti were over and that joint publication was out of the question.

To me this question of avant-garde originality seems a little ridiculous. Debord's elegant little pamphlet has to settle a few translating and publishing scores, and then brag about the reception of *Society of the Spectacle* in Italy before it gets around to the Moro affair, on which it contains barely ten pages. Debord's historical allusions are, as always, rich. And the theory that it was the "occult state" that smelt of this crime is certainly correct, but his essay doesn't have the detail or scope of Sanguinetti's *On Terrorism*. After his big wind-up, Sanguinetti delivers thirty thousand words on the subject. Both Debord and Sanguinetti had read their history on the provocations of the Russian Czar's secret service. But, in addition to his detailed study of what happened in Italy (and we should recall that he was up to his ears in the mess), Sanguinetti offers a general denunciation of terrorism and proposes the theory of offensive (by deluded revolutionaries) and defensive terrorism (by States). The Dutch translator of *On Terrorism,* Els van Daele, supports the view held by others that Sanguinetti detracted from his argument by denouncing all terrorism and imposing his schema on it. Her grounds for this are that the legitimate armed struggles of this world don't fit into Sanguinetti's schema. She cited the *Calls From Segovia Prison* as a case in point—Debord wrote the twelve page introduction (signed: "International Friends") to this pamphlet and ushered it into print via Lebovici's Champ Libre in 1980.

Here Debord called for support for fifty Spanish anarchists—Robin Hoods who had been robbing banks and distributing the funds to strikers, the unemployed and autonomous revolutionary groups around Barcelona and Madrid. These were nonparty "libertarians," many of whom Debord claimed were innocent. They were up on charges for crimes committed by police provocateurs—others had indeed bombed railroad tracks, courts and public buildings. It seems that one guard was killed in an exchange of gunfire, which the author of the introduction compares to so many industrial accidents that kill many more people. Debord didn't call for any specific action, only for a struggle to free the libertarians that went beyond legal petitions. According to Els van Daele, the most guilty were freed from prison right before the military seized power in January 1981.

Although Els van Daele uses this group as an example of legitimate armed struggle to refute Sanguinetti's denunciation of terrorism, Debord was much more skeptical about the activity of the group. Sure, they robbed money, Debord says, but they didn't really know what to do with it other than print their tracts. This is not to say that Debord questioned their extra-judicial legitimacy. What Debord admired was their practical resolve and the fact that they acted autonomously. It should be pointed out that these libertarians were on the offensive, corresponding to Sanguinetti's categorization, if not to his negative judgment. It is interesting that Debord didn't sign his name to the introduction to *Calls From Segovia Prison*. Why? Weren't these, after all, revolutionaries who didn't know how to wait for the right moment? At almost fifty years of age, Debord was ready to start the Spanish Civil War again. They were jumping the gun and Debord knew it. But the point I'd like to stress here is that far from there being a "Situationist party line 'on terrorism'" as Tom Vague asserts in his bibliography to *Televisionaries: The Red Army Faction Story 1963—1993*, Sanguinetti's book is a trenchant, eloquent denunciation of the practice that does indeed differ from Debord. Sanguinetti:

> Whosoever in Italy does not use all the intelligence they have at their disposal to rapidly understand the truth which lurks behind each State lie, whosoever does not do this is an ally of the enemies of the proletariat. And whosoever still claims to want to fight alienation in an alienated manner, through militantism and ideology, will quickly perceive that they have renounced all real combat. It will certainly not be militants who will make the social revolution, or the secret services and the Stalinist police who will prevent it! (*On Terrorism*)

Of his time in Spain, Debord was very laconic. Other than evoking his Spanish lovers, his *Panegyric* contains this suggestive phrase: "I played my part—and perhaps my greatest part—in the follies of Spain." He was perhaps more involved with these autonomous groups in Spain than he is letting on, although at certain points they asserted their autonomy from him, which Debord was forced to accept.* His only other remark on Spain in *Panegyric* was that the Spanish police were the most irrational and incapable of all those he'd encountered in Europe. But Debord certainly loved Spain, and says as much in a note added to his translation to Jorge Manrique's Stanzas on the *Death of His Father* (1980):

---

* According to Lucy Forsyth in her Hacienda Conference speech, February, 1996.

The translator, who never judged it good to frequent universities, isn't, in the slightest degree, a Spanish expert. Only a few circumstances of his wandering life, and of his socially less valued occupations, led him to know the rudiments of one or two foreign languages. But, opposed to all those declaimers who actually make a job out of extolling the pseudo-passions that are in style like false witnesses—proving *ipso facto* that they haven't tried them—the translator has had the habit of feeling at home with everything for which he experiences a real taste. When one has had the fortune to know an authentic Spain, under one or another of the admirable figures that it created in the history of this century, and even earlier, one must also love its language and its poetry.

Manrique was a poet-knight who wrote his *Stanzas* around 1477. Debord was attracted to the work because it encompassed the sensibilities of that age—the decline of the Middle Ages with its experience of life on Earth as a short voyage, the triumph of death and evanescent nature of everything that exists in the world: "The sensation of the flow of time is the universal base of lyrical poetry, in Ecclesiates or Omar Khayyam, as with the poets of the Tang dynasty—the cultural environment of the epoch in which Manrique lived permitted him to express this general reality with particular force; as did Villon twenty years earlier." Debord also admired the "coldness" in Manrique's tone when he spoke of the people his family had vanquished to illustrate the way fortunes change and how insignificant possessions are: "The most beautiful is without doubt the lesson, so indirectly expressed, that one must fight for 'one's real king,' whom one makes oneself." Debord also appreciated the quest for historical glory and the "impersonal" way Manrique reported on his own historical operations.

In 1982, Debord signed on with Lebovici to make another film. This is rather curious given that his "complete" cinematic work had been published, in book form, in 1978. The contract is addressed to Debord in Campot, Bellevue-la-Montagne, a small farm in an obscure part of the Upper Loire in the Massif Central of France. The project was to be a two-to-four hour film on the real Spain, possibly with costumed actors and international stars which would've been a major break from Debord's previous films. The idea was to focus on contemporary Spain and center the film around Andalusia (Debord mentions that he lived in Seville and spent time in Cadiz in *Panegyric*).

Debord was to study the project for eighteen months, during which time he earned 10,000 francs per month with 400 francs per week living expenses. All the first class travel arrangements were picked up by the studio. At the appointed time, April 25, 1984, Debord responded from his home in Arles—a modest, yet comfortable bungalow in a city between Avignon and the Mediterranean Sea where he had been living off-and-on since the late Seventies. Whatever genuine enthusiasm Debord had had for his Spain project vanished when, on March 5, 1984, Gerard Lebovici was ambushed and murdered in a Paris parking garage. This "horrible assassination" will be discussed in greater detail below, but it should be noted that after declaring himself incapable of making the film to Lebovici's widow, Debord allowed that his expenses should be calculated on fifteen rather than eighteen months—perhaps a lesson for those wishing to practice the "mastery of manipulation," as Debord put it in his *Contracts*.

Chapter Twenty-seven

Debord's publisher, producer and benefactor, Gérard Lebovici, was born in Neuilly, in the sixteenth district of Paris in 1932. His Jewish parents were of Italian descent; owners of a boutique. He was described as an intelligent, curious youth who took up drama and became friends with many rising stars. A reporter for *Minute* wrote that Lebovici had no talent as an actor, but no less an authority than Francois Truffaut considered him to be a "fantastic actor," apparently referring to Lebovici's acting behind the scenes. After developing his skills as an impresario, Lebovici purchased the most important agency in Paris when he was only thirty-three. First with Artmedia, and then with Soprofilms (production) and AAA (distribution), Lebovici became the "key man" in French cinema. He sponsored films by Truffaut and Alain Resnais, such as *Le Nom de la rose* and numerous other successes—*Le Dernier metro, Mon Oncle d'Amerique, L'Enfand sauvage, La Balance, Morfalous, Fort Sagane, Vivement dimance!, Emmanuelle 4, Les Comperes,* and others. Jean-Paul Belmondo, Catherine Deneuve, Yves Montand—these were the big names, familiar even to American moviegoers, associated with Lebovici's agency. He invented a system of participation whereby he was able to convince the celebrities to invest in their own films. This participation freed up his own funds to buy the distribution rights to Hollywood classics such as Hitchcock, giving him a cut in seventy percent of all films shown in France. Naturally, it shocked the Parisian film world when, in 1983, Lebovici bought the Studio Cujas in the Latin Quarter to exclusively show Debord's anti-spectacular films.

The May '68 Revolution had a huge impact on Lebovici. He met the writer Gerard Guegan on May 24—the night the stock market was set on fire—at the home of his future wife, "a superb brunette of Turinese origin, noble, rich and engaged in the left," according to *V.S.D.,* one of France's tabloids. Guegan and Lebovici created Champ Libre at the end of 1968, with Guegan's book on the history of bandits in France being the first book they published. An auspicious beginning for a publisher whose death would be preceded by his publication of the auto-biography of the notorious bank robber and jail breaker Jacques Mesrine. After rejecting Guegan's second book, which reportedly had a Debord-like character in it, Lebovici called Gaugan and his crew to a fancy restaurant to ask them to resign. They refused. Lebovici fired them—this was in 1974.

Champ Libre was known for never sending review copies to the press. Another anomaly—when Eric Satie's book won an award, Lebovici refused it. The Champ Libre logo was kept on the fine line of books that continued to be published, first under the name Editions Gerard Lebovici, and then, with the death in February 1990 of Floriana Lebovici from cancer, under the name Editions Ivrea—titles by authors as diverse as Malevitch, Jomini, Groddeck, Clausewitz, W.C. Fields, Karl and Groucho Marx. Perhaps the most famous books published by Champ Libre (other than everything by Orwell and *Society of the Spectacle*) was *The New Clothes of Chairman Mao* by Simon Leys and Khrushchev's *Secret Report on Stalin to the XXth Congress of the Communist Party of the Soviet Union*, which underscores the

fact that the libertarian perspective of Lebovici saved its harshest criticism for the false left of so-called "socialist" states.

On March 5, 1984, around 3:30 p.m. Lebovici was dining with another producer at the restaurant George V when he received a phone call, apparently from Sabrina Mesrine, daughter of the dead bank robber Jacques Mesrine. Lebovici then cancelled all his other appointments for the day and was last seen leaving

Lebovici and Deneuve

his office at 4:30. He didn't mention where he was going. Nine hours later he was found in the underground parking lot on Avenue Foch in the sixteenth district with four bullets in his neck. He wasn't robbed. The murder weapon was a .22 long rifle, a weapon often used by marksmen at the Club Foch firing range—part of this underground garage was reserved for members of the club. Evidently, Lebovici was claustrophobic and never used underground parking garages. A note was found in his pocket reading, "Francois, 6:45 p.m."

Early speculation held that "Francois" was Francois Besse, a comrade of Mesrine who was still one of France's most wanted men. Besse had recently submitted a sixty page manuscript to Champ Libre, but police soon dismissed this lead because Besse wasn't a "killer." Lebovici's preface to Mesrine's autobiography lauded Mesrine as "the perfect symbol of liberty for the French of our epoch," adding that it was an "honor" to publish the book. Mesrine's *Death Instinct* is, incidentally, a masterpiece (bolstered by Champ Libre's editors)—a masterpiece of audacity. Note too, that Lebovici was both Jewish and pro-Palestinian, which wouldn't have been smiled upon by Jews working for Mossad.

Another theory was that the murderer was tied to a gang of fifteen videocassette pirates who had been arrested two days prior to the murder, but this was dismissed on the grounds that Lebovici had only produced five cassettes in two years—he wasn't deeply involved in this area of business. Rumors swirled about Lebovici's gambling and taste for "young girls, beautiful models and luxurious call girls" (*Le Soir*). Inevitably, attention turned to Lebovici's ties with the ultra-left. Rumors were printed that he had funded the Red Brigades, and it was said that he liked to boast that his wife Floriana had once worked for the Italian publisher Giangiacoma Feltrinelli; Feltrinelli was so deeply involved with terrorism that he blew himself up with one of his own bombs in 1972.

Naturally, the journalists and police questioned Debord's relationship with Lebovici; the former by making numerous wild accusations, the later in a formal questioning. In his *Panegyric,* Debord looked back on the episode with the police:

> For an author who has written with a certain degree of quality and knows what it means to speak, it is generally a sad ordeal when he has to reread and consent to sign his own answers in a statement for the police judiciaire. First, the text as a whole is directed by the investigators' questions, which are usually not mentioned and do not innocently arise, as they sometimes hope to appear to, from the simple logical necessities of a precise inquiry or from a clear understanding. The answers that one was able to formulate are in fact hardly better than their summary, dictated by the highest-ranking officer and obviously rewritten with a great deal of awkwardness and vagueness. If, naturally—but many innocents are unaware of it—it is imperative to precisely correct every detail by which the thought that one had expressed has been translated with a deplorable unfaithfulness, it is necessary to give up quickly on having everything transcribed in the suitable and satisfactory form that one used spontaneously, for then one would be led to double the number of those already tiresome hours, which would rid the greatest purist of the taste for being so to such a degree. So then, I here declare that my answers to the police should not be included later in my collected works, because of scruples about the form, and even though I signed the veracious content without embarrassment.

Meanwhile, the Parisian press corps staked out Debord's rue du Bac apartment in an all out effort to get a recent photo of the elusive revolutionary. The latest photo available to the press of Debord was from *In Girum...* showing him at forty-five. It became a point of honor for Debord to evade the press cameras. In the small book *Considerations on the Assassination of Gérard Lebovici,* Debord writes that he wouldn't have been much of an urban guerrilla if he couldn't dodge these cameras, adding with cynicism that he had succeeded in photographing the press photographers. To underscore this triumph over the forces of the spectacle, Debord published a photo of himself in this book—the last photo of Debord given to the public.

Debord wrote in *Considerations* that he didn't care about the press, and even though journalists had defamed him for years, he never tried to respond: "But they never said that I assassinated, or tried to have assassinated a friend. They were wrong to go that far." As soon as Debord sued a few journals for libel (*Journal du Dimanche, Minute and L'Humanite*), they all stopped making these allusions. Debord's lawyer won the case. In addition to the money made on the case, the judge's decision stated that the judgment would be printed in three journals of Debord's choice. All journals

Jacques Mesrine

were equally bad, Debord contended, and he didn't care what their readers thought of him. Debord's response to the way the French press had commented on Lebovici's murder was an act of auto-censorship—his films would never be projected again in France. This was incredibly stoic considering all the names he'd been called: pseudo-philosopher, pope, devil, damned soul, negligible, total cynic, and even an "agent of subversion and destabilization in the service of Soviet imperialism."

It was *Minute* that claimed (citing a book by Montaldo called *Secrets of the Soviet Bank*) that Debord had access to account # 03789-7 where "money comes and goes by the tens of thousands of francs." This type of illegitimate accusation would crop up again in 1989. Debord documented these lies against him that were planted in the press. This documentation should erase the label of "paranoid" in any fair reader's mind and allow us to take him at his word that he never worked for any intelligence service. The 1989 incident involved a *Times of London* story that claimed that the *Village Voice* had run a story about Debord's ties to the C.I.A.—the problem was that the *Village Voice* never ran such a story. My FOIA request to get the C.I.A. file on Debord was turned down on the grounds they could "neither confirm or deny" the existence of such a file.

Chapter Twenty-eight

In 1987, Debord and Alice Becker-Ho published the rules for his *Kriegspiel* board game along with diagrams of a full match as *The Game of War*. Debord had been playing and perfecting his game since the 50s so it's understandable that he took pride in it:

> The surprises of this *Kriegspiel* seem inexhaustible, and I fear that this may well be the only one of my works that anyone will dare acknowledge as having some value.

The book of the moves by the Northern and Southern forces was published by Éditions Gérard Lebovici (including the rulebook first published in 1977 by the Society of Strategic and Historic Games). Five copies of the game were made of metal (pictured in the stills of *In Girum...*), and a cardboard version of the board game was mass produced with wood pieces. The importance of this game in Debord's life was clarified in *Panegyric:*

> I have played this game and, in the often difficult conduct of this life I have utilized lessons from it—I have also established a rule of the game for this life, and I followed it [...] On the question of whether I have made good use of such lessons, I will leave it to others to decide.

The best description of the *Kriegspiel* and its limitations is by its author (translated in its entirety in the Appendix). Like all strategic games, the *Kriegspiel* forces one to think in terms of the deployment of forces, maneuvers, battles, etc. But the supreme importance placed on the need to maintain lines of communication (directly with the arsenal or via transmission units) illustrates the possibilities inherent in the strategy of disrupting these lines of communication. Even very desperate situations, Debord tells us, can be reversed by generalized application of this indirect strategy (which is not to be confused with limited, tactical attacks of communication lines in a different strategy, say, one aimed more directly at the enemy's arsenal). The game is highly mathematical in terms of the firing range and offen-

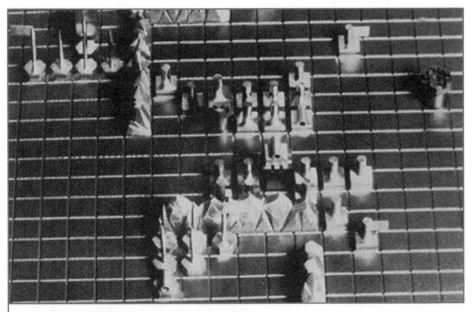

Limited edition of *The Game of War*

sive-defensive coefficients. Even Debord acknowledges that the game is somewhat abstract and gives his strategic thoughts more historical, and even personal, context in his next two books *Comments on the Society of the Spectacle* (1988) and *Panegyric* (1989), discussed in the next chapter.

Chapter Twenty-nine

Debord was obviously attracted to war and its dangers, and of all the writers who wrote about it—Sun Tzu, Archilochus, Thucydidies, Cervantes, Gondi, La Rochefoucald, Machiavelli, Saint-Simon, Stendhal, Jomini, etc.—the one Debord admired most was Clausewitz (1780–1831). Like the first Frenchmen to read Clausewitz, Debord was drawn to the martial spirit of the Prussian soldier who enlisted in his early teens for the Rhine campaign. Clausewitz was a thorough-going professional soldier with a Kantian philosophical bent, which he picked up at the Berlin Academy. In *Panegyric,* Debord writes that he loved to read about the battles of history, the "surface eddies on the river of time," such as those Clausewitz experienced first hand—the Jena campaign where Clausewitz was captured, and the Moscow campaigns of 1812 and 1813 when Clausewitz served with the Russians. Clausewitz would rejoin the Prussian Army and become chief of staff of a corps at Ligny, and the director of the Military Academy at Berlin. While he was best known for his celebrated *On War* where he extrapolated, in a highly rational way, on the implications of advances in techniques and tactics, Debord quotes from his memoirs and letters as well:

> And when I think that these people march side by side, on a long and difficult journey, in order to arrive together at the same place, where they will run a thousand dangers to achieve a great and noble goal, these reflections give this picture a meaning that profoundly moves me.*

Like Machiavelli before him, Clausewitz wanted to discover exactly what war was—an instrument of politics, Clausewitz argues, but also a strategic game using acts of violence to compel one's opponents to fulfill one's will. Debord certainly cultivated the power of his personality to the point that he could impose his will, tastes and desires on others. I'm reminded here of the passage in Michele Bernstein's novel in which she admits that Debord's lucidity and logic compelled her to adopt his seemingly extreme opinions on art and life. Likewise Clausewitz tended to emphasize logical ideals and absolute assertions (which his disciples would develop into the theory and practice of "absolute war," exemplified by the big battles of WWI). Alice Becker-Ho was no less immune to Debord's will, especially when his tastes and desires where expressed with his characteristically fractious language that gives the impression that to disagree with Guy entailed the risk of an attack. Alice obviously mastered Debord's *Kriegspiel,* and she shared other cultivated interests with him, such as their fascination for the criminal poet Francois Villon (1431–1463) and gypsy slang.

In *Panegyric,* Debord states that, "The Gypsies rightly contend that one is never compelled to speak the truth except in one's own language; in the enemy's language, the lie must reign" and in his chapter on his youth, he actually writes in Villon's argot: "... Our acts of violence and our earthly delights are past. Yet I vividly recall my penniless comrades who understood so well this delusory world: when we met in our hangouts, in Paris at night." In her remarkable little book, *Princes of Jargon* (1990), Alice Becker-Ho reveals neglected factors "in the origins of the slang of the dangerous classes," notably the gypsies who traversed Europe in the XVth Century on pilgrimages whose only legitimacy was the word "adventure." There are no heroes in gypsy legend, Becker-Ho tells us, no justification for their errant life. But Villon comes pretty close to taking on legendary status in her essay and glossary—Villon's texts are a main source of the vernacular language of what might be called "thieves' jargon." Obviously she and Guy learned the language together. Becker-Ho's 1994 publication, *The Essence of Jargon,* extends her earlier analysis to many more languages,

---

*   Carl Von Clausewitz, letter of 18 September 1808, cited before the VIth chapter—on war—of Debord's *Panegyric.*

notably German, and develops a model of slang based on the analogy of river deltas whereby the confluence of expressions from diverse origins defies etymology—slang is a "secret language written on water."

To get back to the power of Debord's thought, what Debord practiced publicly was a strategy of dissuasion to detach spectators from the spectacle. He tried to set an example of opposition with his life, which was by this point an established pole of instigation. Alas, he was getting old. At fifty-seven, quoting Massena (the French marshal under Napoleon I, 1758-1817) speaking when he was fifty-seven to the effect that command wears one out, Debord made it clear that he was calling it quits.

And rather than surrounding his enemy, as he had done in *Society of the Spectacle,* Debord was now content to play psychological war games. *Comments on the Society of the Spectacle* (1988—henceforth *Comments*) is a little treatise on the secrets of his time that Debord dedicated to Gerard Lebovici. Here, Debord describes the transformation of the spectacle from pseudo-rival forms (concentrated and diffuse) into the global "integrated spectacle"—his term for the current realpolitik of power in the hands of mafia statesmen, industrial mafia, the spy mafia and the mafia itself. With the fall of the concentrated spectacle of Soviet "communism," his thesis that the spectacle tends to unify and simplify society around the *ideology of democracy* ("the dictatorial freedom of the Market, tempered by recognition of the Rights of Spectacular Man") is verified. Likewise, Clausewitz was one of the keenest observers of the transformation of the international system of 1648–1789 into the next phase (1815–1914). For Clausewitz, empires and nations are the key strategic entities, but Debord has a much broader conception of strategy because he considers himself to be a strategic entity in the battlefield of everyday life. For Debord, it isn't so much a political philosophy of war that he lives, rather the application of strategy to all social relations, including his interpersonal relations. Debord is too much of a *bon vivant* not to let his guard down and behave recklessly every now and then, but "discretion," is the way of life for the author of *Panegyric,* who gives his readers examples, such as speaking with less intelligence than the prodigal amounts always on the tip of his tongue. "Constraint," to put it in our terms—what Machiavelli and Gracian called "prudence"—was the most visible form of strategy in Debord's war with the spectacle. On the other hand, his constant drinking appears to be based on another strategy, the strategy of attaining the most pleasure possible (although this pride at being a good guest at the banquet of life obviously masked a painful addiction). Debord drank like a soldier and then glorified his tragic flaw in writing:

> The hours and their shifting conditions almost always have a determining role in the necessary renewals of the moments of a spree, and each hour brings with it a reasonable preference between all the possibilities that offer themselves.

The portrait that Debord offers of himself in *Panegyric* is of a drunk old vet singing songs sung by Villa's partisans in the Mexican Revolution: "Of that famous Northern Division, only a few of us are left now, still crossing the mountains, finding someone to fight wherever we go." At other moments, however, Debord quotes Archilochus (VIIth Century) who set the example of throwing back drinks and throwing aside his shield and sword. Still, the conditions of daily life in the society of the spectacle were so dismal that war remained a logical, if unrealized, necessity, much the same way it was in Machiavelli's time.

Debord raises the stakes in saying the "unspeakable about the State," as he remarked about Machiavelli in *Society of the Spectacle* by practicing the guile Machiavelli extols in the very lines of *Comments*—the booklet isn't a continuation of *Society of the Spectacle,* rather an unexpected explosion in an elite propaganda war. *Comments* is simultaneously a descriptive mapping of the spectacle's "present *lines of advance,*" and the "practical consequences, still little known, resulting from the rapid deployment of the spectacle during the last twenty years." This tone of supreme confidence seemed designed to let all the mercenaries who conspire for the spectacle know that he, Debord, knew more about them than vice versa.

Readers of *The Prince* will recall Machiavelli's criticisms of the ineffectual and even disloyal mercenary armies—he reportedly dealt with the leading *condottieri* who demanded high pay for questionable security when he was Secretary of the Council of Ten in Florence. The clarity and sweep of Debord's propositions about mercenaries and democracy in *Comments* are reminiscent of Machiavelli, with whom he shared a strategic way of thinking. It's interesting to note that the Greek concept of strategy was an expansive science that encompassed many other sciences, because both Machiavelli and Debord looked for lessons from Greece. Although Machiavelli shared with Debord the "historical consciousness issuing from the democratic communities" of Antiquity, Debord would have reveled in the wine-soaked Renaissance version of democracy that Machiavelli found so disorderly and fragile (Debord, to be sure, would've pressed for more, much more democracy and festivity). Even if Debord insists that he doesn't write like a classical author, he only *reasons* like one, here in *Comments,* more so than elsewhere, Debord uses words like "agora," denoting a quest for ideological legitimacy in the tradition of Antiquity. The pithy formulation "We believe we know that history appeared in Greece at the same time as democracy. We can verify their simultaneous disappearance" ties his historical duty to democracy, but he's no dupe of the spectacular version. Debord's vision of democracy was based on open assemblies, the *ecclesia,* where debate was carried out in public by delegates who were revocable by the base at any time.

Comments and its companion, *Panegyric,* are Debord's theocratical and autobiographical summing up. The spectacle as the "autocratic reign of the market economy which had acceded to an irresponsible sovereignty, and the totality of new tech-niques of government which accompanied this reign" has synthesized its diffuse and concentrated forms (outlined in *Society of the Spectacle*) into the "integrated specta-cle." In 1988, when Debord was writing, Mitterand was still the President of France—his socialist party having ruled since 1981, often in cohabitation with the right. Gorbachev became General Secretary of the Communist Party in 1985, and by 1988 was pulling troops out of Afghanistan like the Romans out of Jugurtha. Rushdie's *The Satanic Verses* hit the stands to charges of blasphemy. Senior PLO offi-cial Abu Jihad and two bodyguards were assassinated in Tunis. Iraq was using poison gas produced with German assistance against the Kurds. A fighter plane from a U.S. aircraft carrier in the Persian Gulf mistook Iran Air A300 Airbus for the enemy and shot it down. Columbia angered the U.S. when it released Medellin cartel leader Jorge Luis Ochoa, who was wanted on wholesale cocaine charges. The chlorofluro-carbon agreement in Montreal. These were the type of diverse events that Debord used to theorize the integrated spectacle, which he characterized by 1) incessant tech-nological innovation; 2) fusion of state and economy; 3) unanswerable lies; 4) the perpetual present; 4) generalized secrecy.

So it is that thousands of plots in favor of the established order tangle and clash almost everywhere, as the overlap of secret networks and secret issues or activities grows ever more dense along with their rapid integration into every sector of eco-nomics, politics and culture. In all areas of social life the degree of intermingling in surveillance, disinformation and security activities gets greater and greater. The general plot having thickened so much that it's almost out in the open that each part of it now interferes with, or worries, the others. All these professional con-spirators are spying on each other without really knowing why; they're colliding by chance and yet not identifying each other with any certainty. Who is observing whom? On whose behalf, apparently? And actually? The real influences remain hidden, and the ultimate aims can only be seen with great difficulty and almost never understood. So that while no one can say he is not being tricked or manip-ulated, it's only in rare instances that the manipulator himself can know if he is a winner. And in any case, to be on the winning side of manipulation does not mean that one has chosen the right strategic perspective. Tactical successes can thus lead great powers down dangerous roads.

According to Debord, the integrated spectacle keeps as its highest ambition the trans-formation of "secret agents into revolutionaries, and revolutionaries into secret agents." Statements like these give the entire work the allure of secrecy by implying that the meaning is only accessible to revolutionaries and agents of the spectacle. The growth crisis in the secret services, "the natural product of the concentration of capital, production and distribution," means that everyone—journalists, historians and novelists—have turned into spies who silence whatever spectacular discourse "finds inconvenient." Whereas the Dada boxer Arthur Craven envisioned a dystopic future when everyone was an artist, Debord had lived to see the day when everyone was a spy. There were so many spies that they were like Keystone Cops in episodes like the French disaster with Greenpeace in Aukland, although this incident was perhaps designed to *appear* inept.

The Greenpeace ship Rainbow Warrior

These arms merchants, statesmen, secret agents and revolutionaries have all disabused themselves of any respect for legality—the mafia is the model for all business, although this doesn't justify the childish fetish for secrecy among those who have nothing to hide. Conditions created by the diffuse and then integrated spectacle favored these mafia-style organizations. Previously, the suppression of witness testimony to neutralize the police and justice system enabled the mafia to rule in the secret sphere of protection rackets and other defensive tactics. But the resignation of the citizenry, the loss of logic and the "progress of venality and cowardice" have enabled the mafia to go on the offensive—first with the booze racket, then with TV, cinema, publishing, movies, etc. The "laws sleep" as the mafia continues to develop new forms of protection and dependence based on agreements of distribution that, according to Debord, "decide everything."

The drug-dealing dictator of Panama was Debord's model of the new Prince. As Debord was writing *Comments,* Noriega was indicted by federal grand juries in Tampa and Miami on charges of accepting bribes from drug traffickers. When the President of Panama tried to oust Noriega as the head of the National Guard, the

President was dismissed by the National Assembly. Noriega's opponents, including the U.S., waged war with strikes and sanctions. On advice from his chief security advisor, a former Mossad officer, Noriega had worked for many years with the C.I.A. against Cuba and informed the U.S. about his drug-trafficking—when the U.S. turned against him, Noriega had the audacity to look to Castro for support.

For his more sympathetic readers, Debord opens *Comments* with an intriguing quote from Sun Tzu, the author of the unsurpassable VIth Century text *The Art of War* whose aphoristic style was certainly close to Debord's heart:

However desperate the situation and circumstances, don't despair. When there is everything to fear, be unafraid. When surrounded by dangers, fear none of them. When without resources, depend on resourcefulness. When surprised, take the enemy itself by surprise.

Manuel Noriega

Sun Tzu's concept of "pure war," whereby the enemy is subdued without fighting any battles, corresponds precisely to the way the spectacle arrived. Therefore it's somewhat surprising that Debord would open his last big attack on the society of the spectacle with these aggressive words by Sun Tzu, who is a more moderate strategist than Clausewitz. One of the messages in *Comments* is that the spectacular occupation and domination of life has been perfected, but it's a fragile perfection that Debord interprets dialectically as presenting revolutionaries with revolutionary conditions. Skipping ahead to the bitter end of the book, to the coda, we find Debord discussing what it means to *work vainly*, which could be interpreted as working without success (as a waste of time and effort); or to *work vainly* in the sense of not being rewarded for work because it wasn't approved (still a waste of time, but the work could nonetheless be good). So even in *Comments*, which purports to realistically describe "what is," Debord reveals his hand in the unity of his opening and closing thoughts by admitting that he chose sides a long time ago— the side facing a desperate situation in which he was likely to work vainly.

In chapter V of *Panegyric,* Debord glorifies his association with people who were spied-on by the police, and gives his first hand account of the national traits of the enemy:

> ... the English police seemed the most suspicious and the most polite, the French police the most dangerously trained in historical interpretation, the Italian police the most cynical, the Belgian police the most rustic, the German police the most arrogant, while it was the Spanish police who proved themselves the most incapable.

Indeed, Debord's police records and files with secret agencies would certainly expand the picture we have of Debord, much the same way Villon's biographers have patched his life together using his *Testament* and police records. Debord liked to mix it up and break the rules in the process, including the rules of the game of war. The spectacle posed a spectrum of obstacles that forced people into constraints, into the "reasonable options" favored by domination. But those, like Debord, who resisted servitude and took risks, found themselves in wartime conditions. This life during wartime doesn't just correspond to an event like May '68, when numerous dispersed bands grouped into heavy units and, operating independently, managed to sack Paris. Debord's resistance included the cultivation of his memory, personality, tastes, logic, vocabulary, syntax, etc.; and, paradoxically, his own tactical constraints that might be rationalized by the freedom inherent in his resistance.

Debord restates the psychological effects of the society of the spectacle in *Comments,* noting the self-denial required to attain status, and the way authentic experience continues to vanish. The allure of the Absolute Knowledge of computers and the act of succumbing to the irrational authority of prestigious celebrities are the drugs of the spectacle that preclude all logic.

> At the level of techniques, when images constructed and chosen by someone else have become the principal connection of the individual to the world that was previously seen by the individual himself everywhere he went, one can't fail to notice that images uphold and withstand everything because inside these images one can juxtapose anything without contradiction. The flux of images carries everything, and equally it's someone else who governs this simplified resumé of the sensible world. Someone else chose this flow, and also the rhythm of what should appear— like a perpetual, arbitrary surprise—without wanting to allow any time for reflection, and completely independently of what the spectator can understand or think about it. The psychological root of the general adhesion to what's there, the adhesion that is itself ipso facto of sufficient value, is found in this concrete experience of permanent submission.

Tiananmen Square, Beijing, 1989

Debord never pretended to have an ultimate strategy, but it's fair to say that he argued with great moral force for the value of a fully lived life over the zombie-like existence generated by the spectacle. This and other latent social conflicts were to be exploited, as were the glaring contradictions in the political economy. At certain times in his life, such as when de Gaulle came to power, Debord was ready for a civil war in the streets of Paris. But he understood that the population was at the center of the struggle, that there was little he and his comrades could do on their own, which is why they used a cultural strategy of creating propaganda as a donation to a project that was much bigger than the Situationist International. It should be acknowledged that Debord's later works, while accessible on the surface to any competent reader, were too elitist in tone to appeal to a mass audience. There were no armies of urban paupers to whom he could offer more radical strategies, such as the forgotten project of council communism (nor is there any explicit mention of "constructing situations" in *Comments*).

As for the last generation of revolutionaries, the ones that succeeded Debord, they had been negated by a generalized lack of trust that Debord illustrates in chapter XXVII by a long quote from Thucydides on political parties foundering on rumors and suspicions, always tending toward oligarchy. History might come back into play, but it's more likely to come back in the form of a farce staged by the agents of surveillance and provocation who have become quite adept in creating poles of negation. The Moro affair, the bombings by militants "at the service of the established order right from the start, even though he may have had quite the opposite intention," and the historic role of the P2 Masonic lodge in Italy—these were all on Debord's mind when he delineated the progression often experienced by the partisans of armed struggle: misguided, provoked, infiltrated, manipulated, taken over, subverted.

In strategic terms there seemed to be little room for revolutionaries to maneuver, but the same quote by Thucydides makes the point that it's easy to overestimate the strength of a formidable foe. And in *Panegyric* Debord gives an example from Herodotus' account of Leonidas, King of Sparta, holding the Thermopylae pass against the invading Persian army under Xerxes in 480 B.C. When outflanked, Leonidas' three hundred troops held on for two days, covering the retreat of the Greek fleet. Debord mentions the story of Loenidas' seer Megistias, who foresaw the defeat but remained with his king. At historic moments, Debord implies, one must act despite the odds. On the other hand, the short-sighted orders by Lord Raglan to the Light Brigade which Debord quotes in *Panegyric,* illustrate how disastrous this blind courage can be. This was during the Crimean War (1853–6), in which Turkey, Britain and France eventually captured the port of Balaclava and later handed Russia a humiliating defeat.

In the last chapter of *Panegyric,* and throughout *Comments,* Debord expressed his disgust for the progress of "decadence" in the service of the empire of servitude. The term "decadence" is a major motif of Nietzsche's autobiographical *Ecce Homo,* which, like *Panegyric,* is basically a self-righteous diatribe. For Nietzsche the word decadence signified degeneration and disease. At one point decadence is the relapse Nietzsche experiences in his long years of convalescence, at another point it's an instinct that contains its opposite—the anti-decadence of a clean mind. Perhaps Debord chose the term because it is one of Nietzsche's more celebrated plagiarisms, this time of Paul Bourget's "Theory of Decadance" chapter in *Essais de psychologie.* Of course, Nietzsche added a few wrinkles to Bourget's theory by hailing Socrates as a decadent who nonetheless symbolized integration in a period of disintegration. For Debord, the disease of decadence now manifested itself in symptoms like terrorism, disinformation, assassinations, etc. (On a practical level, Debord suggests, one should recognize the nuances between "fallacious," "deceptive," "impostrous," "inveigling," "insidious," "captious.") Debord had a deep disgust for the way masters ruled their ignorant servants, and he felt free to hail resistance to domination as a Renaissance-style virtue. The revolutionary perspective was the only logical and mentally healthy perspective for Debord, although he would, like Nietzsche, freely admit that he was decadent.

The "servitude" created by this generalized decadence echoes Etienne de La Boetie's celebrated *Discourse on Voluntary Servitude* (1577), a text sprinkled with classical examples and more contemporaneous historical examples that drew on the experience of Huguenot Protestants in XVIth Century France, such as the St. Bartholomew's Day massacre of Calvinists in Paris by Catholics in 1572. La Boetie's arguments are worth recalling here, especially the central argument that people tend to enslave themselves, and that tyrants fall, not from violent action, but when the people withdraw their support. Even among those raised in subjection, La Boetie contends, even among those trained to adore rulers, there will always be those who refuse to submit because liberty is the natural condition of the people. For La Boetie, change is dependent on the negation of the vast networks of corrupted people who have an interest in maintaining tyranny: "When they lose their liberty through deceit they are not so often betrayed by others as misled by themselves."

Debord's *Comments* echoes La Boetie as it traces the base of generalized decadence to the ignorance of spectators who put up with everything from art frauds to pollution to the entire commodity-driven logic of the spectacle. Conflicts and scandals come and go without much notice: "Secrecy dominates the world, foremost as the secret of domination." Historical falsification is a fact of life that Debord illustrates by the way secret services use terrorists, but also by the way the economy threatens human survival while science gives its rubber stamp to the process. Perhaps nothing irks Debord so much, and nothing signifies the decadence of these spectacular times as much as the eradication of historical knowledge. According to Debord, even knowledge of art history is required to know what's authentic and what's possible. What is history? Ask the poet:

> The memorable, the totality of events whose consequences manifest themselves for a long time. Likewise historical knowledge should endure and aid in understanding, at least partially, the events to come: "an everlasting possession," according to Thucydides. Hence history was the measure of real novelty; and it's now in the interest of those who sell novelty at any price to make the means of measuring it disappear.

Debord considered his grasp of historical and strategic knowledge to be his most valuable asset, so it's predictable that he concludes *Comments* from a historic-strategic perspective. Debord reminds the reader of Clausewitz' distinction between *tactics* (the use of force to win combat) and *strategy* (the use of victories to attain the goals of war). Napoleon Bonaparte's advantage was that he could understand diverse maneuvers from the perspective of battles he figured he'd won in advance, as if on the first assault. Incidentally, it's probable that Napoleon had read Sun Tzu, the author of lines such as "Thus a victorious army wins its victories before seeking battle." Recall Napoleon's use of troops who lived off the land and fired independently in their wide columns to defeat the Austrians and Russians at Austerlitz, to defeat the Prussians at Jena and Russians at Friedland in a series of campaigns from 1805–7; and keep in mind Napoleon's coup d'etat of Brumaire (November 1799) when his cohort Emmanuel-Joseph Sieyes (1748–1836) persuaded the legislative councils to move from Paris to St. Cloud on the pretext of a terrorist plot. Once the councils arrived in St. Cloud, they realized on 19 Brumaire (November 10) that Sieyes was actually the one doing the plotting and a coup had taken place in the capital. Napoleon eventually agreed to speak to the councils, and when he was shouted down and then attacked, his brother Lucien told his troops that deputies were trying to assassinate their general. The hall was cleared, and the remnants of the legislative councils agreed to replace the Directory (the five directors separated from legislative councils who ruled during the last four years of the French Revolution) with a provisional government of three consuls, two of whom were Napoleon and Sieyes. The French population was indifferent to the event because it didn't understand the significance of what had happened. During his Consulate, Napoleon centralized authority by instituting prefects and unifying the civil code that bore his name. No surprise then that he crowned himself Emperor in 1804 and established an imperial nobility. Like Napoleon, the powers of spectacular domination will soon disabuse themselves of any remaining scruples and false strategies. Once these secret powers see just how far they've come and recalibrate how far they can go, they'll go on the offensive. Perhaps the spectacle will find a way to over-extend itself the way Napoleon invaded Spain in 1808 and Russia in 1812, but don't bet on it. Debord predicts that the forces in service of domination will be relieved of command, and this will probably happen without anyone noticing. This "relief" (*rèleve,* which Imrie translates as "changeover") could be ominous for the spectators who think that they're still living in a world that was eliminated many years ago. The fate of the surplus populations around the world seems to be new forms of abject misery, such as those experienced by the skinbags who serve machines or the sweatshop workers whose extended families depend on them not to starve.

Chapter Thirty

This "relief" that Debord predicted in 1988 was arguably well underway by 1989—the uprisings in Eastern Europe led to Yeltsin's victory in the Russian Parliament, the fall of communism in Poland, Czechoslovakia's Velvet Revolution and the overthrow of the Romanian dictator, Ceausescu. Deng Xiaoping resigned his last political post on November 9; and in 1991, Jiang Qing—Mao's widow and the head of the Gang of Four—committed suicide. Debord's Prince, Manuel Noriega, was ousted by elections in Panama in 1989, but he ignored the results and managed to retain power for a moment with an attempted military coup. By 1990, German unification was a reality, and England's conservative Prime Minister Margaret Thatcher was forced to give up command of the ship of state. Iraq's military dictator was duped by the United States into thinking he could invade Kuwait, which led to the Gulf War's sanitation of incredible atrocities using the techniques of the spectacle, including the new "virtual reality" of "smart bombs." United States cold warriors would like think their display of military force engendered the suspension of "communist" rule in Russia, but it's evident to any honest observer that the counter-revolutionary system of the U.S.S.R. simply decomposed in 1991. Voters in Bosnia-Herzegovina chose independence from Yugoslavia in 1992, precipitating the siege of Sarajevo and other hostilities. The following year, scandal finally reached former Italian Prime Minister Giulio Andreotti.

In his last book, *"This bad reputation..."* (Gallimard, 1993), Debord describes these recent events:

Guy Debord

Ubu is king again in Poland in the dynasty of Walesa; the global coalition against Iraq and its devastating non-result; the Russian republics and the development of all their civil wars with the democracy of prevaricators, under Yeltsin; the concentration camps of Serbia, and the ethnic negotiations of Sarajevo that continue during extermination despite the courageous mediation of Europe; the humanity-media landing in Mogadishu that was so laughable; the victory of the right-wing state against Escobar in Columbia, as well as the cleansing accomplished by "deathsquads"; across the sub-continent the formal abolition of apartheid and the massacres of Blacks in South Africa; the Algeria that they'd like to pass off as the only country where the economy doesn't function at all, and perhaps because of Islam; the Italy of Clean Hands that finally established the proof of Andreotti's innocence. Everywhere speculation has, in the end, become the sovereign aspect of all property. It auto-regulates itself, more or less according to the local preponderances around the Stock Markets, States, Mafia: all federated in a sort of democracy of the elites of speculation. The rest is misery. Everywhere, excess Simulation has exploded like Chernobyl, and everywhere death spreads as fast and massively as disorder. Nothing works anymore, and nothing is believed anymore.

Debord doesn't really develop the theme of speculation beyond this. He leaves it to others to develop a critique of this technique that's applied equally to finance and the celebrity rumor mill. The capitalized use of "Simulation" is a tip of the pencil to

Baudrillard, the former teacher's assistant of Lefebvre and major "dissident" social critic who had a pro-situ phase in his thirties when he edited the journal *Utopia*. Perhaps, Debord felt that he had outshined his predecessor Lefebvre, who died in 1991, and that he could afford to recognize the intelligence in Baudrillard's analysis of the orders of simulation without diminishing his own bad reputation. Viewing himself as the last true sovereign of the extreme left, Debord probably thought that he was a diamond shining in the night, and that the others were obscured in darkness. As for rivals, he honestly felt he had none. It's interesting to look at the concept of speculation in relation to academic studies of Debord, such as Sadie Plant's *The Most Radical Gesture: The Situationist International in a Postmodern Age,* which pits Debord against Baudrillard:

> But although Baudrillard's hyperreality seems to be waiting just around Debord's last corner as an ineluctable horizon at which the spectacle will one day meets its own image, there is still a sense in which Debord refuses to follow Baudrillard to the point at which the social world spirals off into a free-floating chaos of meaningless flux. (pp.174–175)

Published in 1992, Plant obviously hadn't read the above quote in Debord's 1993 *"This bad reputation...,"* that includes the line "excess simulation has exploded like Chernobyl..." so she couldn't really know how much credence Debord gave to Baudrillard. And nowhere in *Comments* (the work Plant discusses here to demonstrate the conflicts between the two theorists) does Debord prescribe any meaningful activity for anyone, as Plant implies. In *Situationist International,* Baudrillard gets away with only one mention, that being the mild insult "pro-Chinese." For all we really know, Debord might've been flattered in the way that Baudrillard followed some of Debord's interests in his youth, and Debord appears to agree here with the theory of simulation created by Baudrillard when he was a more mature theorist. Debord certainly didn't consider Baudrillard a "rival" as Plant portrays it, even if Baudrillard encouraged this notion by positing the eclipse of the spectacle by his conception of "obscenity."

In a similar vein, in *"This bad reputation..."* Debord explicitly dates the spectacle to the 20s, which calls into question Thomas Richards' claim in *The Commodity Culture of Victorian England: Advertising and Spectacle 1851–1914* that he takes "up the analysis where Debord leaves it off." Like the Telos roundtable discussion of Debord that always turned back to Adorno, Richards doesn't write about the spectacle so much as its pre-history in the historical minutia of Victorian commerce. Richards' book isn't without merit, but it doesn't extend Debord's analysis as the author claims.

The story of how Debord came to publish *"This bad reputation..."* with Gallimard is of interest because in his youth he insisted that this prestigious publishing house would never buy the rights to any of his books. Not that Debord would ever admit to having been motivated by anything other than his whims, the flurry of publishing with Éditions Gerard Lebovici—*Comments* in 1988, *Panegyric* in 1989, the critical edition of *In Girum...* and Alice Becker-Ho's *Princes of Jargon* in 1990—was probably inspired, at least in part, by the illness (and ultimately the death) of Floriana Lebovici. While they remained friends, Debord's relations with Floriana

were more strictly cordial than had been the case with her deceased husband. It appears that she was still full of good will for Debord—she didn't just publish Debord, she used the same lead type that was used to print the first edition of Joyce's *Ulysses* on Debord's *Panegyric*. Her obituary reports that she was a friendly woman whose book boutique on ritzy rue St. Sulpice kept short hours, and whose tastes led her to publish Dada poets like Arthur Craven, Clement Pansaers, the Spanish novelist Ramon Gomez de la Serna, as well as Roger Lewinter, Mezioud Ouldamer, and Karl Kraus in beautiful editions. Debord didn't like the next generation of Lebovicis, namely Lorenzo, who now has nothing to do with Debord's work at the renamed Éditions Ivrea.

Bill Clinton and Boris Yeltsin

Debord eventually bought up the remaining stock of his books from his old publisher when he signed with Gallimard. But before the formal split, Debord tried to have Gérard Lebovici's former notary, Gérard Voitey, take over the operation of Éditions Gérard Lebovici.

The portrait of Voitey painted by the Parisian press is of a self-made man, a former rock drummer who wound up in publishing due to his love of books. Gérard Voitey would commit suicide a few days after Debord, and although no one knows if he went to the grave to bury some secret, the best explanations of this event seem to be totally unrelated: Voitey was bankrupt. As Jean Jacques Pauvert said of Voitey, no one in French publishing could figure out what Voitey was doing with his various publishing ventures: "He was completely atypical and operated with total incoherence. I didn't understand anything, and I didn't know what cause he served." This same Pauvert, the wise old man of the industry, would facilitate Debord's deals with Gallimard and Éditions Les Belles Lettres. Beginning in 1992, Gallimard began issuing Debord's major works—*Society of the Spectacle, Comments on the Society of the Spectacle* together with *Preface to the Fourth Italian Edition of Society of the Spectacle,* followed by *Panegyric, Considerations on the Assassination of Gerard Lebovici,* and his *Complete Cinematic Works.* The classicist in Debord must've appreciated being published by Belles Lettres because this house publishes the famous bilingual Collection Budé of all the Greek and Latin classics. Belles Lettres published the Debord-Jorn collaboration *Memoires* in a fine edition, and the essay "The Decline and Fall of the Spectacle-Commodity Economy" as a small pamphlet in large type. Debord was well aware that his writing wouldn't be judged simply by what it said, but also by how it appeared. Happy to move into the pantheon of Gallimard and Belles Lettres writers, Debord enjoyed a little of the bittersweet satisfaction from his growing reputation as a classical stylist by displaying his achievements via big houses that had better distribution networks than his previous publisher. Given his pride, it's not too farfetched to assume that he wanted to provide for his wife as well. His writing days were almost over—in 1990, he was diagnosed with peripheral neuritis, a terminal condition found in alcoholics: the nerve ends of his face, hands and feet were burning away.

The only real portrait we have of Debord in these last years is from Merri Jolivet, an elderly, very successful painter whose handicap and style prompts comparisons with Toulouse-Lautrec. According to the account Jolivet published in *Liberation* following Debord's suicide, Debord introduced himself to the painter in a wine bistro in the fourteenth district, and they saw one another frequently from 1990 to 1991. Jolivet describes the way Debord would spend the entire day preparing dinners for them and their wives in his rue de Bac apartment; how Debord never phoned, but addressed invitations by mail. Jolivet goes on to describe the glass-enclosed bookcase in Debord's office where all the books he loved were kept, and how Debord gave him a copy of *Memoires* in the original sandpaper edition. They met day-to-day in the bistros and bars, Alice usually at Guy's side. A taste for provocation still with him, Debord reportedly exchanged "the worst insanities" with Jolivet in front of police headquarters one day.

He didn't have a television and he was curious about everything. He spoke with the same elegance that he demonstrated in his writing. His speech was an extremely precise, never banal. One had the impression of hearing him think before you. His conversation was of a rare quality. Then, when we were in the street, he exercised his talents of observation on everything—publicity, urban decor, architecture, etc. He never missed an occasion to exercise his critical spirit, even if it was at four in morning after a very wet evening, or at noon at lunch. He had marvelous control of the effects of wine. And if we happened to often change cafes, it was also because of the variable quality of wine.

He never made an outpouring of emotion. He was a warm, refined aristocrat. I never knew him to make the slightest vulgarity, the slightest triviality, and with him, I made a grand voyage in one place during this period.

Jolivet learned of Debord's move to Champot, in the Auvergne, by a letter "returned to sender." It must've been a difficult time for Debord. His tranquility had been tested by anxiety in the streets of Arles, where (according to Michel Prigent, one of his English translators who had visited him there in the Eighties) Debord reportedly drank more whiskey per month than the whole rest of the city. The last stop would be Champot. He must've been a little bored in the harsh, desolate farm where he spent most of his time. High in the mountains in three stone buildings behind high stone walls, he manned the fort and commanded the wind and the trees in eternal struggle, only occasionally going out to the local cafe. He had time to do a little writing, and it figures that he would settle a few scores with his last booklet.

The title *"This bad reputation...,"* is a quote from a passage by Gorgias de Leontium (483–375 BC), the Greek rhetorician and sophist: "...I tried to nullify the injustice of this bad reputation and the ignorance of opinions." Gorgias was a proponent of democracy who supplemented the relativism of Protagoras with rationalistic agnosticism. His prose style influenced Isocrates and Thucydides—Vico hailed him as the grandfather of rhythmic prose. His three propositions (anything is not real; if anything were real, it would still be unknowable; if anything were knowable, it would be inexpressible) might've struck a chord of wisdom for Debord at this stage in his life.

The way Debord quotes his detractors at such length in this booklet, and by his glorification of his manipulations in his posthumous *Contracts,* leads one to believe that he felt honored to have his bad reputation. But Jolivet lets on that the criticisms, and perhaps even more so the corrupt praise, did get under his skin. If he could help it, however, the public would only see his implacable mask. In *"This bad reputation..."* Debord wants us to understand that he was a determined individual; determined to live freely above all else.

I understand my times very well. To never work requires great talents. Happily, I had them. I never had any apparent need to work even though I wasn't rich to begin with. I never had the slightest inclination to employ myself in one of the arts in which I was perhaps more capable than others, consenting only one time to take

the least consideration for the actual tastes of the public to the end of accumulat-
ing a surplus. My personal vision of the world didn't excuse such practice with
money, except to protect my complete independence; and thus without engaging
me in anything in exchange. The epoch where everything dissolved greatly facilitated my game in this regard. The refusal of "work" could be incomprehensible and
held against me. I didn't pretend to embellish this attitude by some ethical justification. I simply wanted to do what I like the most. In fact, I sought to know, during my life, a good number of poetic situations, and also the satisfaction of a few
of my vices, ancillary but important. Power didn't figure into my life. I love freedom, but surely not money. As the other remarked: "Money wasn't a desire of
childhood."

In *"This bad reputation..."* Debord displays some of his literary tastes. Kafka, for
example, revealed "a large part of the sinister spirit of this century." But it was Jarry,
Debord insists, who disclosed much more of the XXth Century with the putschists
of King Ubu, which is a surprising point for Debord to make because he hadn't been
a partisan of the project of imaginary solutions when Jorn was obsessed with Jarry.
Debord was also partial to Francis Ryck,* an idiosyncratic French crime-spy novelist, and mentions a Ryck title that featured a character who seemed paranoid to the
point of being slightly absurd, but who—it turns out—had good reason to fear the
State. Debord was more likely to condemn what the mass of spectators applaud, so
it's interesting to see what sort of genius he loved. These rare remarks about literature shouldn't, however, be misconstrued as putting great value on literary enterprise—strategists, such as Debord himself, were the most precious commodity given
the disastrous state of affairs of spectacular democracy. But Debord put leisure too
far above labor to be worth very much: he was happy to simply display talents that
were far superior to his "position" in society. Any sort of status other than what he'd
managed to attain would've been too tiresome to get and to keep.

Debord is predictably critical of the Pompidou Center exhibit on the Situationists
that traveled to Institutes of Contemporary Art in London and Boston in the late
Eighties. The exhibit "concentrated" the history of the S.I. in its spectacular pre-'62
phase in a Stalinesque way, according to Debord; although, viewed dialectically, this
might've been advantageous, because hidden aspects of the history left enough room
for those learning of the S.I. for the first time to form a second opinion. I'd like to
note here that while Debord enjoyed some rock 'n' roll and jazz, his strongest taste in

---

* This Ryck novel, *Le compagnon indésirable,* contains the passage: "Why don't you
write what you know, confide it to a notary and tell him to divulge it if anything happens to you..."

music was for classical French composers such as Michel Corrette, Francois Couperin, Delalande, etc. I mention this because of the way the S.I. has been associated with punk following the publication of Griel Marcus' *Lipstick Traces* in 1989. It's worth recalling that even Marcus came around to the conclusion that there's nothing revolutionary about punk nightclub acts. And if Debord and the S.I. were anything, they were revolutionary. Vaneigem was partial to the improvisation of jazz, but I think it's fair to say that every style of music has as much subversive potential as any other if the content of the lyrics is revolutionary. The few times that Debord collaborated in the composition of songs—with the C.M.D.O. in 1968 and with the Spanish autonomists in the late Seventies and early Eighties—pop tunes were usually used so that the songs could be readily sung. Debord and the Situationists coined the term "masperisation" to refer to falsifications and distortions of Situationist texts and history. The insult "masperisateur" (after the editor Maspero who butchered key documents from May '68) applies to much of the commentary generated around Debord's death. Perhaps another word needs to be created to describe the academics and critics who create false conflicts and affinities to sustain their careers.

Debord liked to boast that *Society of the Spectacle*, which appeared exactly a century after the first volume of Marx's *Capital*, provided an explanation of the existing world right down to its core, but he also conceded in *"This bad reputation...,"* that it may have only appeared to do so. The real merit of *Society of the Spectacle*, as he saw it, was its sustainable aspect—events twenty, even thirty years after it was written have made it more relevant than ever. Reality continues to change, but this change is experienced as an illusion due to the consumption of homogeneous commodity-spectacles. The behavior of each individual is infected by the spectacle—all sensations and memory are sifted through the spectacle by the way time is transformed into the representation of artificial time. In 1968, Debord called for self-management as the alternative to the spectacle; since then, the spectacle spread to the point that all he could do was go against the grain, be contrary to scare off his detractors (and most everyone else if he could), minimize his obligations and be sophisticated. Debord was too wise to be upset by events that he couldn't control, and he seemed to get a sense of serenity from the way the rich always manage to fail at life.

Intelligence was the foundation of Debord's life, and that intelligence prepared him for adversity. Drinking was his Achilles' heel, and even if he degraded himself by drink, he took pride in drinking the way, say, a W.C. Fields would. The master of every situation, he would master death by sentencing himself to it when the moment was right; when he could effectively surround himself with the trappings that would make his influence and power felt as much as possible. Brigitte Cornand, a cinematographer who had made a film on Surrealism that cited Debord, wrote Debord that her forthcoming film *This Situation Must Change* would divert Debord (although she seemed to be referring more to the use of excerpts from films by Gil Wolman and Rene Vienet and from the text of Debord's film *In Girum Imus Nocte et Consumimur Igni* than "diversion" properly speaking). Debord liked Cornand's film, and through a friend, met with her to propose a project. Canal + ("channel plus"), one of France's racier television stations, agreed to finance the 1.2 million franc, anti-television film, setting the stage for Debord's final, explosive *folie de grandeur.*

Debord gave Cornand a list of film and television clips to find—prison workers on the job, excerpts from *Scarface,* student protests in Mexico City in 1968, Chernobyl, the savage attack on a Somali woman by a mob as American soldiers watched. She and her cameraman spent two weeks in Champot in June 1994, and came back for a few days to make final cuts. (Debord reportedly took a long trip to Venice in the meanwhile.) Cornand didn't perceive how ill he was even though the film contained boards about cancer and scenes of desolation: "The film is a testament, right down to the choice of music. Lino Leonardi played the music that he created for the *Testament of Francois Villon.* And I didn't see anything, I didn't understand anything." A little while before his suicide, Debord sent Cornand a letter that contains this passage:

> The illness peripheral neuritis, noticed in Fall 1990. At first almost imperceptible, but progressive. It only became really painful after the end of November 1994.
>
> As with all incurable illness, one wins a lot by not seeking to, nor accepting to cure oneself. It's the opposite of an illness that can be contracted by a regrettable lack of prudence. On the contrary, it requires the loyal obstinacy of an entire life.

The leopard dies with his spots, as Debord wrote in *Panegyric.* He never moderated his passion for booze. All or nothing—that was Debord's style. His passions and ambitions had been the vehicles of self-realization, and maintaining them was the only way he could maintain his self-respect. Life had to be lived to its fullest, which is to say with pleasure and adventure, not pain, emptiness, hopelessness. At sixtytwo, a few weeks shy of his sixty-third birthday, Guy Debord shot himself in the heart. It was Wednesday November 30, 1994, the day before world AIDS day, which meant that he characteristically (some say "perversely") timed his death to coincide with a sort of global funeral. Perhaps more so than any radical of his time, Debord remained faithful to the methods and dreams of his youth. What began with the grandiose auto-destruction of poetry, led to the auto-terrorism of his attempted suicide-by-asphyxiation in his early twenties. There was the auto-dissolution of the S.I. with historical pomp, and the dramatic circumstances that led to the auto-censorship of his films. Finally, his auto-assassination with a gun at the height of his glory, which invites the rereading of passages in *"This bad reputation..."* where he states that he would never kill himself because of the calumnies leveled against him. Death was the remedy to his disease, one that he didn't fear and eventually administered to himself. This voluntary death, to paraphrase Montaigne, depends on one's own will and is perhaps the best way to go.

In November, not long before his death, Death sent the following letter to his friend, the poet Ricardo Paseyro:

At last I found the reference in the honest book by Byron. I'll cite the passage for you: "Cervantes and Quevedo both knew Alonso Alvarez de Soria, the Francois Villon of the Seville area. (...) The last poem by Alvarez was written shortly before his death by the same disease that dispatched Pero Vasquez:

They've given me three hours to live
Those who want to escort me to death
And since the route is long
They insist we leave early...
Ah! the time remaining is short:
He who owes so much can never pay very much.

Early on, Debord realized that life, like art, had to be contested to be fully realized, and in his first masterpiece, the film *Howling in Favor of Sade,* Debord had already remarked that, "The perfection of suicide is in ambiguity." And again in *Comments,* he stated that "We live and die at the confluence of a great number of mysteries." These statements would be verified by the events that followed his suicide. Sometime on the night and early morning of Friday–Saturday, December 2–3, Gérard Voitey—"The Notary," as he was called in the publishing world—shot himself in the head with a P.38 pistol. He was in his car near a lake in Gouvieux, not far from Chantilly. It was first reported that he had been in an auto accident, but the police quickly amended this to say that Voitey was found with the gun in hand and a note indicating that he intended to kill himself. Then it was reported that there was no suicide note. The most troubling aspect of his death was the revelation that a former right wing "negationist" had been appointed to a high post in Voitey's Éditions Quai Voltaire, although colleagues report that Voitey had had no idea about this aspect of the employees' past. Speculation on the Left Bank had it that Voitey had been commissioned by Gérard Lebovici when he was his notary to reveal some secret about Debord upon his death.

Then, on Sunday December 4, Roger Stéphane, a well-known writer-adventurer and member of Combat in the resistance, committed suicide in his apartment. He was the son of a Jewish banker who became known as "Capitaine Stéphane" for leading the commandos who liberated the Hotel de Ville of Paris in the summer of 1944. Co-founder of a newspaper, the author of numerous books on himself, Stendhal and Montaigne (and the editor of selections from Retz' *Memoires*) he became known for his television interviews with his famous friends. He was critical of France's torture and genocide in Vietnam and Algeria, and at one point Francois Mitterrand (then Interior Minister) wanted to imprison him. Stéphane later broke the news about Mitterand's involvement with the Vichy regime in an interview with the future president. Stéphane had been published by Voitey's Éditions Quai Voltaire and was reportedly acquainted with Debord, but there was no evidence of a suicide pact between any of them. French commentators point to these suicides as acts of protest against the vanity displayed by most public figures and cite the note left by Stéphane as proof—it included this quote from Stendhal: "Everything passed simply and decently, with no trace of affectation on his part."

At the time of his death, circumstances suggested that Debord might've been murdered. Situationist literature was discovered in the home of a person involved in a cop-killing spree and city-wide chase in Paris days before Debord's death. Even more ominously, police in the Loire were convicted of staging a suicide by hanging of a prisoner earlier the same week—this in a climate of deep division between the police and Ministry of Justice in France. The journalists who traveled to Champot were only half-assured by local cops that no police had visited Debord's farmhouse the week before his death: "Even if we had gone up there, we wouldn't tell you." The cops did tell reporters that the body had been cremated, and it was reported that the ashes were later scattered into the Seine in a private ceremony. We can imagine his widow and a small group of friends at the point that parts the river like the bow of a ship—Square du Vert-Galant on île de la Cite, Paris—reading a little of Debord's poetic prose: "The spirit goes on its circuits and the spirit returns. Revolutions go down in history, but history doesn't fill up. The rivers of revolution return from whence they came only to flow again."

Guy Debord, His Art, His Time (the black and white film by Guy Debord that was realized by Brigitte Cornand) was shown on television on Friday January 9, 1995 along with *Society of the Spectacle* and *Refutation of All Judgments...* The new film opens with a round table discussion of *Comments* by Parisian intellectuals to show how idiotic they are (one insists that Napoleon and Louis XIV are the spectacle). Debord periodically inserted this motif into the very sullen second half of the film as if to say that they, the do-nothing intellectuals, were responsible for the acid rain, nuclear accidents and other atrocities. The images are accompanied by music, or the commentary of the original television broadcasts. Pascal, the XVIIth Century French mathematician and physicist known for the clarity of his *Pensees,* was diverted ever so slightly by Lautréamont in the phrases that Debord uses at the beginning of *Guy*

Square du Vert-Galant on île de la Cite, Paris

Debord, His Art, His Time: "I write my thoughts with order, with an unconfused design. If they're true, the first to come will be a consequence of the others. It's the real order." I'll leave it to others to develop the endless glosses suggested by Debord—glosses of Pascal (too biblical for my taste), but also Heraclitus, Xenophon, Pierre Mac Orlan, Calderon, Gracian, Tocqueville, Chateaubriand, Orwell, etc. My goal here has been to cover the basic debts, not to develop an esoteric interpretation of some limited aspect of Debord's life and thought in an academic way.

Debord obviously wants us to look at the order of images he used in the film, at the apparent incoherence of the sequence of images. The film is divided into unequal sections—a short segment on *His Art* and the remainder on *His Time.* Brigitte Cornand filmed the manuscript of *Society of the Spectacle,* a few pages of *Memoires,* and stills from *In Girum...* to illustrate Debord's art and his love of Paris whose form changed "faster than the heart of a mortal." The black and white screen of *Howlings in Favor of Sade* makes an appearance, as do Debord's friends (filmed from photos) who influenced his excess, as if to say that the art of friendship was the highest art that he practiced. These friends—Alice Becker-Ho, Ghislain-Gontran, Jacques Herbute, Ivan Chtcheglov, Gil Wolman, Asger Jorn, Toni Lopez Pintor—would appear again (after the section containing the devastating images of *His Time*) at the bitter end on the film. This high value on friendship and remarks by Cornand that the quality of his life (eating and drinking well) was essential to Debord, lead me to believe that while Debord was obviously a hedonist, he might well have been more of an Epicurean that he let on. In *"This bad reputation..."* he's very explicit, stating that he didn't want to save the world, only to help his friends. This begs the question of the posthumous publications of his *Contracts* with its glorification of manipulation of the Lebovicis, people he had once called friends. If it weren't for the almost maniacal egoism of this apology for manipulation, one could argue that he was playing the moral card of the "honest man," who is honest even about his con jobs.

As for the order of the images, they begin with Christo's draping of Pont Neuf as "art," then shift to long segments on desertification and forest fires. The filming of a girl undergoing faith healing in a mud bath allows Debord to heap scorn on the media professionals who would insist that the truth is revealed by this fragmentary image. Inexplicably, the film jumps from the story of female championship wrestlers in Japan to the search for oil in a park outside Paris. The demolition of numerous high-rise apartment buildings prompts Debord to comment that economics isn't the only science of the enemy to be proven "fallacious." Then the audience is told that the most sinister date in the history of the XXth Century is 1933. And after citing the Kennedy assassination, the single protester who stopped tanks in Tiennamen Square, tank commandos in Moscow behind Yeltsin, election violence in Haiti and Algeria, Debord turns his attention to the historical significance of the illiterate, violent kids in the suburbs of France. All of Europe, Debord then insists, has become Nazi. Chernobyl, AIDS in the blood supply—these are detestable tragedies, yes, but nothing disgusts Debord so much as the neo-Dada that forgets its roots in the poet-boxer Arthur Craven, and only wants to produce a mild shock in national palaces. Debord juxtaposes an interview with Italian Prime Minister Berlesconi with a pompous State funeral where the entire French political class is in attendance. Art then comes in for a comparison with cancer creeping along chic Paris streets. There's a long segment of an Arafat speech at UNESCO and a reportage on ACT UP protests in Paris. A river flood washes away an entire village, then turns into a gleaming virtual reality city. Prison work is held up as the most legitimate heritage of work, and the G-7, with U.S. President Clinton jogging ahead of everyone else, decides everything at its meeting in Naples—a fitting place to end my narrative given Debord's thoughts in *Comments* about mafia-statesmen and the "relief" that will take place without anyone recognizing it.

Not only did Debord want to disclose the truth about his times, he wanted to discover the fundamental truths of time. And even if his conclusions about spectacular time become dated, his basic method of sweeping away all servile fears in order to get a clear perspective should continue to inspire those who embark on similar quests in the future. Debord's extreme love of historical glory (the historicity that is the essence of humanity) is only half-apparent in this film. In this first and last gesture to a large audience, Debord chose not to foreground his Hegelian Marxist roots. Instead he used this anti-television film as a way to strike a posture of mysterious and defiant pride, which he augmented with a touch of bravery by falling on the sword. He wanted to be remembered for his books, films, and adventures, so he shrewdly conceived of a way of checking out with enough grandiosity to interest those who would perpetuate the memory of his actions.

Debord attained his unique place in history without ever going to a university or holding a big job. Indeed, Debord may end up being best remembered for his revival of the "I'll never work" of Rimbaud and the "War Against Work" of the Surrealists; and again the critique of exchange that draws on Bataille's analysis of potlatch. Debord will also be remembered as a man who invented a viable revolutionary role that entailed a great deal of hiding out, and whose art reached the level of hiding the art in his works. This was a sound personal strategy that exerted a powerful influence on the events of May '68; a moment when, as Marx wrote over a century ago, "... a situation is created from which retreat is impossible, and circumstances themselves cry: *Hic Rhodus, Hic Salta*. Here is the rose, dance here." For Debord history at its best is a conscious self-creation by historical subjects, and in this light it is always worth recalling that over the last two centuries capitalism has been contested by workers in every industrialized country. As the conditions created by this system of domination worsen, revolutionaries will look to Debord's theories and the way he embodied his thought in May '68. These revolutionaries might encourage the proletariat and sub-proletariat to speak to one another without mediation, and to form assemblies (what the Argentinians are calling *ollas populares*) and practice democracy. As Debord demonstrated, new social values must flourish and life itself has to take the offensive for this to happen. The spectators of the world could find themselves crossing the point of no return where historic interventions or massacres are inevitable. On the distant shore lies Rhodus. Only time will tell if the mass of spectators can make the leap to that distant isle, as Aesop's Swaggerer said he could; or at least throw down the rose and begin to dance to the rhythm of revolt. In what I interpret as a symbol of his implacable refusal of the society of the spectacle, Debord translated this "*Hic Rhodus, Hic Salta*" of Aesop, Hegel and Marx as: "Here is the foot of the wall. Here is the mason." *

---

* Debord's translator's note in Sanguinetti's *Real Report* is an idiomatic French expression normally referring to the quality of the work.

Appendix: *The Game of War*

The game has long been out of print, but those who are up to the challenge can fashion a board game very easily using the diagram and table of pieces at the end of the rules. Just take the diagram of the board to a copy shop, have it enlarged and mounted. Most craft shops sell bags of round and square wooden chips—these can be labeled with stick-on letters to denote the type of piece.

The Game of War
Guy Debord

translated by Len Bracken

Preamble

This *Kriegspiel* puts into play the operations of two armies of equal strength. Each one seeks, by maneuver and battle, the destruction of the adversary's army while being obligated to cover the resources on its territory (indispensable for waging a campaign) and to protect the freedom of its communications.

The whole of strategic and tactical relations is contained in this "Game of War" according to the laws established by the theory of Clausewitz on the basis of classical XVIIIth Century warfare, which were prolonged by the Revolutionary wars and those of the Empire. Thus the nature of tactical units—on foot or mounted—(their conventionally fixed offensive and defensive strength, the proportion of diverse types of units in an army and the support that they can have), also proceeds from this historic model.

I. The Terrain and Goal of War

The Game of War is played on a terrain of 500 squares (25 x 20), divided by a parallel frontier running along the longest side. Each territory thus has a depth of ten squares. The asymmetrical territories of the armies have two arsenal squares each, three fort squares, a mountain pass square and nine mountain squares. Mountains are untraversable and block fire; they block lines of communication between the armies and their arsenals or transmission units.

Each side can freely position all its units in the interior of its territory. One unit occupies one square. The initial deployment of each army is chosen not knowing the disposition of the adversary: at least one of the two sides must write down the placement of all its units on a map, which it places on the terrain after the other side has positioned its units.

The first turn is chosen by a roll of the dice. Each turn is constituted by the movement of five freely chosen units (combatants or non-combatants) and by the attack, resulting from this movement, of an enemy unit that finds itself about to be engaged.

One is always permitted to abstain from announcing an attack. Likewise, an army can move less than five units, or even none.

The goal of each army is the complete destruction of the military potential of the other. This result can be obtained by destroying all combat units, or by taking both enemy arsenals (an arsenal being placed outside use as soon as it is occupied by an adversary's combat unit).

II. Combat Units

Each army, at the opening of hostilities, has 15 combat units—the breakdown is as follows:

9 infantry regiments
4 cavalry regiments
1 foot artillery regiment
1 mounted artillery regiment

The marching speed of each unit is 1 square per turn for infantry and foot artillery, and 2 squares for cavalry and mounted artillery. Each unit can move in any direction. The units that can move two squares per turn, can move in a straight line or in a diagonal, or even by one square in a straight line, then another in diagonal, or vice versa. But the only restriction is that they can only move through empty squares. One is allowed to move these rapid units only one square per turn, according to available opportunities.

Each unit's tactical strength is defined according to each type of arm, which is different depending on whether they are attacking or are being attacked. This tactical force is expressed, in diverse situations, by numerical coefficients.

Infantry regiments have an offensive coefficient of 4, and a defensive coefficient of 6. The defensive coefficient reaches 8 when it occupies a mountain pass, 10 when garrisoned in a fort.

The cavalry regiment has an offensive coefficient of 7 when it charges, which is to say when it is in immediate contact with the square occupied by the enemy that it attacks. It's defensive coefficient is 5; it is not raised if the cavalry unit occupies a mountain pass or a fort. Beyond the charge, cavalry can be employed as infantry in attack, and its offensive coefficient is thus 4.

A cavalry charge is the addition of the offensive weight of all cavalry units aligned horizontally, vertically or diagonally in a series of squares (not necessarily with continuity) behind a unit placed in immediate contact with an enemy unit. Cavalry can't attack, by a charge, a unit of any kind that is entrenched in a mountain pass or a fort.

Artillery regiments (mounted or on foot) have an offensive coefficient of 5. Its defensive coefficient is 8. This defensive coefficient rises to 10 when the artillery is placed in a mountain pass, and to 12 when it is in a fort.

The shots of all units—as well as the charge of cavalry—operate in a straight line (vertical, horizontal, diagonal) with the square occupied by the target unit. The offensive or defensive reach of the artillery is 3 squares in all the columns around it. The firing range of the infantry is 2 squares. The reach of a cavalry unit deployed defensively (or employed as infantry in attack, which is to say when it doesn't make contact with the square under attack, be it immediate contact or be it by the intermediary of another friendly cavalry unit) is also 2 squares. The offensive reach of the cavalry when it charges together in a single column can attain 4 squares for the last of its four regiments, thus the offensive coefficient is felt up to the square arrived at by the first. But if the first regiment is counter-attacked on the next turn, it will not be upheld, other than by its own defensive coefficient, except by those of the two units that follow—the fourth finds itself out of reach.

III. Shock Tactics

To attack an enemy unit is to concentrate fire on the square that it occupies, or in the case of cavalry, it's the charge of a certain number of units within reach of that square.

Add up the offensive coefficients of all units in a situation to attack a square. Then add up the defensive coefficients of all adversary units in position and within reach of fire of the same square under attack (including the unit occupying the square under attack). If the total figure of offensive force is less than or equal to that of total defense, the unit resists. If the offense is two or more points greater, the target is destroyed, and the destroyer must occupy the empty square. If the offense is only one point greater, the target must abandon the square it occupies and this is always the first move of the five moves of units of that side's next turn. The unit fired upon, can't be in an attack for the next move: its offensive coefficient can't be counted that time with the other units of its side and this is so even if it finds itself within reach of the adversary unit that will be attacked. Finally, if a unit is dominated by one unit in an attack and is incapable of leaving its square because the neighboring squares are occupied by the other units, the unit is destroyed.

The obligation to provide for the best defense of each unit is imposed by the fact that a prolonged inferiority in a tactical shock leads to a unilateral numerical weakening. This quantitative weakening, in every case strategically disastrous, can sometimes be quickly transformed on the tactical scheme, in irreversible qualitative inferiority on the front of engagement, as soon as the number of the total offensive force of the army has undergone its losses and fallen too low to permit any effective counter-attack.

IV. Communications

All offensive and defensive value, and the entire mobility of a combat unit is absolutely subordinated to the necessity for it to stay in communication with one of the arsenals of its side. This communication represents the transmission of orders and information and arrival of supplies and munitions and accounts for the internal coherence of the army. An arsenal can only be used by the original side—it can't be conquered to be used, only destroyed to deprive the adversary of it.

A unit doesn't march or fight if it doesn't remain on squares in direct or indirect liaison with one of its arsenals.

Direct liaison is when each arsenal can communicate with its army by alignment of squares (vertical, horizontal, diagonal) that fans out from it (no limit on reach) except when blocked by mountains. For example, all forts are aligned on squares that relay to one of its side's arsenals. On whatever square on its line, this line of communication can be relayed by a transmission unit of the advanced mobile echelon of the arsenal, which is itself sent in liaison (with unlimited range) in all the alignments of squares fanning out from the square it occupies temporarily. A second transmission unit, if placed on a square relayed to the first unit of transmissions of its side, re-sends, in turn, the liaison in the same way from its square.

Each side has a foot transmission unit that moves 1 square, and one mounted that moves 2 squares. These non-combat units have no offensive coefficient and their defensive coefficient is 1 (with a range of two squares). They constitute a good target objective for the adversary so its good to keep them out of range if isolated, or protect them with sufficient force from the combat units. The transmissions units are the only ones capable of moving without liaison with an arsenal, but all moves made this way are done so without relay power.

Indirect liaison is when each combat unit is in liaison with all other combat units in contact with it; that is, placed on one of the eight squares that touch it. This communication is understood by all units of the same side in contact with one of the other units. Thus, for an army or detached corps where all units touch square-to-square, it must be and it suffices that one of the units is in direct liaison with an arsenal or a transmissions unit.

A combat unit can move up to a square where it won't be in liaison. But there (if its liaison isn't reestablished by contact with another unit that is in indirect or direct liaison with the arsenal, or by the movement of a transmission unit that reopens the line of communication) the isolated unit is immobile and deprived of all offensive and defensive force—it can be destroyed without resistance by all enemy units within or who move into range. Meanwhile every unit that stays in liaison and finds itself in range to cover an immobile unit with its shots, lends the immobile unit its defensive coefficient.

A line of communication is cut by all enemy combat units placed on whatever square on the line for as long as it is there.

A liaison broken by the presence of an enemy unit on the line of communication can be reestablished directly if the intercepting unit leaves the square (by itself or if destroyed) or if the transmissions units reopen lines of communication via another alignment of empty squares. The liaison can be reestablished indirectly by friendly units that are free to move and who re-tie the liaison with units with whom the communication had been cut by reaching any square immediately next to one of its units.

If a maneuver of one side surrounds all or part of an enemy army, this side can, at the beginning of each of its moves, use its attacks to destroy, without encountering any resistance, one of the surrounded units within reach of its shot. Resistance can't respond with its remaining units, except when liaison is reestablished. In the case of a detached corps that is surrounded by an enemy who is interposed on all practical lines of communication, the last resort is to try to free it before its complete destruction by means of an "army of rescue" composed of friendly troops who could remain or be replaced in liaison—they must try to pierce the enemy front and make a junction with the surviving units.

Given the vital strategic importance of communications, the strategic goal is often a maneuver against the communications of the adversary rather than an offensive run successively against its two arsenals. This situation also influences tactical engagements and the order adopted in the battle in its diverse moments, to position oneself well for defense and counter-attack, but also cover the lines of communication. An army can, even before its numerical equilibrium is broken, find itself in a disequilibrium situation because its lines of communication are menaced. An army whose lines of battle are confused with the lines of communication quickly loses its tactical hold in the engagement and soon runs the risk of being partially or totally surrounded. The destruction of only one unit can create a break in liaison for an entire part of an army, which will be lost if the contact can't be reestablished. This result of the tactical engagement on only one square is susceptible to bringing about big strategic consequences.

Thus keeping the placement of only one of the arsenals is the necessary condition for a side to fight and win. It's best to keep both for as long as possible even if that means changing the lines of operation of the entire army, or combining the operations of detached corps operating on distinct bases.

V. Particular Conditions

The destruction of an arsenal can be assimilated in an attack. As soon as one side occupies an adversary arsenal by one of the five moves or its units, the blow in which this move was made can't bring an attack against another square. The only way to destroy an arsenal is to occupy it when it is empty of all adversary units. When an adversary arsenal is occupied by an enemy unit, this unit must first be destroyed. On the following turn, the empty arsenal can be invaded.

A transmission unit, being deprived of offensive value, can only destroy an arsenal by occupying it. Likewise, contrary to the combative units, a transmission unit doesn't block the line of communications of the enemy by occupying a square.

A cavalry unit, placed in a fortress, can't attack in a charge except by leaving this square. However, a cavalry can charge from a mountain pass that it occupies.

An arsenal is like other non-mountainous squares, and implies no adjunction nor limitation to tactical employment of units.

A fort, regardless of whose it is, can be used by whoever occupies it: from the moment an enemy unit seizes it, the tactical defensive advantage of the fort goes to that unit. Contrary to arsenals, forts are never destroyed and can change hands several times during a battle.

The territory of the eastern mountain, in its greatest length, oriented perpendicularly to the border, is called the "North Side." The white units are attributed to it.

If the two sides, after a large reciprocal weakening, or for other reasons, simultaneously renounce all offensive maneuvers, they can agree on a non-result without any further delay.

VI. On the Conduct of War

The Game of War, like war itself and all forms of thought on strategic action, tends to impose at each instant, considerations of contradictory necessities. Each side, to the extent that it knew how to keep its freedom of maneuver, finds itself constrained to choose between operations in which it lacks sufficient means in space and time.

Spatially, on one side as on the other, and so long as no break in the equilibrium has been attainted, there are never enough forces. One can't protect oneself everywhere one should. Nor can one attack and supply one's offensive everywhere it would be desirable, not even where necessity to do so is imposed by the adversary. Temporally, the movements of an army are never as rapid as one would like (this represents the "friction" that lessens all the movements of war, the transmissions of orders and the inevitable delays in execution).

One must often choose between opening quickly with few troops, or slowly with more troops to the point where one will have to fight. Urgent movements are often required—making reinforcements march or moving transmission units—by tactical encounters when engaged in combat. Because in each attack there is the need to send the maximum units while assuming the best support against the subsequent move by the enemy, or in recalling the unit that the result of the preceding effort of the enemy had left open.

Each side must strive to keep the initiative and compensate for insufficiencies in the speed of concentration on a decisive point where one must be strongest because strategic victory doesn't succeed except if it can claim victory in a tactical engagement. Defense is itself the strongest—tactically and strategically—but only offense or at least a counter-offensive can obtain success.

Defense can't remain static, except temporarily on a few highly localized positions, which give it the means to counter-attack. As the offensive develops, it goes toward its point of culmination, be it when it encounters superior forces that require it to turn into defense; be it when the counter-maneuver of the enemy begins to make its effect felt on distant lines of communication. This counter-maneuver can be repulsed in turn by the direct defense of friendly troops who block access to that line of communication, or by an indirect defense that menaces the flank of the enemy counter-offensive. The limits and combinations are fixed by the lack of effective force and by the lack of time for the execution of this or that movement.

It is favorable to extend one's front to menace the flanks or rear of the enemy, but the concentration of battle forces is the most imperious necessity. The defeat of the enemy in a major battle is the most direct path for triumph in the ensemble of a campaign, because this defeat can lead to the defeat of the entire defeated army, or at least to an irreversible numerical weakening. If a concentrated army interposes itself between corps of enemy troops that are separated, one of them risks being completely destroyed without the other being able to help; and an army spread out on a thin line can be pierced, which can bring about the preceding situation.

It is advantageous to attack the adversary's communications, protecting one's own, which may be extended. If undertaking a maneuver with a detached corps of troops, this corps must have enough offensive and defensive strength to oblige the enemy to oppose it with a sizable fraction of its forces. But if the detached corps is too well reinforced, it dangerously diminishes the tactical resistance of the main body, which is the pivot of maneuver. A detached corps should remain so for the shortest possible time, and it constitutes a stronger strategic menace if it marches quickly, and will normally be composed of mounted units. But these mounted units are also the shock units, thus the main body of the army can't go completely into battle if the enemy captures them. Plus, these strong offensive units are defensively weak if caught by the enemy and without the infantry for support (the infantry support, which could be adjacent to them, would slow their march). This difficulty is underlined by the fact that the two sides have few arms. The combative forces are limited to the smallest army possible for maneuver and battle. Such an army tied up in a vast territory, authorizes the use of detached bodies that can obtain decisive victories, but at big risks, because the army wouldn't be able to wage war in good conditions without the reciprocal support brought by these three arms.

Parallel to this is the tactical engagement of two armies that are completely reunited. It is best to maneuver to the enemy's flank to close in on his lines of communication or to obtain a concentration of fire by surrounding a wing. But the enemy can use the occasion to do the same on the opposing wing: "What turns, is turned."

The fraction of an army which, having been locally dominated in an engagement, will find itself too weak to continue to mount counter-attacks, will go into retreat to obtain higher concentration, or will try to retire to its reinforcements, or towards a stronger position. For example, a mountain pass or a fort. The victorious army should pursue the loser of an engagement to augment the total number of losses until the loser is reestablished. But this victorious army can only march in echelons of five units in each move so that if they maintain contact with the retreating army, they risk being counter-attacked by the army that regains its superiority in the concentration of its forces and wants to regain the initiative as soon as it can. At the right moment when the tactical exploitation of engagement stops, one must launch the exploitation of victory, for example by operating against arsenals and lines of communication of the enemy, as a function of the new situation created by the retreat of his army, and by the enemy's numerical inferiority, because the enemy's losses had been heaviest after the moment when the balance of power turned against the enemy.

In the *Game of War*, there are numerous bad dispositions and maneuvers, but none of the best maneuvers on which one can decide, at least as long as there remains a certain equilibrium of forces and positions, is assured of being good. It will become so or not according to what is done or not by the adversary. A degree of inattention is present in both sides, and the best calculations depend largely on the modifications introduced by the unforeseeable succession of replies by the adversary, and the responses they in turn create, all more or less correctly understood, and above all, more or less well executed. The permanent interaction of tactics and strategy can bring about surprises and reversals—sometimes at the last instant. The principles are steadfast, their application is always uncertain.

This is a war of movement—sometimes momentarily frozen on a static front, in the defense of a pass or a fort—where the territory has no interest in itself, but only by tactical or strategic positions that are necessary to an army or harmful to its enemy. One can occasionally win without battle, and even win with only very few partial combat situations. One can also win by frontal attack without maneuvers. But outside of these two extreme cases, one normally employs a series of maneuvers, combats, and a principal battle followed by new maneuvers. In the principal battle, maneuver is usually in the form of envelopment, retreat and moves against communications. One must not spare troops or maneuvers, nor dispense with them vainly. He who wants to keep all, loses all. However, he who lets himself lose more than his adversary can no longer contest the adversary.

VII. Absent or Under-represented Factors

To comprehend all the implied uses of the present *Kriegspiel,* it will be useful to consider the principal limitations.

First of all, the study of the summary application of the general theory of war introduces intended historical limitations: this doesn't represent ancient warfare, nor feudal warfare, nor modern warfare transformed by technology since the middle of the XIXth Century (railways, machine guns, armor plating, motorization, aviation, missiles).

Three essential, and more troublesome elements of all wars are absent or under-represented because they don't appear to be able to figure in a conflict that is decided on a checkered terrain, and that excludes all exterior intervention of chance. These are, firstly, climatic conditions and the alternation of day and night; secondly, the morale and strength of the troops; thirdly, the uncertainty in regard to the positions and movements of the enemy.

In the unfolding of this *Kriegspiel,* all time is equal: the solstice of war where the climate never varies and night never falls before the inevitable conclusion of the conflict. This is a serious lack vis-a-vis reality. It couldn't be corrected except at the price of a loss of rigor in the schematic representation of the totality of conflict processes.

The morale and strength of the troops are only summarily accounted for by the effect of instantaneous paralysis of the combative value of all units whose communications have been cut (including the garrison of a fort; so that the forts don't function as a barrier, but only as a point of tactical support). In this sense, it's like the armies of the Seven Years War which were directly dependent on their warehouses and convoys, rather than those of the French Revolution. The limitation of the relative effectiveness of troops, and their irreplaceable character that makes them so valuable, are linked with the military model of the same epoch. One can also consider the offensive weight identified by the depth of a cavalry charge to have an effect on morale—Ardant du Picq having clearly established that a cavalry's action in real combat isn't the mechanical result of the mass multiplied by speed. The usury of morale, which has always had the biggest effects in war (the usury of morale by generals), is susceptible to act here on the command of each army in a grand way. One is frequently given to exaggerate the consequences of a maneuver that one sees sketched by the adversary, although it might only be a fake. One can't effectively have the firm assurance of what to do (and not even always when one has acquired a crushing numerical superiority) because, in certain circumstances, the beaten army can still launch decisive operations on the communications of the victor.

Finally, this game is far from a total representation of war in that it doesn't maintain uncertainty in regard to the position and movements of the enemy, except its initial battle positions, which one doesn't know: but the enemy can only reasonably choose between fairly few zones of concentration, and it is prudent to do likewise. As soon as the operations begin, one instantaneously knows exactly and confidently all the moves that are made by the adversary one is facing: "The east (*ost*) knows what the east is doing" that it has to strike (thus the cavalry doesn't have an exploratory function here; only shock effect, pursuit or raid capabilities).

These restrictions being formulated, one can say that the *Game of War* exactly reproduces the totality of the factors that deal with war, and more generally, the dialectic of all conflicts.

Figures

arsenal = A (best recreated as a transparency so that other pieces can easily move into the same square)

fort = F (best recreated as a transparency)

mountain = shaded area

pass = striped area

foot artillery = FA

mounted artillery = MA

cavalry = C

infantry = I

foot transmission unit = FT

mounted transmission unit = MT

attacked square = AS (best recreated as a transparency)

UNITS		COEFFICIENT		Range (offensive & defensive)	Marching Speed
type	no.	offensive	defensive		
infantry	9	4	OS 6 PS 8 FS 10	2 squares	1 square
cavalry	4	7 in charge 4 as infantry	5	charging calvary: unlimited in the alignment of the charge… non-charging calvary: 2 squares	2 squares
artillery — foot	1	5	OS 8 PS 10 FS 12	3 squares	1 square
artillery — mounted	1				2 squares
transmission unit — foot	1		1		1 square
transmission unit — mounted	1				2 squares

OS = ordinary square • PS = pass square • FS = fort square

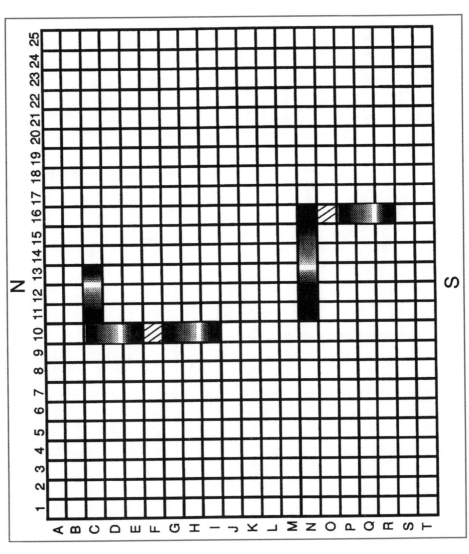

Books by Guy Debord

"Cette mauvaise réputation..." Paris: Gallimard, 1993.

Considérations sur l'assassinat de Gérard Lebovici. Paris: Gerard Lebovici, 1985.

Commentaires sur la societe du spectacle. Paris: Gerard Lebovici, 1979. Paris: Gallimard, 1992. Translated by Malcolm Imrie as *Comments on the Society of the Spectacle.* London: Verso, 1991.

Contre le cinéma. Aarhaus, Denmark: Insitute scandinave de vandalisme compare, 1964. *Des Contrats.* Cognac: Le temps qu'il fait, 1995.

Le Déclin et la chute de l'économie spectaculaire-marchande. Paris: Jean-Jacques Pauvert Aux Belles Lettres, 1993 (originally an essay published in *Internationale Situationniste* number 10, 1966).

Fin de Copenhague (with Asger Jorn). Copenhagen: Bauhaus Imaginiste, 1957. Paris: Allia, 1986.

In girum imus nocte et consumimur igni: edition critique. Paris: Gérard Lebovici, 1990. Translated by Lucy Forsyth as *In Girum Imus Nocte et Consumimur Igni.* London: Pelagian Press, 1991.

Le 'Jeu de la guerre': relevé des positions successives de toutes les forces au cours d'une partie. Paris: Gerard Lebovici, 1987.

Mémoires (with Asger Jorn). Paris: International Situationniste, 1959. Paris: Les Belles Lettres, 1993.

Oeuvres cinematographiques complètets 1952-1978. Paris: Champ Libre, 1978. Paris: Gallimard, 1994. Translated by Richard Parry and others as *Society of the Spectacle and Other Films* (Doesn't include *In Girum Imus Nocte et Consumimur Igni*). London: Rebel Press, 1992.

Ordures et decombres déballés à la sortie du film "in girum imus nocte et consumimur igni." Paris: Champ Libre, 1982.

Panégyrique I. Paris: Editions Gerard Lebovici, 1989. Translated by James Brook as *Panegyric: volume 1.* London: Verso, 1991.

Préface à la quatriéme édition italienne de "La Société du spectacle." Paris: Champ Libre, 1979. Paris: Gallimard, 1992 (published together with *Commentaires sur la societe du spectacle*).

La Société du spectacle. Paris: Buchet-Chastel, 1967. Paris: Champ Libre, 1971, 1983 and 1987. Paris: Gallimard, 1992. Translated as *Society of the Spectacle* Detroit: Black & Red, 1970, revised editions published in 1973, 1977 and 1983 (good translation). Translated as *The Society of the Spectacle* by Donald Nicholson-Smith, New York: Zone Books, 1994, (poor translation).

La Véritable scission dans l'Internationale (with Gianfranco Sanguinetti). Paris: Champ Libre, 1972. Translated by Michel Prigent and Lucy Forsyth as *The Veritable Split in the International.* London: B.M. Piranha, 1974. Revised and republished by B.M. Chronos, 1985 and 1990.

Films by Guy Debord

Critique de la séparation (Dansk-Fransk Experimentalfilmskompagni, 1961). 20 minutes.

Guy Debord, son art et son temps (with Brigitte Cornand) (Canal +, 1994). 60 minute video.

Hurlements en faveur de Sade (Films Lettristes, 1952). 90 minutes.

In girum imus nocte et consumimur igni (Simar Films, 1979). 80 minutes.

*Réfutation de tous les jugements, tant élogieux qu'hostiles, qui ont été jusqu'ici portés sur le film **La societe du spectacle*** (Simar Films, 1975). 25 minutes.

La societe du spectacle (Simar Films, 1973). 90 minutes.

Sur le passage de quelques personnes a travers une assez courte unite de temps (Dansk-Fransk Experimentalfilmskompagni, 1959). 20 minutes.

Bibliography

Adorno, Theodor. *Minima Moralia: Reflections from Damaged Life.* Frankfurt: Suhrkamp Verlag, 1951. Translated by E.F.N. Jephcott. London: Verso, 1978.

_____ *Prisms.* Translated by Samuel and Shierry Weber. Cambridge: MIT, 1981.

Alba, Victor. *Histoire du P.O.U.M.: le marxisme en Espagne (1919-1939).* Translated by Noemie Pages. Paris: Champ Libre, 1975.

Anderson, Andy. *Hungary '56.* London: Phoenix, 1964.

Ariosto, Ludovico. *Orlando Furioso.* Translated by Barbara Reynolds. London: Penguin, 1973.

Atkins, Guy. *Asger Jorn: The Crucial Years, 1954-1964.* London: Lund Humphries, 1997.

_____ *Asger Jorn: The final years 1965-1973.* London: Lund Humphries, 1980.

Avrich, Paul. *Kronstadt 1921.* New York: W.W. Norton & Company, Inc.

Bakhtin, M.M. *The Dialogic Imagination.* Translated by Caryl Emerson and Michael Holquist. Austin: University of Texas, 1981.

Bakunin, Michael. *God and the State.* New York: Dover, 1970.

_____ (see French transliteration: "Bakounine"). *Oeuvres Completes Volumes 1-8* (edited by Arthur Lehning). Champ Libre: Paris, 1973—1982.

_____ *Selected Writings* (Ed. A. Lehning). Translated by Steven Cox. New York: Grove, 1974.

_____ *Statism and Anarchy.* Translated by Marshall S. Shatz. Cambridge: Cambridge University, 1990.

Balestrini, Nanni. *The Unseen.* Translated by Liz Heron. London: Verso, 1989.

Barathon, Claude. *Les Folles idees de Fourier.* Chambray: CLD, 1980.

Bataille, Georges. *La Litterature et le mal.* Paris: Gallimard, 1957.

_____ *Oeuvres completes.* Paris: Gallimard, 1969.

_____ *La Part Maudite.* Paris: Minuit, 1967. Translated by Robert Hurley as *The Accursed Share,* Volume 1. New York: Zone, 1988.

Baudrillard, Jean. *Simulations.* Translated by Paul Foss, Paul Patton and Philip Beitchman. New York: Semiotext(e), 1983.

Bauer, Bruno. *The Trumpet of the Last Judgment Against Hegel the Atheist and Anti-Christ.* Lewiston: E. Mellen, 1989.

Baumann, Bommi. *How It All Began.* Vancouver: Pulp, 1977.

Becker-Ho, Alice. *L'Essence du jargon.* Paris: Gallimard, 1994.

_____ *Les Princes du jargon.* Paris: Gerard Lebovici, 1990.

Benjamin, Walter. *Reflections.* Translated by Edmund Jephcott. New York: Harcourt Brace Jovanovich, 1978.

Bernstein, Michele. *La Nuit.* Paris: Buchet-Chastel, 1961.

_____ *Tous les chevaux du roi.* Paris: Buchet-Chastel, 1960.

Berreby, Gerard, ed. *1948-1957: Documents relatif a la fondation de l'Internationale situationniste.* Paris: Allia, 1985.

Birtwistle, Graham Michael. *Living Art: Asger Jorn's Comprehensive Theory of Art Between*

Helhesten and Cobra (1946-1949). Utrecht: Reflex, 1986.

Blazwick, Iwona (ed.). *An Endless Passion... An Endless Banquet: A Situationist Scrapbook.* London: ICA and Verso, (n.d.)

Bossuet, Jacques Benigne. *Discourse on Universal History.* Chicago: University of Chicago, 1976.

____ *The Jubilee Manuel.* London: Burns & Oates, (n.d.)

____ *Maximes et reflections de Bossuet sur la politique.* Paris: Fuseau, 1964.

Bourget, Paul. *Essais de psychologie contemporaine.* Paris: Plon-Nourrit, 1933.

Bracken, Len (ed.) *Extraphile #1-6.* Arlington: 1993-1995.

____ *The Neo-Catiline Conspiracy and Other Essays,* Arlington: 1996.

Brau, Eliane. *Le Situationnisme ou la nouvelle internationale.* Paris: Nouvelle Editions Debresse, 1968.

Brau, Jean-Louis. *Cours, comrade, le vieux monde est derriere toi! Histoire du mouvement revolutionnaire etudiant en Europe.* Paris: Albin Michel, 1968.

Brecher, Jeremy. *Strike!* Boston: South End, 1972.

Breggin, Peter. *The Psychiatric Holocaust.* London: Libertarian Reprints, no date.

Burckhardt, Jacob. *The Civilization of the Renaissance in Italy.* Translated by S.G.C. Middlemore. London: Penguin, 1990.

Castoriadis, Cornelius. *Cornelius Castoriadis: Political and Social Writings.* Minneapolis: University of Minneapolis, 1988.

Charnay, Jean-Paul. *Essai general de strategie.* Paris: Champ Libre, 1973.

Chevalier, Louis. *L'Assassinat de Paris.* Paris: Calmann-Levy, 1977. Translated by David P. Jordan as *The Assassination of Paris.* Chicago: University of Chicago, 1994.

Cieszkowski, August von. *Prolegomena zur Histriosophie.* Translated from German to French as *Prolegomenes a l'historiosophie.* Paris: Champ Libre, 1973.

Clark, T. J. *The Painting of Modern Life: Paris in the Art of Manet and His Followers.* New York: Knopf, 1984.

Clausewitz, Carl von. *On War.* From the translation by J.J. Graham. London: Penguin, 1968.

Cohn, Norman. *The Pursuit of the Millennium: Revolutionary Millenarians and Mystical Anarchists of the Middle Ages.* New York: Oxford, 1970.

Coordination Des Groups Autonomes d'Espagne. *Appels de la Prison de Segovie.* Paris: Champ Libre, 1980.

Cotta, Alain. *L'Homme au travail.* Paris: Fayard, 1987.

Courier, Paul-Louis. *Oeuvres completes de P.L. Courier.* Paris: Firmin Didot Freres, 1837.

____ *Pamphlets politiques choisis.* Paris: Sociales, 1961.

Champ Libre. *Correspondance Vol. 1.* Paris: Champ Libre, 1978.

____ *Correspondance Vol 2.* Paris Champ Libre, 1981.

Christie, Stuart. *Stefano della Chiaie: Portrait of a Black Terrorist.* London: Anarchy/Refract, 1984.

Cravan, Arthur. *Oeuvres: Poems, Articles, Lettres.* Paris: Gerard Lebovici, 1987.

Dante. *The Divine Comedy Volumes 1-3.* Translated by Mark Musa. London: Penguin, 1981.

Davidson, Steef. *The Penguin Book of Political Comics.* New York: Penguin, 1982.

Descartes, Rene. *Discourse on Method and the Meditations.* London: Penguin, 1968.

Dumontier, Pascal. *Les Situationnistes et Mai 68: Theorie et pratique de la revolution (1966-1972).* Paris: Gerard Lebovici, 1990.

Ehrmann, Henry. *Politics in France.* Boston: Little, Brown and Company, 1983.

Ellul, Jacques. *Propaganda: The Formation of Men's Attitudes.* New York: Knopf, 1965.

Fanon, Frantz. *L'an V de la revolution algerienne.* First published in 1959. Reprinted as Sociologie d'une revolution. Paris: Maspero, 1968. Translated by Haakon Chevalier as *A Dying Colonialism.* New York: Grove, 1965.

_____ Pour la revolution africaine. Paris: Maspero, 1964. Translated by Haakon Chevalier as *Toward the African Revolution.* New York: Grove, 1967.

Ferry, L. and A. Renaut. *La Pensee 68: essai sur 'anti-humanisme contemporain.* Paris: Gallimard, 1985. Translated by Mary H.S. Cattani as *French Philosophy of the Sixties.* Amherst: University of Massachusetts, 1990.

_____ *68-86 Itineraires de l'individu.* Paris: Gallimard, 1987.

Feuerbach, Ludwig. *The Essence of Christianity.* New York: Harper, 1957.

Ford, Simon, *The Realization and Suppression of the Situationist International: An Annotated Bibliography 1972—1992.* Edinburgh and San Francisco: AK, 1995.

Foucart, Francois. *Lacenaire: l'assassin demythifie.* Paris: Perrin, 1995.

Gabel, Joseph. *False Consciousness.* New York: Harper & Row, 1975.

_____ *Mannheim and Hungarian Marxism.* New Brunswick: Transaction, 1991.

Gombin, Richard. *Les Origines du gauchisme.* Paris: Seuil, 1971.

Gane, Mike (ed.). *Baudrillard Live: Selected Interviews.* London: Routledge, 1993.

Gracian, Baltasar. *El Heroe.* Translated by Joseph de Courbeville as *Le Heros.* Paris: Noel Tissot, 1725. Paris: Champ Libre, 1973, 1980. Paris: Gerard Lebovici, 1989.

_____ *The Wisdom of Baltasar Gracian.* Adapted and edited by J. Leonard Kaye. New York: Pocket Books, 1992.

Guilbert, Cecile. *Pour Guy Debord.* Paris: Gallimard, 1996.

Gray, Christopher (ed.), *Leaving the Twentieth Century: The Incomplete Work of the Situationist International.* London: Free Fall, 1974.

Greeman, Richard. "The Permanence of the Commune" in *The Revolution and Reaction: The Paris Commune 1871* edited by John Hicks and Robert Tucker. No City: University of Massachusettes Press, 1973.

Guillaume, Pierre (ed.). *Organe de critique et d'orientation postmessianique.* Paris: 1995.

Habermas, Jurgen. *The Philosophical Discourse of Modernity.* Cambridge: MIT, 1987.

Hampson, Norman. *Saint-Just.* Oxford: Basil Blackwell, 1991.

Hegel, G.W.F. *Introductory Remarks on Aesthetics.* London: Penguin, 1993.

_____ *Lectures on the History of Philosophy.* London: Routledge and Kegan Paul, 1968.

_____ *La production de l'espace*. Paris: Anthropos, 1974. Translated by Donald Nicholson-Smith as *The Production of Space*. Oxford: Basil Blackwell, 1991.

_____ *Le Temps des meprises*. Paris: Stock, 1975.

Po, Li and Fu, Tu. *Li Po and Tu Fu*. London: Penguin, 1973.

Lipovetsky, Gilles. *L'Ere du vide: Essais sur l'individualisme contemporain*. Paris, Gallimard, 1983.

Lukacs, Georg. *History and Class Consciousness: Studies in Marxist Dialectics*. Translated by Rodney Livingstone. Cambridge: MIT, 1972.

_____ *The Young Hegel*. Translated by Rodney Livingstone. Cambridge: MIT, 1976.

Mailer, Phil. *Portugal: The Impossible Revolution?* First published by London Solidarity. Quebec: Black Rose, 1991.

Machiavelli, Niccolo. *The Prince*. Translated by Christian Detmold. New York: Airmont, 1965.

_____ *The Discourses*. London: Penguin, 1970.

Mannheim, Karl. *Ideology and Utopia*. Translated by Louis Wirth and Edward Shils. San Diego: Harcourt Brace Jovanovich, 1936.

Manrique, Jorge. *Stances sur la mort de son pere*. Translated by Guy Debord. Paris: Champ Libre, 1980.

Marcus, Greil, *Lipstick Traces: A Secret History of the Twentieth Century*. Cambridge: Harvard University, 1989.

Marien Marcel (ed.), *Les Levres nues (1954-1958)*. Paris: Plasma, 1978.

Histoire de L'Internationale Situationniste. Paris: Gerard Lebovici, 1989.

Marx, Karl, *Capital* (volumes 1-3). First published in 1867, 1885 and 1894. Translated by Ben Fowkes. London: Penguin, 1976.

_____ *Civil War in France: The Paris Commune*. First published in 1871. New York: International Publishers, 1940.

_____ *Class Struggles in France 1848-1850*. First published in 1850. New York, International Publishers, 1964.

_____ *The Communist Manifesto* (with Friedrich Engels). The Communist League, 1848. Translated by Paul M. Sweezy. New York and London: Modern Reader Paperbacks, 1964.

_____ *Critique of Hegel's 'Philosophy of Right*. Cambridge: Cambridge University, 1967.

_____ *Critique of the Gotha Programme*. Moscow: Progress, 1954.

_____ *Early Writings*. Translated by Rodney Livingstone and Gregor Benton. London: Penguin Books, 1974. (Includes *The Critique of Hegel's Philosophy of Right* and *Economic and Philosophical Manuscripts of 1844*).

_____ *The German Ideology* (with Friedrich Engels). Written between 1845 and 1846. Moscow: Progress Publishers, 1964.

_____ *Grundrisse*. First published in 1859. Translated by Martin Nicolaus. London: Penguin, 1974.

_____ *The Holy Family, or Critique of Critical Criticism* (with Friedrich Engels). Written in 1844. Moscow: Progress Publishers, 1956.

_____ *The Poverty of Philosophy.* Moscow: Progress, 1975.

_____ *The 18th Brumaire of Louis Bonaparte.* First published in 1852. New York: International Publishers, 1963.

Matarasso, Pauline (translator and editor). *The Cistercian World: Monastic Writings of the Twelfth Century.* London: Penguin, 1993.

Mauss, Marcel. *The Gift.* Translated by Ian Cunnison. New York: Norton, 1967.

Mesrine, Jacques. *L'Instinct de mort.* Paris: Champ Libre, 1984.

Monet, Jean-Pierre. *Un peu de bon sens.* Paris: Ivrea, 1995.

Mourre, Miche. *Malgre le blaspheme.* Paris: Rene Julliard, 1951. Translated by A.W. Fielding as *In Spite of Blasphemy.* London: John Lehmann, 1953.

Museum national d'histoire naturelle. *Le Belvedere du Labyrinthe: Une operation de retour de l'invisible au visible au Jardin des Plantes.* Paris: Hachette, 1985.

Negri, Antonio. *Marx Beyond Marx: Lessons of the Grundrisse.* Brooklyn: Autonomedia/Pluto, 1991.

Nietzsche, Friedrich. *Ecce Homo.* Translated by R.J. Hollingdale. London: Penguin, 1979.

Ohrt, Roberto. *If I Wasn't Alexander I Would Like to be Diogenes.* Translated by Ian Brunskill. Seattle: Left Bank, 1993.

Orwell, George. *1984.* New York: Plume, 1981.

Pannekoek, Anton. *Lenin as Philosopher.* London: Merlin, 1975.

Parkinson, Roger. *Zapata.* New York: Scarborough, 1980

Perlman, Fredy. *Against His-story, Against Leviathan!* Detroit: Black & Red, 1983.

Peters, Mike (ed.). *Here and Now: Guy Debord Supplement.* Leeds: 1996.

Plant, Sadie, *The Most Radical Gesture: The Situationist International in a Postmodern Age.* London : Routledge, 1992.

Plutarch. *Makers of Rome.* London: Penguin, 1965.

_____ *On Sparta.* London: Penguin, 1988.

_____ *The Rise and Fall of Athens: Nine Greek Lives.* London: Penguin, 1960.

Porch, Douglas. *The French Secret Services.* New Brunswick: Transaction, 1993.

Poster, Mark. *Existential Marxism in Postwar France.* Pinceton: Princeton University 1975

Potlatch: 1954-1957. Paris: Gerard Lebovici, 1985.

Prost, Antoine, *Petite histoire de la France au XXe siecle.* Paris: Armand Colin, 1979 and 1992.

Ranum, Orest. *The Fronde: A French Revolution 1648-1652.* New York: Norton, 1993.

Raspaud, Jean-Jacques, and **Jean-Pierre Voyer.** *L'Internationale situationniste: Protagonistes/chronologie/bibliographie (avec un index de noms insultes).* Paris: Champ Libre, 1972.

Retz, Cardinal de. *Memoirs*. London: H.S. Nichols, 1896.

Ryck, Francis. *Le Compagnon indesirable*. Paris: Gallimard, 1973.

Richards, Thomas, *The Commodity Culture of Victorian England: Advertising and Spectacle, 1951-1914*. Stanford: Stanford University, 1990.

Rigby, Brian. *Popular Culture in Modern France*. London: Routledge, 1991.

Ross, Kristin. *Fast Cars, Clean Bodies: Decolonization and the Reordering of French Culture*. Cambridge: MIT, 1995.

Sadoul, Georges. *Dziga Vertov*. Paris: Champ Libre, 1971.

Sanguinetti, Gianfranco (as Censor), *Rapporto Veridico sulle opportunita di salvare il capitalismo in Italia*. Milan: Ugo Mursia, 1975. Translated by Guy Debord as *Veridique Rapport sur les dernieres chances de sauver le capitalisme en Italie*. Paris: Champ Libre, 1976. Translated by Len Bracken as *The Real Report on the Last Chance to Save Capitalism in Italy*. Fort Bragg: Flatland, 1997

_____ *Del Terrorismo e dello Stato, La teori e la practica del terrorismo per la prima volta divulgata*. Milan, 1979. Translated by Lucy Forsyth and Michel Prigent as *On Terrorism and the State: The Theory and Practice of Terrorism Divulged for the First Time*. London: Chronos, 1982.

Sartre, Jean-Paul. *Situations I & III*. Paris, 1947 & 1949.

Schade, Jens August. *Des Etres se rencontrent*. Translated from Danish to French by Christian Petersen-Merillac. Paris: Gerard Lebovici, 1978.

Schnapp Alain and Pierre Vidal-Naquet. *Journal de la commune etudiante: Textes et Documents Novembre 1967-Juin 1968*. Paris: Seuil, 1969. Translated by Maria Jolas as *The French Student Uprising: November 1967-June 1968, an analytical record*. Boston: Beacon, 1971.

Scott, Andrew Murray. *Alexander Trocchi: The Making of the Monster*. Edinburgh: Polygon, 1991.

Scott, James C., *Domination and the Arts of Resistance*. New Haven and London: Yale University, 1990.

Semprun, Jaime. *La Guerre sociale au portugal*. Paris: Champ Libre, 1975.

_____ *Precis de recuperation*. Paris: Champ Libre, 1976

Simpson, Christopher. *Science of Coercion: Communication Research & Psychological Warfare 1945-1960*. New York and Oxford: Oxford University, 1994.

Sollers, Philippe. *Le Secret*. Paris: Gallimard, 1992.

Souchy and others. *The May Days of Barcelona 1937*. London: Freedom Press, 1987.

St. Just. *Oeuvres Completes*. Paris: Gerard Lebovici, 1984,

Stirner, Max. *The Ego and its Own*. Translated by Steven Byington. London: Rebel Press, 1993.

Telos #86 (Winter, 1990). "The Society of the Spectacle 20 Years Later: A Discussion" by Russell Berman, David Pan and Paul Piccone.

Thucydides. *The Peloponnesian War*. Translated by Rex Warner. London: Penguin, 1954.

Tocqueville, Alexis de. *On Democracy, Revolution and Society: Selected Writings.*Chicago: University of Chicago, 1980.

_____ *Souvenirs.*Garden City: Doubleday, 1970.

Trocchi, Alexander. *Cain's Book.* First published in 1960. New York: Grove, 1979.

_____ *Invisible Insurrection of a Million Minds: A Trocchi Reader.* Edinburgh: Polygon, 1991.

_____ *Man at Leisure.* London: Calder and Boyars, 1972.

_____ *School for Sin.* Paris: Olympia, 1955.

_____ *Young Adam.* London: Heinemann, 1961.

Tzu, Sun. *The Art of War.* Translated by Samuel Griffith. Oxford: Oxford University, 1963.

Vague, Tom. *Televisionaries: The Red Army Faction Story 1963-1993.* Edinburgh: AK, 1994.

Vaneigem, Raoul. *Adresse aux vivants sur la mort qui les gouverne et l'opportunite de s'en defaire.* Paris: Seghers, 1990.

_____ *Avertissement aux ecoliers et lyceens.* No City: Mille et Une Nuits, 1995.

_____ (as Ratgeb) *De la greve sauvage a l'autogestion generalisee.* Paris: Union Generale, 1974. Translated by Paul Sharkey as *Contributions to the revolutionary struggle intended to be discussed, corrected and principally put into practice without delay.* London: Bratach Dubh Editions, 1981.

_____ (as J.F. Dupuis) *Hisotire desinvolte du surrealisme.* No city: 1977.

_____ Isidore Ducasse et le Comte de Lautreamont dans les Poesies. Bruxelles: no publication, 1956. Pantin: Des Amis du Leopard, 1996.

_____ *Lettre de Staline a ses enfants, enfin reconcilies de l'est et de l'ouest.* Levallois-Perret: Manya, 1992.

_____ *Le Livre des Plaisirs.* Paris: Encre, 1979. Translated by John Fullerton as *The Book of Pleasures.* London, Pending Press, 1985.

_____ *Louis Scutenaire.* Paris: Seghers, 1991.

_____ *Le Mouvement du Libre-Esprit: Generalites et temoignages sur les affleurements de la vie a la surface du Moyen-Age, de la Renaissance, et, incidemment, de notre epoch.* Paris: Ramsay, 1986. Translated by Randall Cherry and Ian Patterson as *The Movement of the Free Spirit: General Considerations and Firsthand Testimony Concerning Some Brief Flowerings of Life in the Middle Ages, the Renaissance and, Incidentally, Our Own Time.* New York: Zone Books, 1994.

_____ *Pas de dialogue avec les suspects. Pas de dialogue avec les cons.* (with J. Strijbosch) Antwerp: 1963.

_____ *Traite de savoir-vivre a l'usage des jeunes generations.* Paris: Gallimard, 1967. Originally translated by John Fullerton and Paul Sieveking as *The Revolution of Everyday Life.* London: Rising Free Collective, 1979. Translated by Donald Nicholson-Smith in

Seattle and London by Left Bank Books and Rebel Press, 1983 and 1994.

van der Elsken. *Love on the Left Bank*. London: Andre Deutsch, 1957.

_____ *Parijs! Fotos 1950-1954*. Amsterdam: Bert Bakker, 1981.

Vico, Giambattista. *The New Science*. Translated by Thomas Goddard Bergin and Max Harold Fisch. Ithaca: Cornell University, 1948.

Vienet, Rene, *Enrages et situationnistes dans le movement des occupations*. Paris: Gallimard, 1968. Translated by Loren Goldner and Paul Sieveking as *The Enrages and the Situationists in the Occupation Movement, May-June, 1968*. York: Tiger Papers Publications, n.d. New York: Semiotext(e), New York, 1990.

Villon, Francois. *The Complete Works of Francois Villon*. Translated by Anthony Bonner. New York: Bantam Books, 1960.

Volosinov, V.N. *Freudianism: A Critical Sketch*. Translated by I.R. Titunik. Bloomington: Midland, 1987.

_____ *Marxism and the Philosophy of Language*. Translated by Ladislav Matejka and I.R. Titunik. Cambridge: Harvard University, 1986.

Vygotsky, Lev. *Thought and Language*. Cambridge: MIT, 1986.

Willan, Philip. *Puppetmasters: The Political Use of Terrorism in Italy*. London: Constable, 1991.

Xenophon. *The Persian Expedition*. Translated by Rex Warner. London: Penguin, 1949.

Yack, Bernard. *The Longing for Total Revolution*. Berkeley: University of California, 1992.

Zerzan, John. *Future Primitive*. Autonomedia & Anarchy: a journal of desire armed. Brooklyn and Columbia: 1994.

New from Feral House

VIRTUAL GOVERNMENT
CIA MIND CONTROL OPERATIONS IN AMERICA
Alex Constantine
Further remarkable revelations from the author of *Psychic Dictatorship in the USA*. *Virtual Government* includes a chapter on the mobster and drug connection to the murder of Nicole Simpson, information that will be used in an upcoming documentary on the infamous crime. "Alex Constantine is the foremost journalist and contemporary historian of the murky worlds of vice and vice-squads."—Donald Freed.
PAPERBACK • 6 X 9 • $14.95

KILLER FICTION
G. J. Schaefer, as Told to Sondra London
Introduction by Colin Wilson
These vile, fetishistic stories were used in court to convict Schaefer of serial murder. Schaefer, recently stabbed to death in prison, received his literary training from novelist Harry Crews, and researched his books practicing the sordid crimes detailed within. Includes illustrations. Adults Only!
PAPERBACK • 6 X 9 • $14.95

THE OCTOPUS
SECRET GOVERNMENT & THE DEATH OF DANNY CASOLARO
Kenn Thomas and Jim Keith
This extraordinary book uses the actual notes of Danny Casolaro, a journalist murdered investigating a nexus of crime he called "The Octopus," since it led a torturous course from software manufacturers to Hollywood to Indian Reservations to the Department of Justice.
HARDCOVER • 6 X 9 • $19.95

The titles above may be ordered from Feral House for check or money order plus $2 each book ordered for shipping. For a free catalogue of publications, send an SASE.

Feral House • 2532 Lincoln Blvd., Suite 359 • Venice, CA • 90291